Unitarianism in the Antebellum South

RELIGION AND AMERICAN CULTURE

Series Editors
David Edwin Harrell
Wayne Flynt
Edith L. Blumhofer

Unitarianism in the Antebellum South

The Other Invisible Institution

JOHN ALLEN MACAULAY

THE UNIVERSITY OF ALABAMA : TUSCALOOSA

The University of Alabama Press
Tuscaloosa, Alabama 35487-0380
uapress.ua.edu

Hardcover edition published 2001.
Paperback edition published 2016.
eBook edition published 2016.

Inquiries about reproducing material from this work should be addressed to the
University of Alabama Press.

Typeface: ACaslon

Manufactured in the United States of America
Cover image: "New" Unitarian Church, Charleston, South Carolina; courtesy of the
South Carolina Library, University of South Carolina, Columbia
Cover design: Michele Myatt Quinn

∞
The paper on which this book is printed meets the minimum requirements of
American National Standard for Information Science–Permanence of Paper for
Printed Library Materials, ANSI Z39.48-1984.

Paperback ISBN: 978-0-8173-5865-5
eBook ISBN: 978-0-8173-9019-8

A previous edition of this book has been catalogued by the Library of Congress as
follows:
Library of Congress Cataloging-in-Publication Data
Macaulay, John Allen, 1964–
   Unitarianism in the Antebellum South : the other invisible institution / John Allen
Macaulay.
       p. cm. — (Religion and American culture)
Includes bibliographical references and index.
   ISBN 0-8173-1086-X (alk. paper)
   1. Unitarianism—Southern States—History—18th century. 2. Southern States—
Church history—18th century. 3. Unitarianism—Southern States—History—19th
century. 4. Southern States—Church history—19th century. I. Title. II. Religion and
American culture (Tuscaloosa, Ala.)
   BX9833.43 .M23 2001
   289.1'75'09033—dc21
                        00-012599

British Library Cataloguing-in-Publication Data available

For my parents

Contents

Illustrations

Acknowledgments

It would be impossible to thank all of the individuals along the way, who, either directly or indirectly, have helped me in the production of this project. Over the course of a decade, smiles, supportive conversations, words of encouragement from family, friends, colleagues, work associates, and even strangers did much to motivate me during particularly difficult, isolating, or nonproductive periods. For those who stuck beside me through the "thick" and "thin" times, I thank you for your patience, understanding, and support.

First and foremost, I would like to thank the staff at the University of Alabama Press, particularly Nicole Mitchell and the editors of the Religion and American Culture series. Not only did they graciously accept the flawed project from the beginning, but also consistently demonstrated great patience with each delay of the revisionary process. Kathy Cummins edited the manuscript with meticulous care and a sharp eye. I am indebted to her talent, generosity, and knowledge of the trade. I would also like to thank Dr. E. Brooks Holifield at Emory University, Dr. Robert M. Calhoon at the University of North Carolina at Greensboro, and Dr. Eugene D. Genovese. Dr. Holifield was kind enough to read the original dissertation and offer helpful suggestions for revision and publication and has since acted as a judicious sounding board for changes and improvements. Dr. Calhoon read the original revision with exact care, researched subtopics, and offered insightful changes or amendments. Dr. Genovese graciously agreed to read the manuscript and challenged me to "strike a better balance" in my arguments against the marginalization of these forgotten liberals and for the rationality of the Southern Unitarian faith. I have learned much from his arguments and I hope that my latest revisions have steered a more moderate course. But sympathies and overstatement aside, I have, as much as possible, allowed these Unitarians to speak for themselves knowing that they understood their beliefs, their distinctions, their outlooks, and their fears, much better than I. That being said, any mistakes, omissions, or blunders in this project are entirely my own and do not reflect the helpful changes these advisors suggested.

I would also like to thank the Department of History at the University of South Carolina for the generous financial support during the last several years of my graduate experience. Without the teaching and instructional assistantships and research and travel fellowships, the completion of the dissertation and the revised manuscript would have been either tabled or delayed indefinitely. I wish also to thank several individuals on the faculty at USC who have extended either time or thoughts to the original dissertation. In addition to acting as Chair of the Dissertation Committee, Dr. Clyde N. Wilson patiently read the first draft of chapters and offered helpful suggestions. He supported my project enthusiastically from its inception and unselfishly extended a department office where I would have enough space to work and write. Dr. Robert Weir, Dr. Donald Jones, and Dr. Mark Smith, though with late notice and prior obligations, graciously agreed to serve as Committee members. Dr. Jessica Kross offered initial acceptance into the History Department and supported me throughout my doctoral candidacy, and for that I am very grateful. I hope one day I too will be able to help a student in the same manner and demonstrate the same level of objectivity that she showed me. Other faculty members have also worked with me in and out of the classroom and I am grateful for those contributions as well.

In addition, I would like to thank the many individuals who have patiently helped in securing primary and secondary sources. A special thank you to librarians and researchers at the University of South Carolina; South Carolina Historical Society; the Unitarian Church in Charleston; Georgia Historical Society; Southern Historical Collection at the University of North Carolina, Chapel Hill; Duke University Archives; First Unitarian Church, New Orleans; Louisiana Department of Archives and History; Virginia Historical Society; Massachusetts Historical Society; and Harvard University Archives. A special thank you to Dr. Allen Stokes at the Caroliniana Library of the University of

South Carolina and Tim Driscoll at the Andover-Harvard Theological Library at Harvard Divinity School.

I am deeply indebted to my parents, Dr. William A. Macaulay and Vivian Jarvis Macaulay, who, through good and bad times, continued to support me during and after graduate school with rent and tuition checks (does this dedication and acknowledgment count at least as partial repayment?), cards, letters, phone calls, and most of all, their love. Thanks also to family members, friends, and countless others who footed the bill during necessary weekend or social excursions, demonstrated token patience and/or feigned interest in the project, inspired me with love and moral support, and made this long journey a much more enjoyable one. Thank you David, Margaret, Sarah, Cynthia, Toby, Acacia, Tolly, Lena, Alex, Brand, Woody, Robyn, Dale, and Carey. For all of those not mentioned who helped in different capacities and at various stages of this project, your efforts have not gone unnoticed or unappreciated.

Unitarianism in the Antebellum South

• Introduction

Recent studies in American evangelicalism have burst onto the eighteenth- and nineteenth-century historical landscape with an almost vengeful force: so much so that dissenting evangelicalism has become, in the words of Jon Butler, "the single most common explanatory device in contemporary American history, outstripping such once powerful but now enfeebled predecessors as Puritanism, the rise of the middle class, industrialization, urbanization, or even the growth of democracy." But alas, the evangelical pendulum has swung too far and too fast. In its rise to preeminence, it has, again in the words of Butler, "obscured the historical realities of eighteenth and nineteenth century America," distorted "the substance of religious experience," and eclipsed the "dynamics of American religious development and change."[1]

What is missing in the wake of dissenting evangelicalism and buried beneath the monument historians have built to it is the vital presence and quiet but steady pulse of the "religious rationalism" of the English and Scottish Enlightenment in general, and Unitarianism in particular. Although evangelicalism and other forces met, meshed, and confronted religious rationalism at different times with varying frequency and force, Unitarianism itself was not killed off in the process, but continued to have a strong presence well into the antebellum period. That its more radical and foreign elements such as Deism and Skepticism disappeared or fell out of favor did not stop the formidable influence that Unitarianism continued to have on the religious landscape of both antebellum America and the South.

As current nineteenth-century Northern Unitarian scholarship ably attests, enlightened religion continued to exist in various forms well into, during, and after the antebellum period. In New England, seeds of

Enlightenment ideals fell on soil already occupied by almost two centuries of a Puritanism that had by the time of the Revolution evolved from a once strict Calvinistic core in the seventeenth century to a comparatively broader Arminian base in the eighteenth. When the time came for a Unitarian harvest, primarily among Congregational churches in the first several decades of the nineteenth century, the American Unitarian Association was founded in Boston in 1825. The liberal flower that grew out of that Association had its own distinct political, philosophical, epistemological, and religious petals, all genetically reminiscent of its Puritan heritage in Massachusetts Bay. Current scholarship documents the narrative of this transformation of Puritanism into Unitarianism, and the continuity of Enlightenment ideals from Revolutionary Boston to Unitarian Harvard.

What is not well documented or understood is the continuity of Enlightenment religion in the Southern states well after the Revolution through both the early national and antebellum periods and right up to the Civil War. The continued influence of Enlightenment ideals upon antebellum Southerners has been overlooked by historians too consumed by the evangelical panacea. E. Brooks Holifield has recently noted, "We hear from the historians that the religion of the Southern people on the eve of the Civil War was 'truly a faith,' not a 'reasoned orthodoxy'; that religious development in the Old South was a transition from Jeffersonian liberalism to revivalistic emotionalism, that the religious Southerner had no ambition to 'perfect a system, or to tidy up a world doomed to remain forever deceptive, changeful, and evil'; that Southern faith was 'almost totally' from the heart, not the head; that strictly the Southerner had no mind, only temperament; that he did not think, he felt."[2] Such distortions of fact, mythic stereotypes, and half-truths are no longer valid and the foundations that once supported them are becoming increasingly less secure.

The few discourses that deal with Unitarianism in the South emphasize the decline of the faith in the would-be Confederate states. Yet, decline has too often been exaggerated and misunderstood. Such rushes to extinction, generalities, and distortions of truth have gone uncontested for too long. Historians have failed to explain not only what happened to Southern Unitarians after they lost their churches, but also how Southern Unitarians were able to sustain their positions of prominence among the South's urban, professional, intellectual, civic, and commercial elite. Did the verbal sticks and stones thrown by orthodoxy kill them off in large numbers? Did they pack up and move North? Did they die off by plague or storm? These are some of the questions historians have failed to address, much less answer.

It is true that for many Southern Unitarian congregations, attacks by zealous evangelicals, tension within their own denomination, and the erroneous association of Southern Unitarians with all things "Northern" proved too difficult. Faced with a Northern faction that fell under the spell of abolitionist fanaticism and evangelical emotionalism, and a misguided Southern orthodoxy who too often erroneously labeled them "Deists" and associated them with the antislavery cause, many Unitarians in the South held on organizationally as long as they could. Out of seven Unitarian churches in the would-be Confederate states, only two, Charleston and New Orleans, managed to remain organizationally active on the eve of the Civil War. Eventually churches in places like Augusta and Richmond closed their doors. But this did not mean that Unitarians completely ceased to exist or abruptly stopped holding their liberal beliefs altogether. It did mean, however, that Unitarians tended to become unreceptive to institutional religion as it presented itself in the nineteenth-century South.

Recent works by Francis Bremer, in his studies in American and English Puritanism, and Elizabeth Clark, in her research with the Origenist controversy, remind historians that in addition to looking for religious traditions where there are recognized religious institutions such as organized churches, it is also important to look for friendships, relationships, and associations that are oftentimes submerged within other institutional forms.[3] Both Bremer and Clark invoke "network" paradigms recently asserted by social scientists and anthropologists J. Clyde Mitchell and Jeremy Boissevain in their respective studies to explain the action and behavior of individuals and groups.[4] For Clark, this means that network analysis "makes probable that an individual's actions are as strongly conditioned by relationships with others in the network as by the ideas that constitute the alleged matter at hand (the Origenist controversy)."[5] For Bremer, such social constructions make it imperative for researchers to identify the "range of a person's friends" who provide the "sources of social influence on the person's behavior and beliefs."[6]

By looking at benevolent societies, lay meetings, professional and civic activity, ecumenical interchange, intellectual forums, business partnerships, literary correspondence, friendships, and other associations in which Southern Unitarians were engaged with other Southerners on a daily basis, one sees a much greater Unitarian presence than has been previously recognized. Hidden just below the surface of organized religion in the South was an "invisible institution" not unlike Franklin Frazier's Black Church, a nebulous network of liberal faith that represented a sustained and continued strand of Enlightenment religious rationalism alongside and within an increasingly evangelical culture—so much so that there were, in fact, two invisible religious institutions in the antebellum South, one in the slave quarters and the other in the urban landscape of Southern towns. Whereas slave preachers rediscovered in music and bodily movement and in themes of suffering a vibrant Christian community, Unitarians witnessed the simple spiritual truth that reason and belief are one unified whole. The two invisible churches had a profound influence on Christianity in the South—one from the lowest rungs of the social order and the other from a privileged position in the urban South—and for both, an influence powerfully out of proportion to their institutional strength.

Southern Unitarians who found themselves without a church building for worship often decided that the most practical option for them was to duck into the more orthodox denominations to better ride out the "evangelical storm." They may not have had a church building with a Unitarian title to call home, but they were able to practice their "old and primitive faith" in local Southern churches that were more tolerant of their theology and with whom they had more in common than their Northern coreligionists. For this reason, it is impossible to determine the number of Unitarians in the South, but it is very safe to conclude that their numbers were much greater than historians have previously recognized.

Accounts by individual Unitarians and even orthodox clergy shed new light on the old "accepted" ideas of decline. They affirm the ease with which Southern Unitarians could move about within orthodoxy, demonstrate the perceived threat that Unitarianism continued to pose to orthodoxy throughout the antebellum period, discredit the notion that Unitarians ceased to exist or were inactive after their churches closed their doors, and reveal that Southern Unitarians existed in those areas in which there never were Unitarian churches. Instead of relying on a count of church steeples to gauge numbers, this project blurs the lines between Southern Unitarianism and orthodoxy by demonstrating how their theologies coexisted and intertwined, assesses the impetus behind and the scope of Southern Unitarian reform, and explores some of the reasons Southern Unitarianism, if not going completely "underground," at least went "behind closed doors" of urban orthodoxy.

From the very beginning as evangelical attacks increased and became more vocal, Southern Unitarians began developing less visible forms of Unitarian life alongside the "visible" institution of the church. Just below the surface of institutional religion, Southern Unitarians embarked on literary careers and endeavors, organized tract societies and intellectual forums, joined benevolent reform movements and voluntary associations, and assumed leadership roles in both civic and professional organizations. In doing so, they forged a place within Southern orthodoxy in which other Southerners would join, and in the process created a haven for retreat for themselves in the event of institutional decline. By the end of the antebellum period, Southern Unitarians had contributed to the rationality of the Southern faith.

Enlightenment religion had a formidable influence on nineteenth-century Southerners both in and out of Unitarian circles well after the evangelical waves were unleashed at Cane Ridge, Kentucky, in 1801, moving from the western backcountries east to the older colonial seaboard establishments. Facing the rising tide of "rural" evangelicalism, urban areas across the South became fortresses of "rationality." Holifield again reminds us, "[A]n influential group of Southern theologians [in towns across the South] . . . inherited, modified, and propagated 'rational orthodoxy'" and "reassure[d] men and women that they were reasonable people living in a reasonable world."[7] But this rationality did not eclipse the "heartfelt" nature of evangelicalism, nor did the high emotionalism of evangelicalism outcry the "rationality" of enlightened religious norms. Southern ministers and theologians of the antebellum period were heirs to both traditions and prudently filtered out the more radical elements of both camps, creating a synthesis of sorts that at its foundation proved more rational than emotional in nature. Southern clergymen believed that rationality should pervade human existence and asserted that reason was the formal criterion even of revelation. According to Holifield, for prominent urban clergy, "theology seemed both a reasonable and a rational enterprise, designed to commend Christian faith to an expanding class of educated and aspiring Southerners."[8]

Though the Anglican Church in the South was hit hard during the disestablishment process of the late eighteenth and early nineteenth centuries, it and the more urban units of the Unitarians and the Presbyterians, particularly, became major vehicles for Enlightenment influence well into the antebellum period. During the colonial period, the Presbyterian Church had gained a respectability that even the Anglican Church conceded and recognized. Richard Rankin concludes that "these concessions were also tacit recognition that Presbyterians were more socially acceptable to the Anglicans than any other denomination."[9] During the antebellum period, even though it lost numbers to Methodists and Baptists, the respectability and the influence of the Presbyterian Church upon Southern orthodoxy in general continued as figures such as James Henley Thornwell and Robert Lewis Dabney came to dominate the religious and intellectual landscape of the would-be Confederate States working diligently to expose and repudiate the errors of Enlightenment Deism and Skepticism. And yet, though the Presbyterian Church was hit harder by evangelical influences than the Episcopal and Unitarian Churches, it nonetheless kept, nurtured, and defended religious rationalism as the foundation of its orthodoxy.

Throughout many towns and cities of the South there existed a core of rational Christianity that was shared by Unitarians and Protestants alike. This core allowed for a certain fluidity and similarity of thought between these seemingly antagonistic groups that can today be seen as orthodox, despite the then frequent cries between them of "Atheist" and "Socinian." While the polemics between Southern Unitarians and the "orthodox" community raged early on, these labels could not stick for long, particularly in larger Southern cities such as Charleston and New Orleans, as the educated classes saw more similarities than differences in their theological, political, and cultural outlooks and their epistemological assumptions.

This was true of the Episcopal Church in the South especially during the entire antebellum period. Not only did Unitarian congregations in the South frequently look to Episcopal seminaries (not to mention Anglican) and churches for clergy for their pulpits, they also frequently found sympathizers and future members among their ranks. The Episcopal and the Unitarian churches were perhaps the least touched theologically, socially, and politically by evangelical influences and many Episcopalians rented pews in the Unitarian churches to attend when convenient and when they so desired. Many urban Episcopal laity and clergy associated and debated with their Unitarian counterparts on a regular and often daily basis. Samuel Gilman for a while spent an hour every morning with Jasper Adams, Episcopal president of Charleston College, reading German biblical criticism. They were not alone. Many of the South's educated elite often flirted with the Southern version of Unitarianism and in the process helped to blur the lines between what constituted orthodoxy and what did not. Louisa and David McCord in Columbia, South Carolina, and judge and United States Representative Robert Raymond Reid in Georgia were Unitarians while William Walker in Nashville, Tennessee, flirted with Unitarianism. While John C. Calhoun and William H. Crawford, Democratic-Republican Presidential nominee from Georgia, espoused Unitarian views, they did not necessarily flaunt them either. Nevertheless, their theological positions did help to assuage the initial hostilities and elevate the liberal faith out of the trenches. Samuel Gilman and other Southern Unitarians took over from there. Dr. Gilman's characteristic equanimity, not to mention literary eloquence, endeared him to both national and Southern circles. Likewise, in New Orleans Theodore Clapp gained great respect and admiration from both the citizens of the city and those well beyond its limits. In what came to be known as the "Strangers' Church," Dr. Clapp had led a sizable congregation made up of former Presbyterians, Universalists, German Unitarians, and New Englanders, with a gallery overhead that could seat up to four hundred "strangers" and visitors to the Crescent City. According to Dr. Benjamin Morgan Palmer, Presbyterian minister in New Orleans and Columbia, "The social and amiable qualities of Mr. Clapp endeared him greatly as a man . . . the large majority of his hearers could not appreciate this clamor about doctrine and many of the truly pious . . . were disposed to sympathize with him as one unkindly persecuted."[10] Thornwell described Gilman as having "a genial sympathy with his kind, a spirit full of love to all that God has made beautiful . . . pure, gentle, confiding, shrinking from the very thought of inflicting gratuitous pain, these qualities are everywhere so conspicuous, that one must not be told, why the circles of Dr. Gilman's intimacy are so devoted to their pastor and friend." Though they may have been small in number, from the orthodox perspective Southern Unitarians were disconcertingly respectable.

Holifield concludes that Unitarians and the orthodox, in their common devotion to what he calls the "understanding" of Scottish Common Sense Realism, were also "committed to shared assumptions that shaped their views of theology." Holifield argues that "town orthodox clergy's presuppositions about rationality and theology were much closer to Unitarian positions than they could have comfortably acknowledged."[11] The very presence of the "nearly twenty [local supply] ministers" in Gilman's Charleston pulpit and the "most friendly relations" that they enjoyed among themselves suggest the level of comfort that town theologians were willing to and did acknowledge with Southern Unitarians.

Southern liberals like Samuel Gilman and Southern conservatives like James Henley Thornwell and Robert Lewis Dabney were indebted to Scottish Common Sense Realism for offering a broad foundation on which to reconcile some of their differences and in essence share a common Southern Christian rationalism. Indeed, according to one biographer of Dabney, Scottish Common Sense philosophy encouraged a rationalistic tendency in him that was never fully reconciled to the authority of Scripture.[12] Scottish Common Sense Realism was largely instrumental in precipitating a correspondence between Gilman and Thornwell in the late 1850s that demonstrated both mutual respect between them and shared theological assumptions and positions. As newly appointed editor of the *Southern Quarterly Review*, Thornwell solicited from Gilman articles on Thomas Brown, perhaps the most Idealist of the Common Sense Philosophers at Edinburgh, and asked for his comments and criticisms on an article Thornwell had written on miracles. Similarly, Thornwell also asked for articles from Dr. Samuel Dickson, a prominent member of Gilman's congregation in Charleston.[13]

Along with an enlightened sense of "understanding" and toleration, Southern Unitarians steadfastly maintained as paramount the sanctity of individual conscience in matters of religion and politics. "Liberal Christianity," Gilman declared, "aims to secure more and more the respect and tenderness of the church towards individual conscience, instead of crushing and absorbing the conscience of the individual in the will and despotism of the church."[14] It is for this reason that Southern Unitarians seldom if ever initiated theological attacks upon the "orthodox" circles, but rather waited until criticism demanded a response, which was defensive rather than offensive in nature. Because they chose to emphasize theological agreement rather than discord, Southern Unitarians were able to rise above what often appeared as petty spatting. Southern Unitarians strove for the "purity" of primitive Christianity, emphasized the rationality of the Christian faith, insisted on a "broad and liberal" foundation that minimized doctrinal and denominational differences, worked tirelessly for ecumenical accord, and diligently sought to "render unto Caesar" by keeping the element of politics out of the pulpit.

Theirs was a benign Christian rationalism that was, much like Thornwell's description of Gilman, "pure," "gentle," and "confiding." As part of the Southern religious landscape, Southern Unitarianism remained dedicated to the Southern way of life and its political economy, and within the boundaries then set for its theological standards. When Southern Unitarians saw Northern Unitarianism lapse into "sensual philosophy," Transcendentalism, and "Puritan Fanaticism," they recommitted themselves to the ideals of first-generation American Unitarianism. Sharing an Arian Christology and an Arminian view of human nature with many other urban Southern Christians, Unitarians felt that outside attacks and "Deist" or "Socinian" labels grossly misrepresented their faith and their theological positions. Paul K. Conkin has recently argued that "what these labels too easily conceal and what critics like to downplay is that all the early Unitarian ministers were avowed, serious, conscientious Christians who simply wanted to reform and purify the church." They believed that the Bible was the Word of God and while they rejected the triune God, they "continued to baptize in the name of the Father, the Son, and the Holy Spirit."[15]

Because of its emphasis on the sanctity of individual conscience, the Unitarian denomination as a whole theoretically tended to be more egalitarian than any other. In practice, however, in both the North and the South, most of its members were urban professionals, members of the higher middle to upper class, and seldom came from the lower classes. Compelled by a democratic theology without a full democratic constituency, Unitarians in the North and the South sought social reforms in many areas of American life and were the pioneers of benevolent reform in the nineteenth century. Yet, there was a stark difference between them, not only in terms of what they sought to change and how they went about implementing change, but also, and perhaps most important, in why they sought change in the first place. Unlike their Northern coreligionists, Southern Unitarians sought reform in their own communities, not beyond, and seldom used the pulpit as a political tree stump. For these Southerners, the venue of choice for social change came by way of benevolent societies and social interaction with prominent Southerners outside of their own ecclesiastical spheres. Because of their high regard for individual conscience, Southern Unitarians never sought to put the stamp of denominational approval on any of their reforms.

For Southern Unitarians, in addition to the written word provided by newspapers, journals, and book and tract societies, social reform demonstrated their religious convictions and gave their otherwise "invisible" faith a visible face that was decidedly Southern. Southern Unitarians worked for many reforms in the South, but their choices for reform, like the organizations and societies they chose to work for reform in, reflected their fundamental commitment to the Southern way of life and the Southern world view. Southern Unitarians attacked what they saw were the isolating and subjective tendencies of industrial capitalism and demonstrated their commitment to a divinely sanctioned, socially responsible, hierarchical world.[16]

While most Southerners believed that religion was a matter of personal conscience and wanted to keep the elements of church and state separate, evangelicals on the other hand tended to want an integration of piety, morality, and society.[17] It was perhaps this difference more than any other that first made the confrontation between Unitarians and evangelicals poignant and oftentimes abrasive. And yet, the element of toleration inherent in Enlightenment religion, made even more so by latitudinarianism and Scottish Common Sense Realism, dictated accommodation, and Southerners of conservative and "rational" orientation found themselves in a continued and ever-present dialogue with evangelicals.[18] While "conservatives" gleaned and filtered out portions of evangelicalism to integrate into their "religious rationalism," evangelicals in turn moderated their more extreme elements to better fit in with the conservative religio-political core of Southern orthodoxy. By the end of the antebellum period, Southern orthodoxy and Southern Unitarians in general still retained the latitudinarian/Jeffersonian emphasis on separation of church and state (though both kept, in varying degrees, opposition against the strict separation of society from religion) even during their collaboration with evangelicals.

Southern Unitarians believed that Northern Unitarians had fallen victim to the "fanaticism" they themselves had originally and initially disdained, particularly the fanaticism associated with "revivalistic" evangelicalism and the blurred line it developed between church and state. Southern Unitarians believed that a great change had taken place within Northern Unitarian ranks. While they themselves were used to and had long advocated a minimization of denominational differences with other Southern clergy and laity, they took pride in the belief that they had worked for it through a more rational approach of "understanding" with Southern orthodoxy, never at an emotionally heightened revival meeting.

For Southern Unitarians, the theological attacks they had endured earlier from Southern orthodoxy did not compare with what they deemed the "Puritan fanaticism" of Northern Unitarians. While attacks by evangelicals prompted Southern Unitarians to develop "invisible" outlets for their faith alongside the visible institution of the church, Southern Unitarians blamed their institutional decline not on evangelicals, but on their Northern coreligionists. Herbert C. Peabody in Mobile declared, "The curse of abolition and Puritan preaching hangs over us—'and will not die down.'"[19] Throughout the antebellum years, Southern Unitarians consistently demonstrated their theological and cultural independence from the North. Though sharing much with their Northern coreligionists, Southern Unitarians took great strides to disassociate themselves from the American Unitarian Association and to align themselves with Southern orthodoxy. Doing this was not easy, particularly when many within Southern orthodoxy continued to erroneously label them "Deists" and associate them with the Northern antislavery cause. But Southern Unitarians were able to do so by assuming a lower profile within Southern ecclesiology, declaring their independence from Northern Unitarians, and developing invisible relationships that tied them more intricately to Southern orthodoxy than to Northern coreligionists. As these invisible relationships matured and their theology developed, Southern Unitarians recognized the stark differences that lay between their religion and that of their Northern counterparts.

It is within this context of Enlightenment-evangelical conflict and Northern and Southern Unitarian tension that the first elements of Unitarianism in the South were planted. Once planted they evolved, and then gradually were transformed from the radical Socinianism, Jeffersonian Deism, and Enlightenment Skepticism of the Revolutionary period to the more moderate Unitarianism of the antebellum period. By the time the Charleston church formally broke from the American Unitarian Association in 1857, Unitarianism in the South had evolved into an invisible "subterranean" network of benevolent societies, lay meetings, professional and civic activity, ecumenical interchange, intellectual forums, business partnerships, literary correspondences and publications, friendships, and associations. In all of these relationships, Southern Unitarianism represented a sustained and continued strand of Enlightenment religious rationalism alongside and within an increasingly evangelical culture.

ONE • A Declaration of Independence

"An aged tree stands as a witness upon the field of history," declared Dr. Orville Dewey in August 1856 to the growing crowd gathered under the Great Elm, a tree that had graced the townscape of Sheffield, Massachusetts, for nearly a century. "Could this venerable Elm tell us what has passed beneath it," he continued, "we should know more than history can teach us now." The crowd grew in both number and noise as the Unitarian minister strained his voice to address the local citizens as they jostled one another to find suitable places for shade and stance beneath the large umbrageous branches of that great arbor. "I have been asked to say something at this year's Anniversary of our 'Old Elm Tree Association,' in a manner somewhat more formal, than the free and easy interchange of thought, which we have had on former occasions," Dr. Dewey exclaimed. "I feel something as a learned professor did, when once presiding at a Literary Festival, who, on being desired to bring forward the set toasts, said, 'he did not want to interrupt the hilarity of the occasion.'"[1]

By that standard, Dr. Orville Dewey failed miserably that day for he got few laughs from the Sheffield crowd, and fewer to none from those Southerners who read his speech in both newspaper and pamphlet form several weeks later. Indeed, many Southerners viewed Dewey's remarks as no laughing matter at all, for he had toured the Southern states on numerous occasions, made many friends wherever he went, and claimed to be "much interested in society there, and strongly attached to it."[2] One Southerner responded, "The occasion was too alluring—the exciting subject, the sympathetic audience, the obvious expectation produced by your sojourn for two winters in the very heart of Southern society. . . . Whatever admiration . . . your Elm Tree oration . . . may have produced in Massachusetts, [it] has aroused among us no other sentiment than aversion and disgust."[3]

This sense of "aversion" and "disgust" was perhaps no more poignant nor was the breach any wider than that between Dr. Dewey and the members of the Unitarian church in Charleston, not only the oldest establishment of its kind in the South, but also one of two remaining Unitarian congregations still in existence in the late 1850s in the would-be Confederate States. This congregation had understandably felt a close bond to many of the Unitarian clergy in the North, particularly during the early period of its existence when the waves of "Trinitarian" orthodoxy had beat against its shores with fervor and force. Not only were Dewey and Charleston Unitarians liberal coreligionists, but they had also shared a mutual respect, admiration, and correspondence during much of the antebellum period. Dr. Dewey had traveled among them, stayed in their homes, taken meals with their families, and preached in their pulpit on numerous occasions. Many years later, looking back on his last visit to the South, Dr. Dewey remembered, "A part of the winter of 1856–1857 I passed with my family at Charleston, S.C. I had been there the spring before, and made very agreeable acquaintance with the people. My reception, both in public and in private, was as kindly and hospitable as I could desire."[4] The Charleston congregation had been equally impressed with Dr. Dewey's "genius" and "eloquence." One member of the congregation fondly recalled, "We opened for him our hearts and our homes. His sojourn with us only tended to strengthen the favorable impression, which his talents had already made . . . When he repeated his visit, we felt the return of a friend, and received him as such."[5]

But to this Charleston congregation, the Elm Tree Oration in Sheffield in late summer 1856 drastically severed the cords of mutual affection and split the religious bonds that had tied Dewey to this Southern "family." Obviously disappointed himself, Dewey later recalled the occasion that had caused the breach. "I made some observations . . . that dashed nearly all my agreeable relations with Charleston. I am not a person to regard such a breach with indifference: it pained me deeply. My only comfort was, that what I said was honestly said."[6] The Unitarian congregation understood his attempt at honesty and "sincerity," but were still at a loss as to his omission of "proper regard . . . for [their] own reputation" and his commission of wrongful "slander." For them his speech warranted no other recourse than rebuke.

> The course which Dr. DEWEY has pursued since his last visit to us precludes all possibility, as we must confess it eradicates all desire on our part, either of seeing or hearing him again. . . . His motives may have been pure; he may have believed what he asserted, and in charity we would, if possible, accord to him the virtue of sincerity. A proper regard, however, for our own reputation, and a correct indignation at a statement, which, however sincerely believed by its author, would nevertheless tend to slander us in the eyes of the civilized world; coming, too, from an authority we had learned to respect, yea, even to love—irresistibly compels us to lift up our voice in rebuke of such unkind and unfriendly treatment.[7]

But in the course of lifting up their voices in rebuke and disdain, the congregation went a step further and took measures that would have great significance in American religious and ecclesiastical history. On Sunday, August 9, 1857, a year after Dr. Dewey's Elm Tree Oration, the managers of the Unitarian Book and Tract Society, on behalf of the Unitarian Church of Charleston, issued a lengthy statement in their thirty-sixth *Annual Report* that constituted a milestone in the history of the Unitarian denomination as a whole. On this date, "in common with almost all other denominations of Southern Christians," the Unitarian Church of Charleston, one of the last remnants of denominational unity in the South, formally declared its independence and split American Unitarianism into separate sectional entities.

> The course pursued by a large majority of our Unitarian brethren at the North . . . has been such, that, to protect ourselves in the quiet enjoyment of our domestic rights, we find it expedient to forego the use of most of their religious publications, and the irksomeness of this course (an alternative which, in common with almost all other denominations of Southern Christians, we have been compelled to adopt) is much enhanced because of our very isolated position. We say this rather in sorrow than in anger; but neither the fanaticism of the North, nor the averted looks of those around us, shall deter us from maintaining our old and

primitive faith . . . the liberal spirit that has distinguished our members, and has never failed to meet every demand heretofore made upon it . . . we surely will not withhold a few dollars, when needed to maintain our independence as a Southern congregation of "liberal Christians."[8]

Five years earlier, in 1852, Unitarian congregations in the border states, in Louisville, Kentucky; Wheeling, Virginia; and St. Louis, Missouri, were absorbed into the Western Unitarian Conference. At the annual meeting of that Conference in Alton, Illinois, in 1857, representatives from these congregations withdrew from the Conference, further sealing the denominational split. In 1865, after the war, with the exception of Louisville, Washington, and Baltimore, no other Southern congregation sent representatives to the newly established National Conference of Unitarian Churches.[9] Unitarians in Charleston, Richmond, Augusta, Savannah, Mobile, and New Orleans, and others scattered throughout the South, had spent years developing an intricate network of relationships with other Southerners and nurturing a Southern Unitarian faith that was very different from that of the "Harvard moralists." It would take more than the cease-fire at Appomattox to reconcile these differences.

The topic that Dr. Dewey pursued under the Great Elm in Sheffield in 1856 was, of course, abolition, and more specifically, immediate abolition. Both sides, Dewey and Southern Unitarians, charged the other with changing their former positions on this issue, thus causing the split. Dewey, a self-proclaimed moderate on the abolition question, who once argued that "mutual recrimination will not settle it: calm reason, candour, mutual respect and brotherly kindness must come into this controversy, or it bodes a woeful issue,"[10] in 1856 charged that "it is not I who have changed, but they. When they say 'make slavery a national institution; make the compact of the Constitution carry it into all the territories; cover it with the national aegis; set it up as part of our great republican profession; stamp on our flag, and our shield, and our escutcheon, the emblem of human slavery;' I say, no, never; God forbid!"[11]

Not too surprisingly, Southern Unitarians reacted strongly to what they saw as Dewey's misplacement of "calm reason, candour, and mutual respect," for these were not only crucial elements in the theology they shared with their Northern coreligionists, but also the foundation by which both sides had previously approached this question politically. Southern Unitarians accordingly lamented the change they felt Dewey had undergone: "We had hoped that the apparently sound and well-balanced mind of our quondam guest would have proved capable of resisting the infection . . . we are forced to believe, from his otherwise unaccountable treatment of those whom he had taught to regard him as their friend, that he, too, has fallen a victim to the prevailing monomania, and will hereafter surrender himself into the hands of the designing and licentious party spirit of Northern fanaticism."[12]

The hesitation here in bringing forth the topic of Orville Dewey's Elm Tree Oration lies not in a clandestine attempt to skirt the issue, but rather is intended to relegate the subject to its proper historical context. It would of course be easy to presume, based on the statements given so far, that abolition was the central cause in the breach between the Northern and Southern Unitarians. This in fact is only half true. A proper reading of the history of Southern Unitarianism will show that while immediate abolitionism was certainly a formidable issue in the split between Northern and Southern Unitarians, it was actually less the cause and more the occasion by which these Southern liberals decided to claim their independence, a position many realized they had been enjoying *de facto* for many years. Dewey's remarks merely called into focus the deep theological, moral, social, organizational, and political issues that had long divided the two regional strains of American Unitarianism.

Today, the "aged tree" no longer stands in that "frontier town" in southwestern Massachusetts. The orator has died, the crowd has dispersed, the controversial issue has subsided, and the split within the Unitarian denomination as a whole has been forgotten, ignored, or relegated to the insignificant. The claim of independence by Southern Unitarians has lost its "witness upon the field of history," and accordingly, nineteenth-century Unitarianism continues to be portrayed not only as a New England phenomenon, but also as one of the last bastions of denominational unity on the eve of the War Between the States. While a few histories of the Unitarian churches in the South have been written, none have dealt at length and in the aggregate with the distinctions that would, in the antebellum period, define American Unitarianism fundamentally in sectional terms.[13] Sydney Ahlstrom, in his monumental *A Religious History of the American People*, erroneously concludes not only that the Unitarians escaped "division chiefly because they did not have a constituency in both regions," but also that as a church that "contributed powerfully to the antislavery movement . . . they [Unitarians] became increasingly unified in their witness."[14] Nineteenth-century Southern Unitarians beg for their opportunity to differ.

Not too surprisingly, recent nineteenth-century Unitarian scholarship, an area that has received significant attention in both United States and American religious historiography alike, has centered its scope almost exclusively on the more fertile New England soil with only a rare nod to the sand or clay of the South. Daniel Walker Howe, Douglas C. Stange, and Conrad Wright, perhaps the most prominent names in this body of literature, have given token recognition to Southern Unitarians in journal articles or book paragraphs, but the thrust of their work still continues to follow Ahlstrom's lead in portraying nineteenth-century Unitarianism not as a denomination with two very different and distinct histories, as in truth it is, but rather as a New England phenomenon with a few Boston outposts in the South and West for its transplanted merchants to have a place to worship.

Historians have forgotten that *English* Unitarianism, especially the writings and activities of Joseph Priestley, was responsible for the very first implantation of Unitarianism in America. Priestley established in Philadelphia what Earl Morse Wilbur declares as "the first permanent Unitarian church in America . . . that is the first to be permanently established, and openly avowing the Unitarian name." Likewise, Priestley's writings and discourses were instrumental in pushing former Anglicans at King's Chapel in Boston toward the Unitarian faith.[15] While these churches are notable in and of themselves, Priestley's Unitarianism also had a direct influence upon the Charleston congregation, which for all intents and purposes became Unitarian in 1817 and formally took that name in its title in 1832.

As early as 1952, Raymond Adams, commemorating the one-hundredth anniversary of the 1852 dedication of the magnificent Gothic-style Unitarian church in Charleston, recognized the significant influence of English Unitarianism upon that Southern congregation. Adams saw in the Charleston church the best example in all of America of how English Unitarianism developed in the United States. To a theretofore unresponsive audience, Adams declared:

> Samuel Gilman . . . found no such [New England] Unitarianism here when he came in 1819. He found here a genuine Unitarianism from another source, the source Franklin and Jefferson knew, the non–New England stream of Unitarianism that has been neglected in our histories but that flowed strongly and early in the Middle States and in the South. We who live in the South and who nowadays rejoice in the renewed strength of liberal religion in these Southeastern states need to know something about this other tradition. And if we will consider the congregation Gilman came to in 1819 and trace its background to its source, we shall have a better chart than most for tracing this other Unitarianism. Indeed, we have in the background of this Charleston church perhaps the very best story in all America of the way Unitarianism sometimes came to this country from Old England with little or nothing of New England about it.[16]

Nevertheless, over the course of the antebellum period, New England Unitarianism did have an influence on the Charleston congregation, just not the one they had hoped for.

TWO • The Enlightened Journey
The Origins of Southern Unitarianism

Unitarianism made inroads in the South from three very different sources. The first source was English Unitarianism as represented by the theology of Joseph Priestley. The second was an indigenous Arminianism within Southern orthodoxy, which for years had been nurtured by the moderating tendencies of Scottish Common Sense Realism and Anglican latitudinarianism. The third and final source was New England Unitarianism. Whereas Northern Unitarianism (with the exception of King's Chapel in Boston and the Unitarian Society in Philadelphia) was a direct descendant of New England Puritanism, Southern Unitarianism at its center in Charleston was produced by the implantation of English Unitarianism in a soil already occupied by a native liberal Arminianism imbedded within Southern orthodoxy. Over the years, Southern Unitarians reformed and neutralized the more radical elements of English Unitarianism and created a core of "rational Christianity" that many within Southern orthodoxy embraced and supported. The Southern Unitarian faith was broad and liberal at its foundation, it strove for the purity of Christian truths, it insisted on the rationality of the Christian faith, and it sought to minimize doctrinal differences within the Protestant church. In the spirit of ecumenicism and with a shared core of "rational Christianity," Southern Unitarians and Southern orthodoxy alike often resisted and checked the mission work of Northern Unitarians on Southern soil. While Southern Unitarians welcomed Northern missionaries and literary and theological works from the American Unitarian Association in Boston, they did so on their own terms, censoring, rejecting, and returning on a regular basis those items and ministers that were not congruent with the Southern brand of liberal faith. It is not surprising then that of the three, the New England source of Unitarianism was the least influential in the South.

The seed of English Unitarianism was first planted in the South in Raleigh, North Carolina, by Joseph Gales, close and lifelong friend of the English Unitarian Joseph Priestley. From there it was scattered to Washington, D.C., where Gales, his son, Joseph Gales, Jr., and Robert Little, another English Unitarian and friend of Priestley, organized the First Unitarian Church in the capital city.[1] From Raleigh the English seed was carried on the back of Scottish Common Sense philosophy to Charleston, where it flourished within the first Unitarian church organized in the South. From Charleston, the English seed and the Unitarianism it helped to produce blossomed into churches in Savannah and Augusta, Georgia, and from there spread to Mobile, Alabama, all the while influencing individual Unitarians throughout the South during the entire antebellum period. No other church in the South was as successful in influence, in missionary activity, and in maintaining a theological and intellectual standard for Southern Unitarianism as the Charleston church.

ENGLISH UNITARIANISM

Joseph Priestley and the Spread of English Unitarianism in America

Joseph Priestley was born near Leeds, England, in 1733 and at an early age took up Latin and Greek at Daventry, a dissenting academy, where he committed himself to the Christian ministry under the auspices of a liberal education. After several years of disappointing parish assignments and teaching and tutoring in some of England's chief dissenting academies, Priestley moved closer to home in 1867, back to Leeds, where his wife, Mary, in failing health, could have better medical attention. In Leeds, as the minister of the Mill Hill congregation, Priestley openly embraced Socinianism. Although faced with opposition from many in the congregation, he remained minister there for almost five and a half years. In December 1772, he became librarian to Lord Shelburne, and while in Leeds, Priestley, along with Theophilus Lindsey, a lifelong friend and patron, helped to establish a small British Unitarian movement. All the while he dabbled in scientific experiments, especially electricity, under the guidance and direction of another friend, the by then famous Benjamin Franklin. Priestley's scientific achievements and religious independence endeared him to a small circle of English and American radicals (including Franklin and the dissenting minister Richard Price) who met in London yearly and who welcomed him into their fold. Priestley continued his experiments and soon gained world renown, especially for his work involving the separation of carbon dioxide as well as for the isolation of what is now known as oxygen.[2]

In 1781, Priestley moved to Birmingham to become pastor of the largest dissenting congregation in England. A year later, he published perhaps his most influential and controversial religious treatise, *An History of the Corruptions of Christianity*. This publication, combined with his support for the American Revolution and the early stages of the French Revolution, provoked a violent response from officially organized mobs in Birmingham. On Bastille Day 1791, his house, his books, his church, and his laboratory, virtually his entire life's work, were burned. Under the danger of arrest and in the midst of political tension, Priestley and his wife, longing for greater freedom, decided to emigrate to America in 1794. They were enthusiastically greeted in New York as martyrs to the cause of liberty and welcomed by Governor Clinton and the Bishop of New York.[3]

Though welcomed warmly, Priestley was not invited to preach. Obviously disappointed, he soon decided to move to Philadelphia, where he received a warm welcome and a testimonial from David Rittenhouse, president of the American Philosophical Society. But Priestley did not like the political distractions of Philadelphia, then the nation's capital, and in July 1794 decided to join his son at Northumberland, Pennsylvania, where he would spend the remainder of his life. In 1801 his health began to fail, but he was able to continue writing, up until an hour before his death. He died in Northumberland on February 6, 1804.[4]

When Priestley arrived in Pennsylvania, he was invited to teach chemistry at several Philadelphia colleges, but declined. Instead he built a residence and a laboratory, hoping to settle and "pursue his favorite calling as a preacher, and his favorite recreation as a chemist." In 1795, during three months in Philadelphia, he delivered twelve lectures on the

"Evidences of Christianity" and a sermon on Unitarianism to large audiences, including many members of Congress.

While in town, Priestley met regularly with other English radicals who had also emigrated and who shared his religious views. In the summer of 1796, fourteen English Unitarians met and formed the First Society of Unitarian Christians in Philadelphia. The group included Priestley, Joseph Gales, John Vaughan, from a prominent Unitarian family in England and America, and Ralph Eddowes. Eddowes, a former pupil of Priestley who would later return to England and become a Member of Parliament, was a leading spirit of the group.

When Priestley was not in town, the members conducted services as readers. After an initial setback from a yellow fever epidemic, the growing congregation agreed to call William Christie as minister. Christie was a Unitarian minister from Glasgow who had taught school for a while in Winchester, Virginia, before following Priestley to Northumberland. After a few years Christie broke off from the group and established his own short-lived church because he feared that the members had more power than the minister. Eddowes assumed pastoral responsibilities until 1825, when, after twenty-nine years of lay preaching, a minister was settled. In 1813, a church building had been erected with English aid, and according to Earl Morse Wilbur, this was the "first church building bearing the name Unitarian to be erected in America."[5]

Influenced by the new, "mechanistic" science of Isaac Newton, Priestley believed in an essential universal "necessity," a necessity completely consistent with God's providence. In his *An History of the Corruptions of Christianity* (1782), Priestley asserted the workings of God's providence, believing, with an optimism that never left him, that God, the Supreme Governor of the Universe, was preparing the way for a great reformation already in progress. In this reformation God himself would play an active part in the reemergence of early pristine Christianity, a Christianity uncorrupted by the trappings that had enveloped the faith over the centuries. Priestley's *Corruptions of Christianity* had a profound impact on the religious thought of Thomas Jefferson especially, who became a Deist Unitarian.

Priestley began *Corruptions of Christianity* with what he believed was the greatest corruption, Christian polytheism, or Trinitarianism. He rested all doctrines on one essential truth—the complete unity of God —a doctrine anticipated by the Polish reformer, Faustus Socinius. Paul Conkin argues that "Priestley believed that this monotheism was the most important article of faith in both the Old and the New Testaments, an article always affirmed by Jesus . . . who always identified himself as the son of man."[6] For Priestley, Jesus was in all respects a man and nothing more than a man.

Priestley believed that Jesus, as the promised Messiah, although he did not have a divine nature, did have a special mission. His mission was to clarify what God expects of human beings and to demonstrate both what salvation requires and the level of obedience God demands, even to the point of martyrdom. According to the mission, Jesus personified what God promises, namely a resurrection to eternal life for those who imitate his life. But in arguing for the resurrection, Priestley rejected the doctrine of the atonement, the belief that Jesus' death was a sacrifice necessary to cancel the inherent sinfulness of humanity. He did this several ways. First, he argued for the eternal and inherent benevolence of God. Second, he rejected the doctrine of original sin and human depravity, and third, he denied the belief in separable souls, arguing that human beings, including Jesus, were holistic beings whose minds, souls, and bodies could not be separated, even at the point of death. By denying a separable soul, Priestley, like Thomas Hobbes before him, was not only able to reject incarnation, which allowed Christ to assume a human body, but he was also able to deny that any of the purported saints in the Catholic tradition, including Mary, could intercede with God in behalf of living human beings because they were fully and holistically dead in the ground. Only Christ could do so, not out of any inherent divine powers of resurrection, but because God had raised him from the dead and reconstituted him as a person.[7]

Not all English Unitarians were as radical in their Christological views as Priestley. Coming from a decidedly "dissenting" tradition and without the restraints of an established church, Priestley really stood outside the center of English Unitarianism as it was produced by latitudinarianism within the Anglican establishment. Nevertheless, because of his unique position as a political refugee from the English government and because of his subsequent religious writing in the United States, he stood as the American representative of English Unitarianism in all its varying degrees and complexities. Southern Unitarians, heirs to Priestley's liberal seed, accepted Priestley's message of "dissent" and relied on the latitudinarian emphasis upon the separation of church and state, but rejected any Deist notions. Along with other first-generation Unitarians, including those in the North, Southern Unitarians moved toward the more moderate Arian Christological position.

Thomas Jefferson and the Ideal of Separation of Church and State

Because of its advocacy for toleration, Enlightenment religion in general was tied inextricably to political issues. For Southerners especially, religion was an issue of conscience untouchable by the state; it was an individual matter beyond the government's interest. The advocacy of separation of church and state by figures such as George Washington and Thomas Jefferson, both nominally Anglican and both products of Anglican latitudinarianism and English Unitarianism, and James Madison, more a product of Scottish Common Sense Realism, had a profound influence on the religious and political landscape of the newly formed American Union in general, and its Southern section in particular.

Though nominally Anglican, Thomas Jefferson was theologically a Deist Unitarian. Priestley's charge that Hellenistic theologians had "Platonized" and corrupted primitive Christianity struck a chord with Jefferson, who read Priestley's books repeatedly. For Jefferson, it confirmed his conviction that the "incomprehensible jargon" and "artificial scaffolding" of Greek philosophy stood in the way of true discipleship. Jefferson took this "uncorrupted" theology in the direction of Deism, believing that by discarding the Platonic "vagaries" that lay behind such absurd doctrines as the Trinity, the virgin birth, and the resurrection, one could find the true historical Jesus.

But Jefferson's faith has too often been associated with the New England Unitarian impulse. Early on, he himself often aligned and corresponded with New England Unitarians. Yet, he was perhaps too sanguine about the differences between his brand of Unitarianism and that of New England. He did urge Harvard Unitarians to venture southward and predicted that the movement would sweep the country: "Missionaries from Cambridge would soon be greeted with more welcome, than from the tritheistic school of Andover," he wrote.[8] But as he was both a

Deist Unitarian (and the purest if not most extreme product of Enlightenment religion in the South) and, perhaps more important, an ardent libertarian, Jefferson's religion did not easily mesh with that of New England liberals. Not only were New England Unitarians then more Arians than true Deists, they also were more Federalist in their political orientation. Moreover, because of their Puritan heritage, they also tended to hold what Jefferson came to regard as a dangerous "priestly" power that was anathema to the libertarian Jefferson and his ardent devotion to the principle of separation of church and state. The Congregational clergy in New England had such "a smell of union between church and state," Jefferson wrote, that it would be difficult for them to get it out of their system.[9]

As both the author of the *Statute for Establishing Religious Freedom* in Virginia in 1786 and the leading proponent of the First Amendment to the Constitution of the United States, Thomas Jefferson remained a staunch champion of religious liberty throughout his life. Before the Revolution, the priestly power of the Anglican Church most worried Jefferson. After the war, evangelicals, especially Presbyterians, assumed this position, particularly as their influence over the state universities of both North and South Carolina increased. As President of the United States, Jefferson always kept a watchful eye to any encroachments of the power of the church upon the state. This position manifested itself again when a group of Baptists from Danbury, Connecticut, asked the newly elected President to set aside a day of fasting so that the nation could have the opportunity to heal the wounds made during the recent bitter presidential campaign. Jefferson's political enemies had condemned him during the campaign for being opposed to religion and for being an "atheist," "infidel," and "archdemon." Jefferson was unwilling to set aside such a day with its clear religious overtones in spite of the fact that he knew his position would be a "great offense to the New England clergy." In his letter of reply Jefferson expressed his belief that religion is a matter that lies solely between man and his God. He declared, "I contemplate with solemn reverence that act of the whole American people which declared that their legislature should 'make no law respecting an establishment of religion, or prohibiting the free exercise thereof.'"[10]

Even after his two-term presidency Jefferson remained steadfast in this position. In a letter to Jared Sparks, minister of the Unitarian church in Baltimore, Jefferson wrote, "If the freedom of religion, guaranteed to us by law in theory, can ever rise in practice under the overbearing inquisition of public opinion," then and only then will truth "prevail over fanaticism."[11] As heirs to this libertarian tradition, Southern Unitarians would keep and nourish this petal of their faith throughout the antebellum period. And it is to this petal of libertarianism that Southern Unitarians would appeal in their fight against the "fanaticism" of the North. Whereas Jefferson believed that the ideal of separation of church and state was most threatened by the growing wave of evangelicalism, by the middle of the antebellum period, Southern Unitarians reserved that distinction for their Northern Unitarian coreligionists. For them, it would be the politicalization of Northern Unitarianism more than the attacks by Southern evangelicals that would spell institutional decline.

Joseph Gales and the Origins of Southern Unitarianism

The son of the village schoolteacher, Joseph Gales was born in Eckington, England, in 1761 and was apprenticed to the printer's trade at Newark-on-Trent. After meeting and marrying Winifred Marshall, a cousin of Lord Melbourne, Joseph Gales founded the *Register* in 1787. Champions of such liberal movements as the cause of labor, the abolition of imprisonment for debt, the emancipation of slaves, and the adoption of manhood suffrage, Joseph and Winifred Gales established their home as a haven and rendezvous for free-thinking liberals. However, Gales's criticisms of the conservative government of William Pitt the Younger soon caused him to be ousted from England and in 1795 he and his family settled in Philadelphia, then the new Union's capital, where he purchased the *Independent Gazetteer,* changing its name to *Gales's Independent Gazetteer.* In addition to keeping up the spirit and the voice of his liberal views, Gales began to assert his liberal religious beliefs as well. As an influential editor in the new Union's capital, Joseph Gales quickly established a name for himself and became an important leader among Philadelphia's intellectual elite.

As the "Revolution of 1800" approached, Nathaniel Macon and the Republicans in North Carolina, to counter the monopoly the Federalist newspaper, *The North Carolina Minerva,* had in that state, persuaded

Gales to relocate to Raleigh and edit a Republican organ there. On October 22, 1799, he founded the Raleigh *Register* (named after his first paper in Sheffield) and the next year, 1800, he was elected the state printer by the victorious Republicans, an office that provided a substantial subsidy and that he continued to hold for thirty-two years. In addition to being the editor of the state's leading newspaper, Gales was also mayor of Raleigh for nineteen years.

Through familial connections, lifelong friendships, a broad subscription base, and sharp, intelligent expression, Gales's influence upon politics and religion in the South and throughout the rest of the country was formidable for much of the first half of the nineteenth century. In addition to increasing his paper's circulation by sending out gratis copies to prospective subscribers, Gales kept close ties with other editors of the nation's leading newspapers, thereby creating not only a journalistic circle of leading thinkers and publishers but also a broad national base of readers. When Gales first decided to move to North Carolina, he had sold his Philadelphia paper to Samuel Harrison Smith, who in 1800 transferred it to Washington and renamed it the *National Intelligencer*, under which name it became the country's leading newspaper in the nation's new capital. In 1807, after graduating from the University of North Carolina, Joseph Gales, Jr., the son of Gales, joined the *National Intelligencer* as reporter of Congressional debates. Gales Jr. later acquired the newspaper in partnership with William Winston Seaton, who had married one of Joseph Gales's daughters.

Throughout their marriage and their lives Joseph and Winifred Gales maintained friendships with many influential religious figures: Joseph Priestley, Jared Sparks, Daniel and Jonathan Whitaker, Thomas Cooper, Horace Holley, and Samuel and Caroline Gilman, just to name a few. Over the years, these friendships, and the influence they engendered, would have great significance in the development of Unitarianism in the South. Bringing their Unitarianism with them from England, the Galeses renewed their friendship with the "virtuous, the pious, and the unassuming advocate of Truth, Dr. Priestley." While in Philadelphia, both Priestley and Gales were the founding organizers of the First Society of Unitarian Christians (1796), with Gales being the first lay reader of the group.

In Raleigh, Gales organized and taught a nondenominational Sunday school and worshiped in Episcopal, Presbyterian, and Baptist churches. He gathered congregations in the State House to hear sermons by Jared Sparks, Samuel Gilman, Jonathan Whitaker, and Daniel Whitaker, who supplied Gilman's pulpit in Charleston on numerous occasions and who along with Gilman would be responsible for initiating the Unitarian congregation in Augusta. Clement Eaton characterized the Galeses' type of liberalism as "Jeffersonian" because it "did not generate an intolerance of points of view different from their own, such as the conservative attitude toward revealed religion. They tried to see all sides of a question and avoid the partisan approach which is frequently indifferent to truth." In practical implementation, this type of liberalism, according to Eaton, advocated a "separation of church and state and of church and college, the exclusion of the clergy from politics, the emphasis on morality rather than theology, and on physiology rather than spirit in the interpretation of human nature."[12]

An Indigenous Arminianism

The road from Joseph Priestley's revolutionary enlightenment to Samuel Gilman's antebellum rational orthodoxy was certainly not a smooth one. The most formidable obstacle on the journey was dissenting evangelicalism, whose extreme adherents did not hesitate to attack those faithful liberal pilgrims who decided to tough it out and stay on its meandering path. For most of the liberals, however, whether in a Unitarian church or not, survival meant early on leaving behind the baggage of Deism and Skepticism that tended to weigh down their cause. To this end they were greatly aided by an indigenous Arminianism in the South, which enveloped both Anglican latitudinarianism, which Priestley was reared in, and also a way of thinking and a set of assumptions known as Scottish Common Sense Realism. Both of these traditions were prevalent not only within the Charleston congregation and other Southern churches, but also within American religion in general as well.

For colonists and later citizens of the tidewater region of Virginia and the low country of the Carolinas especially, the weight of the baggage of Deism or Skepticism was not as heavy as it could have been. Even though the Anglican Church was solidly established in those areas, it had within its own ranks nurtured a conciliatory latitudinarianism that aided in the disestablishment process and also alleviated the harshness of theological disagreements within the Church. For years many Anglicans had flirted with the more liberal elements of the English, Scottish, and Continental Enlightenment, such as Socinianism, Arianism, Deism, and Skepticism, and had incorporated them into the broad purview inherent in latitudinarianism. In the process, latitudinarianism helped to produce English Unitarianism on its rather wide and extended intellectual foundation. But when transplanted to American soil, the more radical elements of the English and Scottish Enlightenment especially were often tempered, neutralized, and transmuted into what Sydney Ahlstrom describes as a "benign, optimistic, and utterly respectable Christian rationalism,"[13] a rationalism that had many adherents within orthodox American denominations.

Although the Anglican Church in the South was hit hard during the disestablishment process of the late eighteenth and early nineteenth centuries, it and the more urban units of the Unitarian and the Presbyterian Churches, particularly, would be major vehicles for English and Scottish Enlightenment influence well into the antebellum period. These denominations were the least touched theologically, socially, and politically by evangelicalism, in part because of the influences of Scottish Common Sense Realism and latitudinarianism.

Latitudinarianism

The term *latitudinarian* has its origins in the seventeenth century and referred to a group of students and disciples of Cambridge Platonists who did not conform to any particular opinion or standard and who did not insist on doctrinal correctness. In many ways, latitudinarianism grew in response to the Church's adoption of the theological tenets espoused by the Synod of Dort in 1618–1619 and the Westminster Confession of Faith in 1647. With the Church plagued by divisions, a rather large and influential group of Englishmen offered themselves as mediators on various fronts. Theologically, they stood between Arminians and Calvinists. They insisted that the Anglican high church position— the view that the Episcopal polity was essential to the being of the Church—was wrong. Although most latitudinarians were firmly attached to the Church of England, they did not necessarily see the Church as a divine institution, and they therefore maintained that Dissenters and those who followed other forms of government and worship were not to be excluded from Christian fellowship. In regard to theological questions many tended to side with Episcopius, perhaps the most liberal follower of Jacobus Arminius, who as a student, had taken his mentor's theology in the direction of Universalism. By establishing themselves as mediators, latitudinarians hoped to demonstrate that the contending parties of Arminians and Calvinists had no reason to oppose each other with such animosity because, even though they differed over the means of salvation, both parties hoped and worked for its common end.

Episcopius was professor of divinity at the University of Leiden and during the Synod of Dort in 1618 was the principal advocate of Arminianism. Arminius was also a professor at the University of Leiden and a distinguished Dutch pastor whose theological training had been thoroughly Calvinistic. While the doctrine that bears his name has come to represent the very antithesis of Calvinism, Arminius, throughout his life, considered himself a strict Calvinist on all issues except that of predestination.

High Calvinists claimed that God ordained Adam's fall in order to save the elect from the "mass of perdition." To this group, God then provided irresistible grace, which He denied to those not chosen. For Calvinists, all humanity was totally depraved and election to salvation depended on God's unconditional eternal decree, a decree that dictated that Christ die as an atonement for the sins of the elect. The grace given to the elect was both irresistible and complete. Grace would enable the elect to persevere and not fall from its hold.

For Arminius, as well as his Calvinist opponents, the doctrine of predestination was biblically sound. But Arminius debated the basis by which predestination takes place. Arminius believed that predestination itself was based on God's *foreknowledge* of those who would later have faith in Jesus Christ. His opponents on the other hand believed that faith itself is the result of predestination, that before the foundation of the world, the sovereign *will* of God decreed who would have faith and who would not. Arminius agreed that the decree of predestination dictated that Christ would be the mediator and redeemer of mankind, a decree in no way dependent on human response, but he believed that the decree itself was based not on the will of God, but rather on divine foreknowledge. It was not that God willed who would have faith and who would not, but rather that God merely knew from the beginning of time the final destiny of each individual and how that individual would respond to the offer of salvation in Jesus Christ.[14]

Arminius died in 1609 and his followers, including Episcopius, carried his theology to its logical completion. They argued that the whole system of predestination was an affront to the wisdom, justice, and goodness of God. For them, God decreed to save all believers. Christ died for all humanity, not just the elect. Faith was the fruit of grace, and the human will had no power to believe unless it was empowered by grace, but, they believed, all had sufficient grace to accept the gospel, even though some would resist.

The next year, 1610, followers of Arminius issued a document or a "Remonstrance" (thereafter Arminius's followers were more commonly known as "Remonstrants") that attempted to defend their position. The document itself contained five articles, each dealing with the issues under debate. The first defined predestination in rather ambiguous terms, especially in light of the distinctions made by Arminius. It affirmed that God determined before the foundation of the world that those who believed in Christ would be saved, but it did not delineate whether that would be accomplished through God's will or God's foreknowledge. The ambiguity of the omission was consistent with the final paragraph of the Remonstrance, which declared that belief in Christ was all that was needed for salvation and that "it is neither necessary nor useful to rise higher nor to search any deeper." The second article affirmed that Christ died for all human beings, but declared that only believers actually received the benefits of the atonement. The third article dealt directly with the accusation that Arminians were Pelagians. According to the consensus of the seventh-century Church, Pelagius had denied the concept of original sin and believed in the perfect freedom of the human will, though Pelagius himself may have never held this view. To clarify their position, Remonstrants declared that human beings can do nothing good on their own account and that grace is needed in order to do good. However, in the fourth article, the Remonstrants rejected the Calvinist notion that the grace of God is irresistible. They asserted that the will could resist grace and continue to sin, arguing that in Scripture, "it is written that many resisted the Holy Spirit." The fifth and final article declared that a greater scriptural understanding was needed to establish whether or not it was possible for one to fall from grace, that is, to lose the grace that one had previously received. But for many Arminians, if one could resist grace, the human will had sufficient power and was itself responsible for the resistance and the sin that resistance engendered. Therefore, there could be no perseverance of the saints. The Synod of Dort disagreed with all five of these articles and defined Arminianism as a heresy.[15]

Though latitudinarianism initially sought to mediate between Arminianism and Calvinism, by the time of the Restoration in 1660, most within its ranks had sided with the Arminians. From there many would go on to a decidedly rationalistic theology, including a fully mature Unitarian belief. Indeed, many Anglicans and Episcopalians were not too surprised when the Athanasian Creed was quietly dropped from the Book of Common Prayer. For years, latitudinarians were labeled "atheists," "deists," and "Socinians" by Calvinists within the Church. But the restoration of Charles II in 1660 hastened the eclipse of Calvinism, and latitudinarians enjoyed a considerably greater degree of esteem within English ecclesiology. Thereafter, Arminianism became the standard teaching of most Anglican clergymen. Holifield concludes that while early English Arminians believed in original sin and divine grace, "they rejected predestination as a slander on God's goodness." Rather than being a precise set of doctrines, early English Arminianism was more a "mood and temper," and soon it "merged imperceptibly with an easygoing latitudinarian attitude toward doctrine, while still resting on an "unshakable confidence in the benevolence of God."[16]

In America, latitudinarianism had an equally esteemed following within the established churches, especially in the Virginia tidewater and the Carolina low country areas of the newly formed United States. But in the end, its effect for the Episcopal Church would be less conciliatory than it had been for the Church of England. Because the translation of their views over form of government and church worship dictated a strict separation of church on American soil, latitudinarians in general, though certainly in positions to do so, did little to contribute to the restoration of the Episcopal Church in America. In fact, so great was the ideal of separation of church and state that even though two-thirds of the signers of the Declaration of Independence were nominally Anglican, the most constructive leadership for the restoration of the Episcopal Church still came from those areas where the Church of England had not been established.[17] For Southern Unitarians, the ideal of separation of church and state, an ideal born out of latitudinarianism and English Unitarianism, continued to raise its head throughout the antebellum years and many believed was the central cause in their protracted separation from Northern Unitarians. But the rationalistic theology of latitudinarianism was not entirely self-sufficient and isolated within the Anglican and Episcopal Churches, especially throughout the disestablishment process. Latitudinarianism also drew heavily upon the philosophical resources of the Enlightenment and the Scottish renaissance, particularly the ideas inherent in Scottish Common Sense Realism.

Scottish Common Sense Realism

Common Sense Realism was itself a product of the Enlightenment and in many ways was a reaction to its extreme tendencies. Common Sense Realism was first developed in the eighteenth century by Presbyterian Moderates who controlled the Kirk of Scotland and the four Scottish universities, which were then at the height of their vitality and influence. The founder of this school was Thomas Reid of Aberdeen and later Glasgow University, with his disciple Dugald Stewart of Edinburgh University. The first great exponent in America was John Witherspoon, who left Scotland in 1768 to become president of College of New Jersey. As it was digested and spread by others it achieved a wider influence in America than any other philosophical school. For the first two-thirds of the nineteenth century it became the chief philosophical support for theological and apologetical endeavors North and South as it rose to dominance among Unitarians, Episcopalians, Presbyterians, Congregationalists, and Lutherans, as well as many individuals unaffiliated with any particular denomination.

Scottish philosophy was ubiquitous as an ethical system as it reached beyond denominational and regional lines. Recent works by E. Brooks Holifield and Daniel Walker Howe reflect the uncanny ability of Scottish Realism to cater both to Southern orthodoxy and Boston Unitarianism. Holifield concludes that Scottish philosophy was able to permeate American intellectual life in the early nineteenth century because of "its applicability to both epistemology and ethical problems and partly because of its flexibility. Realism was not so much a set of conclusions as it was a way of thinking that could commend itself to a variety of thinkers."[18] Presbyterians could use the works of Reid to expound their Calvinist sense of duty while Boston Unitarians were able to use Scottish philosophy in their constant search for a rational justification for principles of natural rights. Howe identifies the "essential thrust behind Harvard common sense philosophy" as the urge to justify morals, religion, and what every man sees with his eyes to be true. He declares, "Harvard philosophers admitted that such behavior was perfectly natural, but this alone did not seem adequate justification for it. They wanted to find, in the structure of the universe itself, rational justification for doing these things."[19]

Scottish Common Sense Realism was characterized by a commitment to the ultimate meaningfulness of what human beings know, feel, desire, and decide. It rested on three epistemological assumptions: (1) observation is the basis of knowledge; (2) consciousness is the medium of observation; and (3) consciousness contains principles that are independent of experience and impose order on the data of experience. Thus, consciousness was anterior to experience and regulated what the mind and body saw, felt, heard, etc. These constituents of consciousness composed what was known as "common sense." They were not innate ideas in the sense that men and women were born believing them, but rather ideas that, once presented, would seem self-evident. This kind of epistemology influenced religious consciousness just as it did every other cognitive endeavor, imposing with it a desire for order and logic to everything the mind entertained. Unlike proponents of the Skepticism of David Hume and John Locke, Common Sense Realists believed that the consciousness strove for both understanding and order, revealing that a "natural and original judgment" accompanied one's perceptions of the world.[20]

Hume believed that if one based knowledge on the evidence of the senses, as Locke had done, then the structure of knowledge will disintegrate because no sensations can be found to account for certain concepts that tie our experiences together, such as the concept of causality. Hume argued that while we may have observed a sequence of events many times in the past, we still have no assurance or proof from the evidence of the senses that the sequence itself is inherent in the grand scheme of things and will happen again in the future. Skepticism such as this threatened the entire theological structure of the Age of Reason since Christians and even Deists believed that the universe itself was the *effect* of which God was the *cause.*

Scottish Common Sense Realists argued that Locke was wrong in supposing that knowledge was a matter of the agreement or disagreement of ideas in the mind. If that were the case, Scottish Realists argued, then it would be difficult to explain whether or not there is any correspondence between the idea in the mind and the external reality of which the senses take account. Therefore, Scottish philosophers argued, our awareness of the external world as being what we experience it to be is a basic intuition, a "consciousness," which is self-evident and self-validating and not dependent on argument.

It was in this sense and in these terms that Scottish Common Sense philosophy sought to reconcile discrepancies and tensions between science and theology and reason and revelation. Scottish Common Sense Realism produced, in short, precisely the kind of apologetic philosophy that Christians in the Age of Reason needed. For Southern denominational theologians, Scottish philosophy enabled them to put aside their "divisions," which "were as deep as those of the Northern university faculties," and "unite in their confidence that Realism could solve the pressing dilemmas of both epistemology and ethics, and thereby . . . demonstrate the congruity between thought and behavior and prove the reasonableness of faith."[21] For Southern Unitarians especially, Common Sense Realism provided not only the tools needed for a "rational orthodoxy" and a "scientific theology" but also a means by which to legitimize their "Christian" status among Southern orthodoxy and push for ecumenical reform among the various denominations.

During the late eighteenth century, students of John Witherspoon established an extensive network of academies, colleges, and seminaries that became centers for the diffusion of Scottish thought throughout the Southern religious landscape. In North Carolina, David Caldwell began a backwoods school in 1767 that introduced more than fifty ministerial graduates to the Scottish ideas. Samuel McCorkle, another of Witherspoon's students, started an academy that trained at least forty-five more clergy in the Tar Heel state. Princeton-trained clergy, joined by their own students, carried the Scottish philosophy to Transylvania

University and Centre College in Kentucky; to Martin Academy, Tusculum College, Blount Academy in Tennessee, and Davidson College in North Carolina. Throughout the antebellum period, prominent Southern theologians were influenced by the practicality of Scottish thought, the flexibility of its tenets, and its theological soundness. Presbyterian schools and seminaries were full of Realist suppositions. James Henley Thornwell lectured on them at Columbia, R. J. Breckenridge at Danville, and Robert Lewis Dabney at Union Seminary.[22]

Witherspoon's Scottish Realism reached the Charleston congregation almost on a regular basis throughout the revolutionary and antebellum periods. David Ramsay, William Hollinshead, Isaac Stockton Keith, William Tennent, and other prominent clergy and laity of the First Congregational Church in Charleston were all Princeton graduates and came under the influence of the Scottish school. But it was perhaps through the theological training of its minister Anthony Forster that the influence of Scottish Realism played a direct role in developing Unitarian belief within that congregation, which was already accustomed to its central tenets. While the Scottish influence initially precipitated a Unitarian belief within the congregation, over the course of the antebellum period Realism also allowed Southern Unitarians to move toward the orthodoxy of those around them who also embraced and used its principles.

New England Unitarianism: The Exception to Mushrooms

The final source of Unitarianism in the South was a result of Boston mission work and the American Unitarian Association's supply of tracts, pamphlets, and ministers to such places as Mobile and Nashville, just to name a few. The A.U.A. was formed on May 25, 1825, and was committed to supplying "missionaries, especially in such parts of the country as are destitute of a stated ministry."[23] But even before the A.U.A. was formally organized, ministers from Harvard came to such places as Baltimore, Washington, and Charleston through an informal missionary policy of the yet unorganized A.U.A. Men like Jared Sparks and Samuel Gilman came to promising Unitarian societies in Baltimore and Charleston, respectively, that were already well organized and well attended by Southerners, and whose liberal roots existed independently of New England missionary activity.

During the late 1820s and early 1830s, however, the zeal of Northern Unitarians to propagate their faith throughout the South and West was real and strong. Behind these actions and agents was the determined but misguided conviction among many in the A.U.A. that Unitarianism could not grow without the aid of its ministers and its pamphlets. James Freeman Clarke, then of Louisville, Kentucky, wrote to a friend,

> "I don't understand you when you say that Unitarianism will spread just as well without our aid—I know of no other good thing that will grow without human aid (except mushrooms, and Unitarianism has proved itself to be no mushroom). It strikes me that we should aid it more than we have ... Only Unitarians or something equal to it under another name, *can ever bring the people of [the Mississippi] valley to God.*"[24]

Clarke was not alone. Charles Briggs wrote to the A.U.A. two years later when he attempted to start a second Unitarian society in New Orleans, "My only fears are that there is not enough of the salt of NE [*sic:* New England] in the place. A new society cannot be started anywhere in the West or the South unless there are a few good Yankees at the bottom of it."[25] Indeed, in most cases, with little or no regard for either the prior existence or the independent nature of the Southern Unitarian congregations and individuals whom they encountered, the A.U.A. boldly, aggressively, and proudly absorbed them into its own fold for convenience and self-aggrandizement, despite Southern protests, hesitations, and acts or notices of independence.

Even considering the activity of the A.U.A., the greatest success of Northern Unitarian missionary activity in the South came in those areas that were on the geographical periphery of the would-be Confederate states. But more often than not, these Northern efforts fell on soil already occupied by indigenous liberal seeds, or by this seed mixed with the seed Charleston produced and spread through the South. This pattern has been ignored by Unitarian historians who have too often exaggerated the extent of Northern influences upon the South and portrayed Southern Unitarian churches as nothing more than "missionary outposts" of Boston.[26]

Eventually, churches on the Southern border, where Northern efforts are credited with their greatest success, were increasingly seen by the A.U.A. as springboards to the West rather than as inroads to the South. Even by the 1840s there was sufficient tension between the Northern and Southern ranks for many in the A.U.A. to give up on activity in the South altogether and to concentrate on the West where many saw more fertile and "salty" soil for their New England seeds. Indeed, because of its geographical position, the A.U.A. viewed the New Orleans church as a gateway to both regions. Even so, the congregation in Mobile, though claimed to be founded by James Freeman Clarke on behalf of the A.U.A., looked to New Orleans and to Charleston, rather than Boston, for theological, financial, and spiritual support.

With its strongest congregations coming directly from non–New England origins, from the theologies of Joseph Priestly and English Unitarianism in Charleston and from Mississippi Presbyterianism in New Orleans, Southern Unitarians from the outset recognized the fact that their faith was decidedly Southern, and it became even more so in the mid to late antebellum period. With a Christology, epistemology, and cultural outlook becoming more similar to Southern orthodoxy than the latter camp was willing to admit, Southern Unitarians realized they in fact had more in common with Southern clergy and laity than with their Northern coreligionists, a realization not precipitated by the abolition question, but by an innate consciousness of accepted sectional differences, distinctions, and norms.[27]

URBAN BEGINNINGS

Charleston

Sparked by the theology of the English Unitarian Joseph Priestley, the Second Independent or Congregational Church of Charleston was incorporated as a separate organization in 1817 under the guidance of its minister Anthony Forster. It acquired the title the Unitarian Church of Charleston fifteen years later in 1832 under the pastorate of Samuel Gilman. Its origins were directly and inextricably tied with the history of the Independent or Congregational Church of Charleston, which it grew with and in for well over a century. The church had taken solid root in ecclesiastical soil that prided itself on a "broad and dissenting bottom," a forceful independence "from all foreign shackles," and a rigorous freedom "to act upon the . . . most liberal principles."

Founded in the decade of 1680–1690, the Independent church originally gathered a broad faction of many of the dissenting religious groups in Charleston: French Huguenots, Scotch and Irish Presbyterians, and Old and New Englanders. But with an early Huguenot secession, the congregation soon came under the leadership of a Presbyterian faction that would continue to assert a forceful influence upon the congregation for some time, in spite of the fact that many of the more strict Presbyterians withdrew in 1732 to form the Scotch or First Presbyterian Church of Charleston. Even with this secession, many Presbyterians remained and the congregation continued to insist upon the freedom to be called "Congregational, Presbyterian, or Independent—sometimes by one of these names, sometimes by two of them, sometimes by all three . . . [so that] no moderate person of either denomination might be afraid to join." So great was the congregation's zeal for religious freedom that they declared: "The constitution of this church is to have no absolute, invariable form, but to act upon the freest and most liberal principles, as occasion may serve, and edification direct."[28]

By the late colonial period, the congregation could boast increasing numbers and such notable figures as the Presbyterian minister and ardent patriot William Tennent and the historian David Ramsay, who along with other students of John Witherspoon, president of the College of New Jersey, "the first real ambassador" of Common Sense Realism in America, carried the Scottish philosophy to "academies, colleges, seminaries, and churches all over the country."[29] Demonstrating his indebtedness to the enlightened ideals of separation of church, the belief in Anglican disestablishment, and the religious liberty of the congregation he represented, William Tennent, in a 1777 speech to the South Carolina House of Assembly, repeated his convictions for the separation of church and state. "We contend," he declared, "that no legislature under heaven has a right to interfere with the judgment and conscience of men in religious matters, if their opinions and practices do not injure the state." Tennent believed that no one had the "right to dispose of my conscience, and to lay down for me what I shall believe and practice in religious matters."[30]

Because of the growth of the congregation before the Revolutionary

War, plans were set in motion for a second edifice to house the crowds of worshipers, but that building on Archdale Street was not completed until 1787. It was dedicated in October of that year because the war and British occupation had devastated the city of Charleston, displacing many of the congregation's leading families and individuals. After the war and Anglican disestablishment, the number of members again began to grow and under the leadership of Dr. William Hollinshead from Princeton, the congregation soon began to enjoy the fruits of its labor.

Being one corporate body with two church buildings, the Congregational church was able to establish a co-pastor within a year of the dedication of the Archdale Street building. The Rev. Isaac Stockton Keith, a graduate of Princeton and a student of Witherspoon, joined Dr. Hollinshead, and the two became co-pastors at that time. Each minister was to preach every Sunday to both congregations when demand was sufficient to fill both sets of pews, seating between five and six hundred people each. Though unusual, the arrangement was "harmonious" and apparently advantageous, for both churches grew in number and strength. In 1806, to replace the so-called White MeetingHouse, a new brick church was built, also on Meeting Street. It soon came to be called the Circular Church because of its shape. Rev. Keith served the congregation efficiently and faithfully for twenty-five years until he died in 1813. After the congregation sent letters of inquiry to Princeton, Andover, Yale, and Hampden-Sydney, Dr. Benjamin Morgan Palmer was secured as temporary pastor in 1814 to replace the deceased Keith, a decision made with considerable opposition (72 in favor, 37 opposed). With the fear that the Arminian-Calvinist disputes between church members and Hollinshead and Palmer would "[sow] seeds of discord and disunion [and] might lead ultimately to the dismemberment of the Church," the laymen of the church took formal steps toward reconciliation soon thereafter and the ministers themselves followed, with the result that Palmer became co-pastor.[31]

In April 1815, because of ill health (and one can only speculate whether there were perhaps theological reasons), Dr. Hollinshead asked for and received a leave of absence with full salary until the end of the year. The Rev. Anthony Forster from North Carolina was invited to become a temporary supply. When Dr. Hollinshead's illness appeared to be greater than originally anticipated, Forster was practically though not formally invested with the office of co-pastor. The choice of Forster, like Palmer before him, demonstrated some of the theological divisions within the congregation, which eventually precipitated a Unitarian secession. Such a decision was accepted grudgingly by members in both camps, but was one that many found more palatable given the liberal nature of the church itself and the historical inclination of each group to gravitate naturally more readily and regularly to one of the two worship buildings that the church owned and provided.

Because the Congregational Church of Charleston had enjoyed a long history of ecclesiastical freedom, many in the church felt it "wise and necessary" that the church propose three articles of its own to the 1778 State Constitution of South Carolina, a constitution drawn up in the middle of Anglican disestablishment. Article Thirty-Eight of the state constitution declared that "the Christian Protestant" was to be "the established religion of the state, and that all denominations were to enjoy equal religious and civil privileges." Historian George N. Edwards explains that in accepting the new constitution, the church added three articles of its own covering "Scripture Doctrines of Grace" already held. The first article stated the doctrine of the Trinity, the second the fall of man and the need for atonement, and the third the substitutionary doctrine of the atonement. After the application was made to the state, the church was incorporated on October 9, 1778.[32]

The adoption of the proposed articles strongly suggests the continued influence of the Presbyterian faction within the congregation as a whole. Eventually, however, it became clear that while a good number within the congregation may have believed the central tenets of the added articles, many others felt that they were unnecessary, especially given the zeal for religious freedom the church had so long possessed. According to Edwards, "there were [still] many in the society who had never approved either the rule requiring subscription to the Creed and Articles, or the double character of the organization. Many felt neither was consistent with the principles of Congregationalism, or the position of independence which the Church had so often assumed and insisted on."[33]

It is this constituency to which Anthony Forster tailored his message. When he refused to subscribe to any articles except those that "were offered to him simply on the principles of the gospels," he dissolved his connection with the society altogether. This of course precipitated a crisis in the congregation and finally a plan of separation was agreed upon. In the spring of 1817, seventy-five subscribers followed Forster to the Archdale Street church and sixty-nine remained with Palmer at the Circular Church on Meeting Street. Unfortunately, Forster became ill soon thereafter and retired to Raleigh, North Carolina, in 1819, where he died in 1820.

Raised in the Episcopal Church, Forster was grounded in the broad theological foundations of Anglican latitudinarianism. After receiving his degree from the University of North Carolina, Forster, for reasons unknown, sought theological training from the Presbyterian minister and educator Dr. William McPheeters of Raleigh. McPheeters had been a student of Rev. William Graham at the Augusta Academy (later name Liberty Hall) at Timber Ridge, just outside of Lexington, Virginia. Graham, who later wrote the first important scriptural defense of slavery to appear in the South in the late eighteenth century, had been a student of John Witherspoon at Princeton and was an avid and faithful proponent of Scottish Common Sense Realism. This undoubtedly influenced his decision to establish a course of study at the Augusta Academy similar to the one he had pursued at Princeton.[34] Along with the indirect influences of latitudinarianism within the Episcopal Church, Forster's professional theological training came under the direct auspices of Scottish Realism through his mentor, Rev. McPheeters of Raleigh.[35] Forster's training in Scottish Realism was matched by many in the Charleston congregation. Tennent, Hollinshead, and Keith were all Princeton graduates (as was David Ramsay), with Keith studying directly under Witherspoon.

Anthony Forster's wife was a daughter of Joseph Gales. Though trained in the moderate Calvinism of Scottish Common Sense Realism, Forster did not accept his in-laws' theological positions and initially set out to refute them, asking his father-in-law for the books upon which he based his views. But Forster soon fell sway to Priestley's arguments, which constituted the bulk of the borrowed library, and he found himself in the middle of a spiritual crisis in which he felt the "ground sinking beneath" his feet.

Without assuming the name Unitarian, Forster began to preach to his Charleston congregation on those things "that are common to all

Christian denominations, and in which, he felt confident, lay the essential elements of salvation and of the Christian life."[36] Undoubtedly comfortable in this church that had long prided itself on independence from "all foreign shackles," Forster quite naturally attracted a sizable liberal following in the Charleston congregation who wanted to remain true to the church's founding principles. Members of the Charleston congregation adhered to a recognizable set of principles that had many adherents within Southern orthodoxy. It was Arminian in nature, advocated the goodness of humanity, believed strongly in personal and collective "progress," rousing men and women to live lives of virtue and constant improvement, emphasized the simplicity and "purity" of the Christian faith, denounced historical "trappings" of tradition, and strove for ecumenical accord. To a great extent, these Enlightenment beliefs, including those of the more radical English Unitarian Joseph Priestley, were conservative in their views of scriptural authority and the centrality of miracles.

In March 1818, Forster and the members of the congregation adopted a series of rules of government for the newly formed church. In the Enlightenment tradition of Jefferson, the members "solemnly assert[ed] for ourselves, and as fully allowing to all others, the right of private judgment and freedom of opinion in all things pertaining to the conscience." In the first article, the congregation affirmed the primacy of biblical revelation: "Article First. We receive the written Word of God, contained in the Scripture of the Old and New Testaments, as our only rule of faith and practice."[37] For the remainder of the antebellum period, despite contrary tendencies of some of their Northern coreligionists, the church never swayed from that adoption. It became the centerpiece of its theology and assisted the church in moving the liberal faith closer to the "orthodoxy" of those around them.

Faced with the untimely illness and death of Forster, the congregation took the name Second Independent or Congregational Church of Charleston and appealed to President Kirkland of Harvard for a replacement. Samuel Gilman, a young tutor there and an avowed Unitarian, was chosen by Kirkland and in the spring of 1819 came to Charleston to officiate at the Archdale Street church. Samuel Gilman and his wife, Caroline, married in 1819 just before coming to Charleston. The former Caroline Howard had met Samuel Gilman at a party in Cambridge in 1810 and between the time they met and married, she spent each winter in Savannah with her merchant brother, Samuel Howard. During that time she became accustomed to the Southern way of life, and although born a New Englander, she would, for the rest of her life, remain a Southerner by heart and by choice. In addition to writing and editing many articles and books on a variety of subjects, Caroline worked diligently with other women of the church in a variety of tasks.[38] After a trial period, Samuel Gilman was unanimously elected pastor, and in December 1819, was ordained by Jared Sparks, Unitarian minister in Baltimore (and later president of Harvard), Joseph Tuckerman, Boston's first Minister to the Poor, and the Reverend M. Parker, pastor of the Saltketcher Presbyterian Church in South Carolina.

The faith of this liberal Charleston congregation stemmed from an indigenous Arminianism that had been watered over the years by Scottish Common Sense Realism and the ideals of Anglican latitudinarianism within the colonial establishment. Many ministers and members of the congregation had been directly or indirectly touched by the epistemology and theology of Scottish Realism, which in turn was responsible for establishing both a moderate theological position and a relative fluidity of thought and movement between and among Southern orthodox believers, especially those of urban, professional, academic, and literary persuasion. The history of the Second Independent Church within that of the First Congregational Church of Charleston and the personal theological journey of their first pastor, Anthony Forster—from the Episcopal Church to the Presbyterian and ultimately to Unitarian faith—also demonstrates both the indebtedness this congregation felt to Southern orthodoxy and the degree to which they would go to protect and defend the religious freedom they had long enjoyed and that many felt were part and parcel of their Southern experience. The extent to which Samuel Gilman, himself a New Englander, inherited this distinctly Southern faith and was shaped by it over the course of the antebellum years suggests strongly the different directions that American Unitarianism would take on the two sides of the Mason-Dixon line during the nineteenth century. Within a few years of the beginning of his ministry, there would be other indications of that as well. Gilman would remain in Charleston for the next four decades until his death. His ministry would be the center and the golden age of Southern Uni-

tarianism. By the early 1840s, the initiative for establishing and supporting Unitarian churches in Augusta and Savannah, Georgia, and even
Mobile, Alabama, rested almost entirely on the back of the Charleston
congregation, and most of these churches sought affiliation with the
Charleston church rather than the A.U.A.[39]

THREE • The Uni-Uni Connection

Peripheral Universalism in
New Orleans and Richmond

With Charleston at the center, Unitarianism on the geographical periphery of the would-be Confederate states, in places like New Orleans
and Richmond, often flirted with a Universalism whose strength fluctuated with the theology of whichever minister happened to be in the
pulpit. In New Orleans, the mixture of Theodore Clapp's Universalism
with Unitarianism and his ecumenical zeal aided in his decision to
change the name of his church from the First Congregational Unitarian
Church to the more general Church of the Messiah. In Richmond,
the Unitarians and Universalists came together to form the Unitarian-
Universalist Society, commonly known as the "Uni-Uni" Church, blend-
ing the theology of both faiths. While the New Orleans and Richmond
churches existed outside of the Charleston-centered association that
Gilman tried to establish for Southern Unitarian congregations, all of
these Southern churches shared a commitment to a broad liberal gospel.

And yet throughout the antebellum period there remained fundamental differences between Unitarians and Universalists. Paul Conkin
argues that class differences between Unitarians and Universalists were
more prevalent between the two groups than urban-rural distinctions,
and the Richmond and New Orleans examples tend to support this
claim.[1] Unitarianism never had the broad appeal that Universalism
seemed to have. Unitarianism appealed to the urban professional classes
whereas Universalism enjoyed a wider class range. While Unitarianism
and Universalism both shared a disdain for evangelical revivals, Universalism existed outside of the Enlightenment influences of latitudinarianism and Scottish Common Sense Realism that helped produce Unitarianism in the South. Clapp was called both a "Restorationist" and a

Trinitarian and he came upon a Universalist theology from his own personal biblical interpretation, independent of Enlightenment and/or Unitarian influences. His views continued to be a thorn in the side of Unitarians in the North who tried desperately to distance themselves from the "deviance" of his views. While New England was slow to realize that its religious liberalism would eventually align with the Universalism they then disclaimed, Clapp recognized the similarities between his Universalist faith and that of his English coreligionists. "The most distinguished Unitarian ministers of London," he declared, "expressed to me their deep regret and astonishment that the liberal clergymen of Boston were not the open and decided advocates of that system . . . which teaches the final restoration of all men to holiness and happiness."[2] While Clapp affirmed divine revelation over human reason, he negated the concept of original sin. Gilman on the other hand was indebted to Scottish Realism, the relational qualities of moral philosophy, biblical criticism, the latitudinarian tradition, and the Southern landscape to provide the "right balance" for a Christian faith still grounded in God's revelation and Christ's divinity. He never entertained Universalist notions or allowed Universalist theology to shape his view of human sin. Gilman scolded Northern Unitarians for formulating "rosier" views of human nature and argued against Transcendental notions of human sufficiency.

But the Unitarian churches in New Orleans and Charleston did share many similarities. Just as the Charleston congregation served as the primary springboard for Unitarianism in Southern states along the Atlantic, so did the congregation in New Orleans serve, perhaps to a lesser degree, as a liberal gateway to cotton-belt states of the Gulf of Mexico. The New Orleans and Charleston congregations also shared non–New England roots, the Presbyterian background of their first ministers, similar patterns of growth and name change, financial independence, the independence of their theological positions from Boston, and an ultimate split with the American Unitarian Association. Though the split was less dramatic for New Orleans than Charleston, it was still real and significant nonetheless.

As was the case with the Charleston church, the founding of the Unitarian church in New Orleans stemmed from the conversion of a Presbyterian minister, Theodore Clapp, in the early 1830s, and from the liberal roots of the founding of the church itself in 1818. By the time of Clapp's conversion and expulsion from the Mississippi Presbytery in 1832, the liberal faction within the church had grown to compose the majority of the congregation. They decided to remain loyal to Clapp and to his theological beliefs, despite the secession of a few strict Calvinist Presbyterians.

In 1803, when the Louisiana Purchase was signed, New Orleans was a growing port city at the mouth of the Mississippi River whose inhabitants possessed a unique blend of French and Spanish character. Before the Purchase, according to the original French charter, non-Catholic churches were forbidden to organize. That tradition had been respected by the French and Spanish officials who had governed there over the years. Only in 1805 when Americans entered the area was the first Protestant church established in New Orleans: the Episcopal Christ Church. Fifteen years later, on January 22, 1818, Sylvester Larned, a young Presbyterian minister and recent graduate of Princeton Theological Seminary, arrived and was given the task of establishing the second Protestant church in New Orleans.

Before Larned's arrival, however, a growing society had already been developing and by February of 1818, Larned had secured commitments from eighty individuals to organize a church. Within a month he had developed a full program of services and secured land from the city council for the building of a church. Built in a plain Gothic style, the church was located near St. Charles "in the heart of the newly developing English section of the city," and according to the church historian, Meg Dachowski, its cornerstone was laid on January 8, 1819, before a crowd of seven thousand people.[3] Unfortunately, as was the case with the Savannah church, illness and death struck this burgeoning Southern congregation early and quickly. During the summer of 1820, as another epidemic of yellow fever swept through the already ravaged city, Sylvester Larned died on August 31, his twenty-fourth birthday.

The bereaved congregation looked to Theodore Clapp, a graduate of Andover Seminary, as its second minister. After seminary training, Clapp had served as an educator in New England and Kentucky. After Clapp preached two trial sermons in February 1821, the New Orleans congregation invited him to be its permanent minister. While considering this option, Clapp discovered that the congregation was forty-five thousand dollars in debt, and he refused to accept the position until the debt was paid. After raising twenty-five thousand dollars through a state lottery, the congregation was able to raise the rest of the money through the generosity of a local philanthropist. Judah Touro, a Jewish merchant, continued to support the congregation throughout the antebellum years even though he remained loyal to his own faith. Touro bought the church building outright for twenty thousand dollars and allowed the congregation full use of the property and rent for church pews as long as the church remained in the same location. With the debt paid and the church's finances in order, Theodore Clapp accepted the call.

Although it was the intent of the congregation that first called Larned to form a Presbyterian church, this was not accomplished until after Clapp's arrival. On November 23, 1823, the church was formally organized along Presbyterian lines. It adopted Presbyterian standards and petitioned the Presbytery of Mississippi to be enrolled as "The First Presbyterian Church in the City and Parish of New Orleans." The petition was accepted and in the spring of 1824 delegates from the church, including Clapp, attended their first Mississippi Presbytery meeting. But trouble had been brewing from the start.

There were early signs that the members themselves, including Clapp, were more liberal than their Calvinist coreligionists. During Clapp's first year as pastor, Judge Workman, a member of the congregation, approached Clapp to ascertain the biblical foundation for the concept of Hell. When Clapp found no scriptural justification, he immediately set out on a personal journey to reread the Scriptures. In the course of his study, without having "seen or read any of the writings of the Unitarian or Universalist divines, not even those of Dr. Channing," Clapp was convinced of the error of his earlier theological position.[4] As his biographer tells the story, Clapp's "religious development was solely the result of his inquiring mind, his broad experiences, and his constant and avid study of biblical sources."[5] When Clapp believed that his initial discovery was confirmed in his search, he declared, "Among all the Unitarian and Universalist writings which I have seen, no work as to expansion or liberality of spirit and sentiment is comparable with the New Testament, especially the Sermon on the Mount, the Acts, and the Epistles." For the next three decades Clapp would hammer out a theology that upheld biblical centrality and the "final happiness of all mankind in the eternal world."[6]

Even during his first session with the Mississippi Presbytery in 1824, problems between Clapp and his Calvinist coreligionists began to surface. At the meeting rumors had circulated among the delegates that despite their affirmation of the Westminster Confession of Faith, Clapp and some members of his church entertained theological notions that did not conform to those of the Presbyterian church. Even so, no serious attention was paid to these rumors until Dr. John Rollins presented specific allegations against Clapp in the fall of 1826. A committee was established to visit New Orleans and investigate the matter.[7] Formal charges soon followed.

For the next six years, until 1832, when Clapp was convicted of heresy, controversy and tension continued between Clapp and the Mississippi Presbytery as they exchanged charges, recantations, and rewordings of statements. In 1832, Clapp was brought to trial on two counts: doctrinal heresy and unchristian (immoral) conduct (the latter was dropped soon after). Drawing from an arsenal it had built up over the years, the Presbytery charged that Clapp "rejected the doctrine of original sin, denied the Trinity, did not hold the doctrine of 'decrees of God,' denied the deity of Jesus, regarded the observance of the Sabbath as optional, and did not believe in intercessory prayer."[8] After a sensational trial, Clapp was suspended from the ministry on December 22, 1832. The Presbytery also decided that his suspension could be lifted if he showed signs of repentance. This was an unlikely option for Clapp.

Considering the ethnic and cultural makeup of the city of New Orleans, it was not too surprising that the members of Clapp's congregation did not themselves readily conform to the strict Calvinism that the Presbytery upheld. As the controversy escalated over the years, most members began to show support for Clapp. On February 26, 1833, the congregation voted by a margin of 86 to 26 to continue with Clapp as their pastor despite the Presbytery's actions. As a result, the majority retained the church property and immediately formed the First Congregational Church of New Orleans. For all intents and purposes, Clapp's church operated as an independent church from that point on, even though it did not outwardly bear the name Unitarian until 1853 when its charter was renewed as the First Congregational

Unitarian Church of New Orleans. But even then the Unitarian title only lasted two years until 1855 when Clapp changed the name to a less sectarian one, The Church of the Messiah. After the split with the Presbytery in 1832, the remaining members who did not follow Clapp withdrew and reorganized to form the First Presbyterian Church of New Orleans, which now traces its roots back to both Larned and Clapp. With these troubles behind him, Clapp began to focus his attention on his ministry and his church's place in the community.

But Northern Unitarian clergy soon noticed the differences between their faith and that of Theodore Clapp. G. W. Hosmer, a Northern Unitarian minister visiting New Orleans, described Theodore Clapp as a "trinitarian, though he does not own the name—he is a restorationist."[9] Charles Briggs relayed the same message to the A.U.A. "[Clapp] will let Mr. Eliot & myself preach in his church in afternoons (when nobody goes to church)," Briggs lamented, "if we will preach practical sermons & not Unitarianism as such."[10] For a good portion of the late 1840s, the *Christian Register* carried exchanges of letters between the editor and Clapp concerning his "deviant" Universalism. The editor charged, "Your argument . . . is based on the Edwardean theory of the will (which is the same as Priestley's) and not on the moral freedom of the human will as maintained by Channing. . . . I do not know that any of our ministers teach that the good works of Christianity . . . merit an endless reward of happiness beyond the grave." The editor concluded that such a reward was the gift of God and that inasmuch as good works are the "manifestations of a *character* of goodness, they are inseparably connected with endless happiness." "I trust you perceive the difference," he declared. "I think, however, you still labor under some disadvantages from your old Calvinistic notions of grace."[11]

RICHMOND

Although general secretary Charles Briggs of the A.U.A. claimed to have founded the Richmond church, the church was not cited in its first listing of Unitarian congregations in the United States, published in 1846, nor was it listed at any other time during the antebellum period.[12] It was, however, included in what appears to be the first history of the Unitarian churches in the South written, officially sanctioned, and pub-

lished by the A.U.A. at the turn of the twentieth century.[13] After the
Civil War when the church building was sold, the proceeds were split
between the Unitarian and Universalist denominations.

After the tragedy of a sudden fire that engulfed the Richmond Theater and claimed the lives of seventy-two citizens on the night of December 26, 1811, the community turned to the spiritual for comfort and
understanding. In the wake of Anglican disestablishment there appears
to have been an awakening of sorts among the citizenry that renewed
interest in organized religion throughout the city. On the theater site
the citizens of Richmond erected the Second Episcopal Church as a
memorial to those who perished. The next year both Presbyterians and
Roman Catholics organized while Baptist and Methodist churches began to attract new worshipers. Although the excitement engendered by
the disaster waned over the years, the emphasis on organized religion
remained.[14]

In 1824 William Hagadorn, the first of several Northern Universalist
missionaries to visit the state, spent six months in Richmond preaching
the tenets of his faith, though no attempt was then made to organize a
church. The next year, Edward Mitchell gained followers in Richmond
after he preached there, but like Hagadorn before him, neither he nor
his adherents made any attempt at forming a church. In 1830, however,
John Bovee Dods, who had preached for several years in Levant, Maine,
spent ten weeks in Richmond and finally brought together scattered
Unitarians and Universalists in the city. Through his leadership, forty-
two men organized the Unitarian-Universalist Society of Richmond,
commonly called the Uni-Uni Church.[15] While there were Universalist
congregations in the South, mostly in rural areas, no other single congregation had yet formally merged these faiths and been so bold as to
bear both names in its title. Members of the society urged Dods to
become their minister, but he declined and recommended John Budd
Pitkin from Baltimore for the position. Dods returned to Maine and in
1836 moved to Provincetown, Massachusetts, where he preached Universalism and founded a school. He later became interested in psychic
phenomena and joined the spiritualist movement.

In the summer of 1830, the society in Richmond contacted Pitkin,
a native of Massachusetts, who was then living in Baltimore and who
had been converted to Universalism through a close friendship with

Otis Ainsworth Skinner. Skinner, originally from Vermont, had become a Universalist minister in Baltimore in 1826, and along with Pitkin published the *Southern Pioneer and Gospel Visitor*, which among other things contained "reports of the dedication of Universalist churches, the ordination of Universalist ministers, and the publication of Universalist tracts."[16] On April 21, 1831, Pitkin delivered his first sermon to the Unitarian-Universalist Society in Richmond and soon thereafter accepted the society's offer to become its permanent minister. A year later, on May 22, 1832, the "First Unitarian-Universalist Society of Richmond" purchased a piece of property on Mayo Street and construction of a church building began shortly thereafter. In January 1833, the members dedicated their new building and during the same service Pitkin was ordained as a Universalist minister by Skinner.[17] Using the occasion advantageously so as to reassure the community of its Christian status and to minimize the theological differences of its members, the society adopted a new and more neutral name: the First Independent Christian Church of Richmond. The selection of Pitkin and the fact that Pitkin and Skinner engaged so actively in Universalist publications during the first years of Pitkin's ministry in Richmond suggest that, at least early on, the Universalist element within the society was the dominant force, if not the driving force, behind organization and consolidation.

Even so, it appears that the Unitarians supported these measures at each stage. In return, Universalist followers often catered to their fellow Unitarian members. In one of his first steps as minister, Pitkin recognized the strength and legitimacy of his Unitarian parishioners. He wrote to the editor of the *Unitarian,* a Boston publication, that the Richmond church was in a healthy and flourishing condition.[18] Unfortunately, as with the New Orleans church, the health of their first minister was not as strong as the reported state of their church. Early in January 1835, because of poor health, Pitkin left Richmond for St. Augustine, Florida, only to die there on February 9. The stunned congregation looked fervently for a replacement. Before he left for Florida, Pitkin himself, anticipating the inevitable, had written the A.U.A., "Let me urge you to interest yourself in our behalf in procuring a supply; and let me also hint to you the propriety of having the preacher well furnished with letters to the most respectable Gentlemen in Richmond."[19]

The A.U.A. quickly responded. General secretary Charles Briggs was already on a tour of the Southern states and he stopped by Richmond to assess the situation. It is not certain when Briggs arrived, but by February 23, two weeks to the day after Pitkin's death, Briggs wrote confidently that not only had he increased the number of pew renters threefold, but also that he could claim the yet "unorganized" society for the A.U.A., regardless of the independent history of the church itself and of the original forty-odd subscribers. "When I came here there were but a dozen pews rented; and now there are about 40—and the tide of public sentiment is beginning to react and set in our favor," Briggs declared. "I intend before I leave to form a church & organize a Sabbath School."[20] After Briggs departed, he wrote that the "deviant faction" within the church no longer posed a theological threat to the standards of the A.U.A. "And I think," he prematurely declared, "there will be no danger of Universalism getting the upper hand."[21] To make sure this did not happen, Briggs, in a letter to Gilman, suggested that Stephen Bulfinch of Augusta gather Pitkin's papers together "to make up a little volume mostly of practical and devotional character . . . showing that he was a Unitarian and not a Universalist."[22] During the summer and fall of 1835, Charles A. Farley, a recent graduate of Harvard Divinity School, supplied the pulpit, but he soon went to St. Louis where he was ordained in 1837. After that he would serve congregations in Illinois, Maine, and Connecticut before retiring in Savannah, where he established a private school.[23]

While the congregation had no luck initially finding a Unitarian minister they were successful in finding a Universalist minister, whose career in Virginia appears to have marked the golden age for the Richmond congregation. Edwin Hubbell Chapin, a Universalist minister from upper New York, first preached in Richmond in May 1838, and then after a trial period of three months, Chapin, aged twenty-three, agreed to become the second permanent minister of the First Independent Christian Church.

While the churches in New Orleans and Richmond had Universalist tendencies, they were cited as *Unitarian* churches by the A.U.A., which tried many times to hammer out their "deviant" theologies. For all intents and purposes, Charleston's Unitarianism remained relatively consistent throughout the antebellum period. And yet, like that of Charleston at the center, the Richmond and New Orleans churches on the Southern geographical periphery, and even factions within churches in the border states in Baltimore, Washington, D.C., and Louisville, Kentucky, would break from the A.U.A.

FOUR

Urban Unitarianism and the
Invisible Tradition

During the antebellum period the Southern economy remained dependent upon seaport and river towns to export cotton and other hin-
terland and lowland staples to Europe, the North, and the outside
world. Because of the nature of the agrarian economy, Southern urban
culture ebbed and flowed, as a town's population fluctuated, with the
waves of the seasons and on the hands of an agricultural clock. Southern
towns like Charleston, New Orleans, Augusta, Savannah, and Mobile
typically slept from late spring to early fall, awoke with the arrival of the
first cotton or tobacco shipments, and arranged their social and cultural
calendars around the staple markets. When harvests peaked in October
and cold snaps killed off disease-carrying mosquitos, farmers and country shoppers flocked to town to restock their homes and stores while
boats carried short- and long-staple cotton and lowland rice to city
docks. Commerce bustled until Christmas, enjoyed a small pause, and
then from January through April, seafaring vessels jammed the harbors,
hoping to make the mid-January rush to European destinations in order
to be back by mid-April for their second cargoes. By June, business
slowed down and many Southern urban dwellers retreated to the country, the hinterlands, their plantations, the North, or to European destinations. In Savannah Unitarian minister J. Allen Penniman lamented
that "many members are absent from the city for business and health."[1]
While diseases like yellow fever and "country fever" were influential in
the seasonal ebb and flow, the waves of people in and out of Southern
towns reflected both agricultural and market changes as well as malady.

During the course of the antebellum period, Southern towns quietly
grew in size and significance. In 1860, J. D. B. De Bow, founder and

editor of both the *Commercial Review of the South and West* and *De Bow's Review*, commented on the growing significance of urban life for the South: "Within the last forty years country life has quietly and almost imperceptibly undergone great changes. . . . the country [has] become more and more dependent on the town. Whether in pursuit of business, pleasure, or information, men leave the country and visit some neighboring city . . . Our bodies . . . are in the country, our souls in the town."[2] In the mid-1840s, De Bow had opened the pages of the *Commercial Review* to town boosters and publicists who lauded the physical advantages of town life, proclaimed the urban gospel, praised reform efforts, and spoke of the "spirit of improvement," the "intellectual achievements," and the "public taste" of Southern towns.[3] But as custodians of cosmopolitan life in a predominately agricultural economy, the professional classes of Southern towns remained drawn to the agrarian appeal. Expressions of gentility loomed large over the urban and rural landscape of the antebellum South, and "planter" status continued to be a formidable force in Southern social circles. By mid-century, Southern towns had become magnets for doctors, lawyers, writers, merchants, editors, ministers, and teachers. Although their numbers remained small when compared with the rest of the Southern population, the high visibility of the professional classes in towns, combined with their growing economic power and visibility, ensured their influence and political force. To secure their new-found status, the South's urban professionals, whenever possible, looked to the planter class for guidance, duplicating land and slave purchases and cultivating intellectual improvement and genteel customs, all as tried and true standards for prestige and power. For many Southern merchants especially, commercial and capitalistic enterprises were oftentimes only stepping-stones to the planter lifestyle. Historians William and Jane Pease have argued that many urban tradesmen used their profits not for furthering their businesses or increasing their incomes, but instead to buy land, plantations, and slaves, if not for themselves, in many instances, for their children. Rather than seeking individual capitalistic gain, the Peases argue, many Southern merchants bartered their urban wares for such intangible country values as social prestige, gentility, and political power. In Mobile, in addition to his work in agricultural commodities exchange, cotton merchant

Herbert C. Peabody owned vast tracts of land and numerous slaves, as did George E. Gibbon in Charleston and John Leeds in New Orleans, just to name a few.

But merchants were not the only ones who sought elements of agrarian distinctions and social prestige. The South's growing number of urban professionals aspired to various levels and elements of planter status. In the late 1820s, Augusta Unitarian minister Daniel Whitaker gave up the pulpit and became a planter in the South Carolina low country, devoting himself to the production of the Southern staples of cotton and rice. Other town ministers like Samuel Gilman in Charleston and Theodore Clapp in New Orleans, though not investing in large tracts of country land, purchased or rented slaves for domestic betterment and social prestige. In Unitarian congregations throughout the South, both ministers and laity owned slaves and land. In New Orleans, Unitarian member Samuel Bell owned thirteen slaves, member Henry D. Richardson owned six, J. J. Day, four, A. M. Holbrook, thirteen, Samuel Stewart, four, John Leeds, six, Thomas Adams, fourteen, and Samuel Kennedy, six. In Savannah, Unitarian minister Dexter Clapp wrote that there were slaveowners in every Southern Unitarian congregation and that in nearly all of these churches, almost every member owned slaves.[4] In Charleston, at the funeral service of slave trader Z. B. Oakes, fellow church members of the Unitarian congregation praised the life and integrity of one of its most prominent members.[5]

Throughout the urban South, the possession of slaves served both symbolic and functional purposes for Unitarians. Slaveownership served as a symbol of prestige and gentility, and when coupled with their own professional careers, helped to determine the social relationships, associations, and organizations in which Southern Unitarians would lead and join. These relationships and associations tied Unitarians closer to other Southerners, to a growing sense of sectional consciousness and Southern identity, and helped them, when under attack, to shape an underground network of liberal faith hiding just below the surface of institutional religion.

Slave ownership, land, power, and prestige also strengthened the distinctions of class and fueled the established intricacies of a hierarchical society. Hierarchy in Charleston, New Orleans, and other port cities in the South defined what David Moltke-Hansen calls the "channels of intercourse, the conventions of discourse, and to a great degree, cultural expectations and values." According to Moltke-Hansen the community and literary culture of Charleston was "dominated by Episcopalians and Presbyterians of British and Huguenot extraction, plantation heritage, [and] cosmopolitan education and prejudice."[6] As Episcopalians and Presbyterians controlled first- and second-place positions in towns across the South, Unitarians came in a very close third.

As was the case with the cities in which they lived, the influence of Unitarians on the religious landscape of the antebellum South remained greater than their numbers. Although cities contained only a small part of the South's population during the antebellum period and Unitarians appeared to comprise only a small fraction of the South's religious groups, both cities and Unitarians more than made up for their size. Unitarianism attracted some of the urban South's most influential literary, professional, commercial, and mercantile classes who were impressed by the "rationality," simplicity, purity, and unity of its faith. Prominent doctors, lawyers, writers, editors, mayors, corporate officers, and merchants espoused Unitarian beliefs and were drawn to Southern cities not only for their own vocations, but also for the intellectual stimulation, opportunities for benevolence, and greater sense of freedom these urban areas engendered in allowing them to practice the rationality of their faith. While larger towns like Charleston and New Orleans drew the largest numbers, Unitarians were also scattered in smaller towns like Apalachicola, Florida; Montgomery, Alabama; Columbus, Macon, and Milledgeville, Georgia; Wilmington and Raleigh, North Carolina; and even small crossroads like Kabletown, Virginia.[7]

By 1850, the South had 7711 lawyers, 8559 teachers, and over twice as many doctors. These urban professionals identified themselves both in terms of their social and cultural milieu and their professions in general, expanding professional opportunities, facilities, standing, and numbers as the nineteenth century progressed. Unitarian contributions to all of the professional vocations remained disproportionately strong throughout the antebellum period as Unitarians ascended through the South's professional classes and formed close associations with other Southerners, often assuming prominent national and local roles. In addition to serving as president of the Bank of South Carolina, the Honorable

Thomas Lee of Charleston was also United States District Court judge for South Carolina. And the same Charleston congregation boasted at least ten doctors, one of whom, Dr. James Moultrie, Jr., served both as vice-president and president of the American Medical Association. In addition to Dr. Moultrie, Dr. Samuel Henry Dickson, Dr. Joshua Barker Whitridge, Dr. Jacob Ford Prioleau, Dr. Albert Mackey, Dr. Samuel Logan, Dr. William S. Monefeldt, Dr. Joseph Stevens, Dr. D. D. Graves, Dr. A. B. Rose, and Colonel Thomas Roper dominated medical advances, medical philanthropy, and medical education throughout the antebellum period. In Savannah, Dr. Richard Arnold served as the first secretary of the American Medical Association, mayor of the city for six terms, founder of the Savannah Medical College, and head of the Board of Education. In New Orleans, Theodore Clapp not only served as minister of the Unitarian church, he was also designated "chair of the Adjunct Professor of Anatomy" at the medical school of the University of New Orleans (which later became Tulane University). During the summers when epidemics ravaged the city, Clapp devoted countless hours to attending to the sick and bereaved.

In Clapp's congregation, Christian Roselius served as attorney general of the state of Louisiana while Henry Babcock practiced law locally in New Orleans. Unitarian merchants and businessmen also dominated the commercial and monetary activity of the Crescent City. As heads of leading trade firms, Joseph Oglesby and Samuel H. Kennedy controlled much of the Western trade from their seats in New Orleans and were influential in the development of railroads into and outside of Louisiana, Texas, and Mexico. Oglesby was elected president of the Louisiana National Bank and president of the Commercial Insurance Company, and elected mayor of the city of New Orleans (though he ultimately declined the offer). Thomas A. Adams served as president of the Crescent Mutual Insurance Company while Samuel Bell, Isaac Bridge, John Leeds, Abijah Fisk, Peter Laidlaw, William G. Hewes, and James H. Leverich controlled much of the city's market business.

Unitarians in the South were also prominent professional writers, literary contributors, and educational leaders. Winifred Gales, wife of Joseph Gales in Raleigh, North Carolina, wrote *Matilda Berkeley, or Family Anecdotes*, published in 1804. Mary Elizabeth Lee of Charleston, wife of U.S. District Court Judge Thomas Lee, was both a poet and a writer, publishing *Social evenings, or, Historical tales for youth* in 1840. Caroline Gilman, wife of Unitarian minister Samuel Gilman, became one of the most popular women writers of her day. In 1832 she began to edit one of the earliest children's papers in the United States, the *Southern Rosebud*, which was renamed the *Southern Rose* the next year. Her husband, Dr. Samuel Gilman, along with Dr. J. B. Whitridge, college president Martin Luther Hurlbut, Dr. Samuel Dickson, Dr. James Moultrie, Jr., Rev. Charles Taggart, and countless others made regular contributions to national periodicals and journals in the areas of literature, poetry, medicine, science, education, and moral philosophy, just to name a few.

Some of the South's most distinguished editors of newspapers and journals were also Unitarians. Daniel Whitaker edited the *Southern Literary Journal and Magazine of Arts* and the *Southern Quarterly Review* and made frequent contributions to the *National Intelligencer,* the *Christian Register,* the *Charleston Courier,* and the New Orleans *Times.* Edgar Allen Poe wrote of him, "Whitaker is one of the best essayists in North America, and stands in the foremost rank of elegant writers."[8] After selling the *National Intelligencer,* Joseph Gales edited the Raleigh *Register* and served as mayor of Raleigh for nineteen years. His son, Joseph Gales, Jr., along with William Seaton, Joseph Gales's son-in-law, later regained and co-owned the *National Intelligencer.* John Moncure Daniel was a prominent and controversial editor of the *Richmond Examiner,* L. W. Spratt edited the *Charleston Standard,* and A. M. Holbrook edited the *New Orleans Picayune.* In addition to his work in medicine and mayoral responsibilities, Dr. Richard Arnold published *The Georgian.*

As part of the new professional class in the urban South, Unitarian ministers frequently enjoyed the most intimate association with these powerful and influential Southerners. Their own intelligence and equanimity and the fact that they were privileged to minister to such an array of prominent laymen all brightened the ways in which they were perceived by the outside community and the ways in which they perceived themselves. Unitarian ministers often met regularly with other ministers for theological and academic discussions and in most instances enjoyed the "most friendly relations" with them. Samuel Gilman and Jasper Adams, Episcopal president of Charleston College, met regularly to read German Biblical criticism together. Gilman was a frequent and regular speaker at various clubs and organizations in Charleston and was part of that city's social and literary elite. By 1850, he could declare that "with the clergymen of this city . . . it has ever been my good fortune to hold the most friendly relations."[9] Meanwhile, Theodore Clapp moved among denominational circles on a regular basis, ministered to the sick and bereaved of the Crescent City, and was esteemed by all citizens of New Orleans.

While Samuel Gilman and Theodore Clapp enjoyed the "most friendly relations" with other ministers in Charleston and New Orleans in the last half of the antebellum years they understood that these relations had come at a high price. For many Unitarian congregations, the price they paid was often their ecclesiastical visibility. As evangelical attacks increased and became more vocal during the early antebellum years, Southern Unitarians began developing less visible forms of Unitarian life alongside the "visible" institution of the church. But Southern Unitarians realized that their unique prominence among the South's urban professionals assured their vocational status (no matter what happened to their church buildings) and provided the perfect forums for their own religious expressions, forums that in many instances were lingering just below the surface of organized religion and that were already firmly intact within the South's growing urban culture. In addition to their private reform efforts and those organized through benevolent societies, Southern Unitarians embarked on literary careers and endeavors, organized tract societies and intellectual forums, wrote newspaper and journal articles, and assumed leadership roles in both civic and professional organizations. In doing so, they forged a much needed space within Southern orthodoxy in which other Southerners would join, and in the process created a haven for retreat for themselves in the event of institutional decline. Even though they had fewer churches in the late 1850s than they had in the thirties, Southern Unitarians believed that their weaknesses had enabled them to remain pure and true to the truths of Christianity. Even though they did not rely on the church pulpit for the heartbeat of their religion, Southern Unitarians believed that they had never lost their faith. For that, they argued, they could thank the Unitarians in the North.

In Baltimore in 1821, Dr. Samuel Miller, professor of ecclesiastical history and church government at Princeton, declared to the members of the First Presbyterian Church that the "system of the Unitarians is nothing less than a total denial and subversion of the Christian religion."[10] In 1830 in Virginia, David Henkel published a pamphlet entitled *Against the Unitarians* attacking Unitarians for claiming Christian status.[11] Seven years later in Charleston the editor of the Baptist journal *The Southern Watchman* printed a scathing article on the "religious delinquencies" of Unitarianism and the threat that it posed to the "Christian world." "Unitarians," the editor declared, "in the esteem of all but themselves, have descended . . . in the scale of error [and] have plunged many fathoms in the gulf of impiety."[12] These were not isolated charges. Accusations against Unitarians mounted in the early years of the antebellum period as churches sprang up in urban areas across the South. Toward the end of his ministry in Charleston Samuel Gilman recalled the heated climate both he and members of his congregation had earlier faced: "The very name Unitarian bore with it an offensive odor. . . . Bitter speeches . . . were daily circulated against us with the activity of current coin. . . . Most persons . . . seemed to shrink from the employment of the epithet Unitarian."[13]

As the new kids on the block, Unitarians in both the North and South faced the difficult task of explaining their theological positions to the more established Christians, who often tended toward *odium theologicum,* and many of whom had become fully aroused by both the presence and number of Unitarian churches popping up on the religious landscape of urban America. Among conservatives, Unitarians were often called "atheists," "deists," and "Socinians." In 1825, the American Tract Society was founded, in large measure as an evangelistic and missionary extension of the Second Great Awakening. The society published literally millions of copies of religious and devotional volumes, moral tracts, hymnals, and periodicals.[14] But the founding of the American Tract Society came only after Unitarians in both the North and South had already organized similar societies. In 1821, Jared Sparks started the *Unitarian Miscellany* in Baltimore and soon had agents scattered throughout the South. There were agents in Washington, Charlestown, Winchester, Eastville, Petersburg, and Dickinson's Stone, Virginia; Raleigh, Charlotte, and New Bern, North Carolina; Nashville, Tennessee; Charleston, South Carolina; Paris, Cane Ridge, Georgetown, Lexington, Louisville, and Hopkinsville, Kentucky; and Pensacola, Florida, just to name a few places.[15] In 1829, the American Unitarian Association, founded in 1825, listed tract agents throughout the South: E. Picket at Wheeling, Virginia; Joseph Gales and son at Raleigh; Samuel Gilman and Thomas Cousins at Charleston; Thomas S. Metcalf at Augusta; Thomas M. Driscoll at Savannah; B. A. White at Milledgeville; B.C. and J. Keiser at Lexington, Kentucky; James A. Fraser at Louisville; Wilkins Tannehill at Nashville; Odiorne and Smith at Mobile; F. Beaumont at Natchez; and M. Caroll at New Orleans.

Facing mounting opposition, Unitarians in the early 1820s, in both the North and the South, had started utilizing tracts and pamphlets instead of revivals to cater to the head over the heart—so much so that Unitarians in general, according to one historian, became the most able and "capable group of writers in the history of American religion."[16] But for Southern Unitarians, the task of defending their theological position to orthodoxy was more difficult than for their Northern coreligionists. Not only did they have to defend their *Christian* name to Southern orthodox clergy, but they also had to combat the association of Unitarianism with all things Northern, an increasingly difficult chore. Many Southerners erroneously associated the Unitarians around them with the "fanaticism" of New England abolitionism. Accordingly, Southern Unitarians edited and sent back those religious publications from outside the South that generated theological discord, that delved into political areas that many believed were beyond the realm of the pulpit, and that tended to compound the problems they already faced.

In the early 1820s in Raleigh, North Carolina, Joseph Gales, through a variety of means, gathered a sizable number of North Carolina subscribers to the *Unitarian Miscellany* of Baltimore and later to the *North American Review.* In his own paper, the *Register,* he published a prospectus of the *Unitarian Miscellany* and proposed to Jared Sparks that the *Miscellany* turn over some of its overflow material for him to publish so that "these [and other Unitarian] extracts may find their way into newspapers and other periodical works . . . without [many] suspecting they contain the favorite sentiments of the Sect which is every where spoken against . . . and Prejudice may in this way be undermined."[17] Throughout the early 1820s, Gales published numerous Unitarian pamphlets, blanketing Raleigh and the surrounding area. Within a few years, he declared, "I believe we have put a stop to the preaching of our Clergy on the subject, for, as we could not give them Sermon for Sermon we published a Pamphlet for every Sermon they preached."[18]

With mounting opposition facing his ministry, Samuel Gilman declared, "We know of no better mode by which Unitarians can counteract its annoyances . . . than by giving our publications as wide a circulation as may be consistent with fair and proper measures."[19] In 1821, four years before the founding of either the A.U.A. in Boston or the American Tract Society, he and members of his church formed the Charleston Unitarian Book and Tract Society, the first organization in the United States for the circulation of Unitarian literature. In Augusta, members of the church, without the aid of a minister, formed the Augusta Unitarian Book and Tract Society in the mid-1820s. When Stephen Bulfinch became minister, he continued to push for increased activity of the Augusta Book Society and called for a wider circulation among the general public. In a letter to the A.U.A., Bulfinch stressed the need for Southern congregations to clarify theological issues and for increased funding for publications. "The progress of Unitarianism here and elsewhere at the South has not been without opposition, and this opposition is certainly manifesting itself more decidedly."[20] Though often besieged by orthodoxy, Bulfinch realized that not all those outside of his congregation aligned themselves with those who issued the attacks. A week before his September 20 letter to the A.U.A., he also wrote of the importance of theological clarification, and he had a notable example to offer, for one never really knew who would be touched by the effort, even a Presidential candidate:

> To illustrate the importance of letting our views be understood, a member of our congregation told me that the other day, he had recently visited Judge Crawford, the late candidate for the Presidency, and in conversation Mr. C said something against the Unitarians. His visitor inquired if

he knew anything about them, and being answered in the negative, explained the doctrine to him.

At the end of the conversation, Bulfinch continued, "the Judge discovered that he had held Unitarian sentiments for years."[21]

In an attempt to diminish both the real and perceived gap that divided his congregation from the orthodox churches, Bulfinch began a literary periodical called the *Unitarian Christian* to assert what he described as "their Christianity and their right to fellowship among Christians and to serve as an outlet for more general literary material." The periodical boasted articles on such topics as temperance, Sunday schools, the origin of the doctrine of the Trinity, and the faith of the apostles, and contained poems of Bulfinch and Caroline Gilman. Though the periodical lasted only a year, the Augusta Unitarian Book and Tract Society continued to forge ahead.

In Charleston, the mission of the book and tract society met with unforeseen success. In 1831, on the tenth anniversary of its founding, Gilman declared that the society had not only retained its ground, but increased in "favor and usefulness, far beyond the expectations of its original projections." "It began with about 30 subscribers," he recalled, "but during the last six years, its average number of members has never been lower than seventy. About 200 different works have been distributed among us since the commencement of our transactions."[22]

In countering attacks by zealous evangelicals through local papers and book and tract societies, Southern Unitarians realized the great importance and utility of the written over the spoken word. They believed that the written word kept the sanctity of individual conscience intact, helped keep politics out of the pulpit, and aided in maintaining "reasonableness" over the emotional zeal of evangelical preaching and revivalism. For Southern Unitarians, the written word allowed an individual to be more reflective, sound, and reasonable in matters of faith and allowed them a quiet forum for arguing their positions. It catered to the head over the heart and assumed a much lower profile than the visible signs of a church steeple or the audible strains of an emotional minister. The written word formed the basis for intellectual cultivation, which for them was the backbone of personal improvement and social reform. In short, the written word provided the perfect tool for a faith that was becoming unreceptive to institutional religion and one whose "invisible" forums were maturing in the underground of the South's religious landscape.

Unitarian ministers did much to contribute to the written forums of intellectual cultivation in the South and in their respective cities. In addition to their sermons, they published numerous and significant articles and books on topics in religion, literature, moral philosophy, theology, and science, and these publications became an index of their clerical success and prestige. In moral philosophy, Samuel Gilman wrote extensively on Scottish Common Sense Realism, especially on the writings of Thomas Brown, publishing numerous articles on the subject: "Brown's Philosophy of the Human Mind" in the *Southern Quarterly Review* in 1829; "Brown's Philosophy of Mind" in the *North American Review* in 1824; "Cause and Effect" in the *North American Review* in 1821; and "Character and Writings of Dr. Brown" in the *North American Review* in 1825. Gilman's most noteworthy sermons were also published: *Revealed Religion: A Dudleian Lecture Delivered in the Chapel of the University at Cambridge*, Boston, 1848; *A Sermon on the Introduction to the Gospel of St. John*, Charleston, 1825; *The Old and the New: Discourses and Proceedings at the Dedication of the Re-Modeled Unitarian Church*, Charleston, 1854; and, perhaps his most famous discourse, *Unitarian Christianity Free from Objectionable Extremes: A Sermon Preached at the Dedication of the Unitarian Church in Augusta, Georgia*, Charleston, 1828. In addition, Gilman published two major works, *Contributions to Religion* in Charleston in 1860 and *Contributions to Literature* in Boston in 1856. Meanwhile, Charles Taggart's "The Diversity and Origin of Human Races" appeared in the *Southern Quarterly Review* in October 1851, and a collection of his sermons and those of Anthony Forster were published posthumously. In 1834, *Poems by Stephen Greenleaf Bulfinch* was published in Charleston, followed by *Manuscript book of poetry and prose* sometime later. During his ministry in Georgia, the Augusta Unitarian Book and Tract Society published several of Bulfinch's sermons. In Richmond, Edwin Hubbell Chapin contributed several poems to the *Southern Literary Messenger* and also assisted with the editing of that magazine.[23] In New Orleans, in addition to writing a series of articles for the *Christian Register* in the 1840s and having several of his sermons published, Theodore Clapp published *Autobiographical sketches and recollections* in 1857, followed in 1859 by his *Theological views, comprising the substance of teachings during a ministry of thirty-five years, in New Orleans*. Moreover, A. M. Holbrook, editor of the *New Orleans Picayune*, published Clapp's sermons on the front page of his paper on a regular basis.

"Ambassadors of Heaven"

While their own natural gifts, education, publications, eloquence, and equanimity did much to elevate many Unitarian ministers in the eyes of Southerners, Unitarian ministers never perceived themselves as lone custodians of intelligence among ignorant parishioners, nor assumed their primary responsibilities lay in intellectual pursuits. While Gilman and other Unitarian clergy believed that "a clergyman ought to be somewhat in advance of the general standard of information prevailing in the community," including "every variety of topic . . . for the general edification of a modern Christian congregation," Unitarian ministers believed their main purpose was the spiritual interests of those entrusted to their care, and that to "them must be devoted the main energies of [a minister's] being." Unitarian clergymen in the South saw themselves as ministers to the sick, poor, troubled, and bereaved, "ambassadors of heaven" to their parishioners and communities, and along with their own parishioners, as part of a larger liberal cause in the struggle for the purity of faith and the truths of Christianity.

Much attention has recently focused on the role of clergymen in the South in general and Samuel Gilman's ministerial legacy in Charleston in particular. Bertram Wyatt-Brown sees Southern urban clergymen as vulnerable cultural intermediaries between a world of intellectual cosmopolitanism on the one hand and proslavery defensiveness on the other. E. Brooks Holifield views urban clergymen as rationalist intellectuals immersed in Scottish Common Sense philosophy. Daniel Walker Howe asks of Samuel Gilman, "How . . . [does] a northern intellectual . . . pursue gradual progress within such an intolerant society as antebellum South Carolina?" Arguing that Gilman was homesick for New England, Howe attempts to demonstrate that "the career of Samuel Gilman was that of a talented and conscientious man enervated by a stifling environment. . . . he [had] a debilitating inner tension between a desire to exercise moral leadership and the hyperconventional, placatory role thrust upon him in Charleston."[24] While Howe sees Gilman as a bridge between the worlds of "New England moralism and South Carolina aestheticism," he also scolds him for his "lack of social involvement and acceptance of responsibility."[25]

But Gilman had a very different view of his role as minister and his place within the Southern community. While he believed that intellectual cultivation and moral responsibility were important for every clergyman, and did much to advance himself in both regards, he felt that intellectual betterment as a virtuous requirement was better achieved as part of a group. In light of the many gifted professionals who weekly graced his pews, Gilman argued that intellectual cultivation, at least for him, should come below the primary assignments of "servant," caregiver, and spiritual leader. As moral leaders, Gilman believed that ministers could assume those responsibilities more effectively in private devotion rather than public commitment, and through quiet deed over loud pulpit admonitions. For Gilman, these "behind the scenes" priorities reflected the nature in which Unitarianism in the South was developing its "underground" and "invisible" associations and networks. The same was certainly true for Theodore Clapp, who risked his life almost every summer to minister to the sick, dying, and bereaved as fevers plagued New Orleans. Because they saw their primary responsibilities as spiritual caregivers, much of these ministers' real contributions have remained hidden and unnoticed by historians who have too often viewed them through the "stifling" lenses of proslavery ideology or equated the role of minister with literary or scholarly significance. While Gilman believed that intellectual cultivation and moral leadership were important, he saw the role of minister more as that of compassionate servant and an "ambassador of heaven":

A very extensive and varied mental cultivation is not generally desirable for the profession of a clergyman. . . . even on the secular days of the week, his position necessarily renders a clergyman the servant, or minister of all. It is difficult, if not impossible for him to pursue large plans of comprehensive study, or engage in the production of elaborate literary performances, while faithfully attending to the immeasurable minor details which encroach upon his attention and his time. The tale of private sorrow must be permitted to reach his ear; the requests of humble poverty must find in him a ready counselor and assistant; the perplexities of the troubled conscience must obtain from him some soothing attempts at relief. . . . Feeling himself a subject of those solemn retributions which he professionally inculcates on others, the more prudent and self-distrusting ambassador of heaven will willingly forego the glittering distinctions of time, looking forward to the period, when they that be wise shall shiver at the brightness of the firmament.[26]

THE ACTIVE LAITY

In their appeal to the professional classes, Unitarian ministers worked alongside Unitarian laity in a combined effort to turn the tide of "emotionalism" amidst mounting evangelical waves. E. Brooks Holifield has argued that town pastors engendered the ideals of "gentility" and "rationality" in formulating their versions of orthodoxy to the professional and planter classes in the urban South,[27] and Unitarian ministers proved to be no exception. What was exceptional, however, was the extent to which Unitarian ministers were aided in the process by the educated professionals in their own congregations. For Samuel Gilman and other Unitarian ministers in the South, "it [was] not enough for a clergyman to contemplate his relations and duties from his own point of view. He must naturally be very much assisted in the task by borrowing . . . sentiments [from] enlightened and conscientious laymen."[28] For Gilman, one's relations with others made for a more "enlightened" perspective, one that was both balanced and in harmony with other rational opinions.

But being assisted by "enlightened" and "conscientious" laity did more than bring balance and harmony to rational opinions. It also fueled the fire of the Unitarian faith by suffusing the liberal tradition to points outside of the pulpit. In Augusta, members of the Unitarian church started the Book and Tract Society without the aid of a minister, and for twenty years after the departure of Rev. Stephen Bulfinch kept the society alive through periodic meetings, gatherings, and tract society publications. In Charleston, much of the groundwork for the book and tract society was laid before Samuel Gilman had even arrived. In Mobile, Unitarian laity kept the congregation together for years after they had a full-time minister, holding their own services and securing their own supply ministers. In Richmond, without a minister, Robert Poore, Samuel S. Saunders, and William W. Dunnavant published a pamphlet "for general and free distribution" to profess their faith in Christianity and to vindicate their Universalism from the "false and injurious aspersions" leveled against them.[29] In Charleston, Dr. Joshua Barker Whitridge of Gilman's congregation in Charleston took his turn in the theological debate and in expounding the "rationality" of the Unitarian faith. In response to charges by the editor of *The Southern Watchman*, Whitridge declared:

> The republications of such vile statements . . . [are] no doubt intended to bring a whole denomination of Christians into disrepute. . . . [These Christians] have shed lustre upon the scriptural, harmonious, and beautiful system, which is distinguished by the simplicity and sublimity of its great characteristic doctrine of the unity of God—and which passes under the enviable name of Unitarianism. A name which Mr. Hall and others would fain deprive us of . . . [30]

URBAN GENTILITY

For Southern Unitarians, the "rationality" of their faith reflected a fundamental world view that they believed was not only "natural" and "reasonable," but also one that stressed the importance of "balance," "simplicity," "symmetry," and "harmony," as Whitridge indicated in his response to the editor of the *Watchman*. As Unitarian laity and ministers worked together in expounding their religious rationalism to the public at large, they carried the same notions of harmony, symmetry, and balance into their ideas of "gentility." Like other Southern intellectuals, Southern Unitarians embarked on literary endeavors that promoted ideas of gentility in letters, diaries, journals, books, poems, and articles. In addition to being exceptional ministers, conscientious caregivers, and accomplished writers, Edwin Hubbell Chapin, Stephen Greenleaf Bulfinch, and Samuel Gilman were also nationally acclaimed published poets, and Gilman's wife, Caroline, was perhaps even better known as a poet than her husband. Samuel H. Dickson, Mary Elizabeth Lee, and Mary Whitaker (wife of Daniel K. Whitaker) were also prominent poets throughout the South. For these and other Southern Unitarians, "gentility" engendered not only notions of virtue, piety, and natural beauty but also "relational" qualities, such as balance, harmony, and symmetry, and they reflected these ideas throughout their writings and publications. In 1845, J. B. Whitridge spoke of the important balance in the relationship between father and son in his published reflection, *Letters, advice, &c., from a father to his son, preparing for college.*[31] Throughout her poems, verses, and prose Caroline Gilman spoke eloquently about the virtue of family and of harmony in the relationships between husband and wife, mother and daughter, and father and son.

Beyond the poetical genre, Southern Unitarians also cultivated notions of "gentility" through laudatory biographies. E. Brooks Holifield has argued that clerical biographies "fused the aristocratic 'life and letters' tradition with an older style of spiritual biography, and thus combined a literary genre that catered to and memorialized men of rank and station with another genre that preached of piety and humility and exalted the virtues of the simple Christian."[32] While clerical biographies were important for the elevation of clergy in other denominations, Southern Unitarians included laity in the genre, embracing prominent statesmen especially: men like George Washington, John C. Calhoun, and even the Roman emperor, Julian—men who chose to keep their liberal faiths to themselves, out of politics, and "hidden" just below the surface of their public lives. In addition to Jared Sparks's momentous biography of George Washington, Samuel Gilman continued to extol the gentility and virtues of George Washington as chaplain of the Washington Light Infantry in Charleston. On the 125th anniversary of the birth of Washington, Gilman addressed both members of the infantry and those of his church in a sermon later published in Charleston. Gilman related most with and admired the "hidden" and "invisible" qualities of Washington. Advocating the virtues of character in the "shade" over those seen in the "sunshine," Gilman's remarks struck a chord with those whose faith was being nurtured underground and invisibly. "No merely human character could constitute a better study and model for earnest imitation than that of Washington," Gilman declared. He continued: "It is to Washington in the shade that I would point as to one of the dearest treasures of humanity. . . . It is Washington contending with difficulties, rather than Washington waving his glittering sword of conquest . . . that ought to be habitually contemplated and prized by every youthful American."[33]

When Charleston Unitarian layman A. G. Mackey spoke before the Grand and Subordinate lodges of Ancient Freemasons in Charleston in 1852, he bestowed on Washington elements of freemasonry and championed him a leader in the cause. Upon the death of John C. Calhoun, Samuel Gilman was chosen over William Gilmore Simms to write the poetic eulogy, and he expounded the same qualities in Calhoun as he had in Washington. Likewise, with the help of fellow church member *Picayune* editor A. M. Holbrook, Louisiana Attorney General Christian Roselius, along with other leading citizens of New Orleans, memorialized the life of Calhoun in their combined published work, *A history of the proceedings in the city of New Orleans, on the occasion of the funeral ceremonies in honor of Calhoun, Clay and Webster.*[34] In the same tradition, Richmond *Examiner* editor John Moncure Daniel praised the character and leadership of one of the Confederacy's most honored and revered generals in his *The life of Stonewall Jackson.*[35] Charleston minister J. R. McFarland revered the faith and bravery of one of Rome's famed emperors in his published discourse, *Julian, Emperor of Rome, commonly called Apostate.*[36]

Unitarians also frequently eulogized and lauded the lives of their own clergy and laity in published funeral discourses and in biographies attached to posthumously published sermons. When church member U.S. District Court Judge Thomas Lee passed away Samuel Gilman's reflective discourse on his "life and character" was published and circulated widely throughout Charleston and South Carolina. Joshua B. Whitridge published in 1842 *A Tribute of respect to the memory of Mrs. Eliza Crocker,* a fellow church member in Charleston, while Gilman published a biographical memoir along with *The poetical remains of Mary Elizabeth Lee* in 1851. With an unusually high death rate among their young clergymen especially, funeral discourses of young ministers peppered Southern Unitarian literature, praising the lives and fortitude of these liberal pioneers taken before their time. In Charleston, layman Martin Luther Hurlbut published a biographical sketch of young Anthony Forster attached to a collection of his sermons. Decades later, John H. Heywood extolled the same virtues in his published memoir and collec-

tion of sermons of the Rev. Charles Taggart. In Augusta, Stephen Bulfinch wrote and published memoirs of Richmond minister John Budd
Pitkin along with a collection of fifteen of his sermons. When William
Vincent Thacher died suddenly in Savannah, Richard Arnold's paper,
The Georgian, relayed the bereavement of the congregation and fondly
remembered the young minister who had just accepted their full-time
call. When Samuel Gilman died in 1858, Unitarians throughout the
South grieved over their bright "anchor" in Charleston. In Mobile, Alabama, Herbert C. Peabody wrote, "a recent dispensation of Providence
in removing one of our dearest friends has awakened a new desire to
endeavor to perpetuate the excellent Christian character and steadfast
faith of [these] dear departed spirits. . . . The bright examples of Sparks
at Baltimore, Gilman at Charleston, Pierpont at Savannah . . . are of
themselves sufficient to inspire them." Closer to home, the Charleston
community was stunned by the sudden death of Gilman, and his death
was mourned not only statewide but also throughout the South. The
editor of the Charleston *Courier* declared: "Seldom, has our city witnessed an occasion of more sincere, wide-spread and spontaneous utter-
ance of grief and sorrow. . . . Never, since the solemn deposit of the
body of Calhoun, has such a scene passed before our observation. . . . It
will be the melancholy office of the citizens of Charleston, in varied
relations and associations, to do honor to such exemplary worth and
merits." When Theodore Clapp died, New Orleans church member
and editor A. M. Holbrook wrote in the *Daily Picayune,* "And who that
lived here with him were not his friends? Who could fail to be such to
one who was the friend of the otherwise friendless, of the stranger and
solitary. For the whole of his life here it was his peculiar self-imposed
duty to watch and wait on the sick during every epidemic which came
upon our city."[37]

Because of their professional status in the community, Unitarian
ministers, along with other Southern urban clergy, were expected to
participate in a variety of secular organizations that stimulated intellectual cultivation and cultural activity. For Unitarian ministers, involvement in these organizations provided "hidden" opportunities for clerical
interchange that formal denominational exchanges on the surface could
not. These opportunities thrust Unitarian ministers into close relations

with other town pastors and urban professionals, tying them more intricately to Southern orthodoxy, albeit in less visible clerical forms. Throughout the South, Unitarian ministers and professional laity became leaders in the literary development and intellectual cultivation of the South and of their respective cities. Southern Unitarians believed that their learning should have practical uses and that mercantile, industrial, and agricultural growth would make possible a more cultured and satisfying life for the community at large. Quoting popular German historian Arnold Heeren, Samuel Henry Dickson maintained that the "exchange of merchandise led to exchange of ideas; and by this mutual friction was kindled the sacred flame of humanity." Dickson and other Southern Unitarians fostered intellectual activities and along with other professional Southerners placed learning and intellectual pursuits at the center of the civilized man's life. Dickson concluded, "The progress of man in civilization, his advancement in knowledge, will be found as distinctly impressed upon the character of his reactions, his favorite amusements, and upon his occupations and serious pursuits." In Charleston in the early part of the antebellum period, intellectual activity and production increased as citizens sought to reform and to modernize their city, restore growth, and make it more competitive. Unitarians in Charleston, along with Episcopalians and Presbyterians, led the way. In addition to his activities as chaplain of the Washington Light Infantry, Samuel Gilman was also an active participant in the New England Society, the Marine Bible Society, the Charleston Private Club, and the Philosophical and Classical Seminary of Charleston, just to name a few. In Savannah, from the beginning of his ministry there in 1839, William Vincent Thacher attempted to make the Unitarian church a focal point in the cultural and intellectual life of the city. He invited guest lecturers, organists, and ministers, including Samuel Gilman, to speak and perform. And as with the Augusta congregation farther inland, he made strenuous efforts to organize a Sabbath School in that coastal Georgia town. A decade and a half later, in February 1855, John Pierpont, Jr., began a series of historical lectures in Savannah under the auspices of the Georgia Historical Society. During the week, when the building was not used for worship, Unitarians in New Orleans often opened their church doors for educational and intellectual enterprises. The congregation welcomed numerous lecturers into the building and used the proceeds for various social causes, including relief for "Destitute Orphan Boys." In 1832, a "Mr. Wheeler lectured on astronomy," while "Mr. Chapman" lectured on writing.[38] In 1835, "Dr. Powell" lectured on phrenology at the church and members of the medical community declared, "his lecture [was] one of the best they had ever heard."[39]

In Southern cities like Richmond, citizens openly and warmly embraced the lyceum movement that emerged in America in the late 1820s, imitating the British mechanics institutes. After the completion in 1826 of the imposing lecture hall in Norfolk, Virginia, citizens of Richmond constructed a similar edifice in that state capital and began holding weekly meetings. When Edwin Hubbell Chapin assumed ministerial duties in the Unitarian church in Richmond, he was well received in the urban community at large and quickly rose in the ranks of that city's literary and professional elite. On April 3, 1839, he addressed the anniversary meeting of the Richmond Lyceum and made such a favorable impression that the lyceum invited him to deliver a series of lectures. The series, entitled "Duties of Young Men," was published and was in use throughout Chapin's long career. At the request of the Richmond Light Dragoons, the Washington Grenadiers, and the Scarlett Guard, he delivered a Fourth of July oration in 1840 to the citizens of Richmond in which he extolled the virtues of the founding fathers of Virginia.

David Moltke-Hansen has recently argued that intellectual cultivation in Charleston was by its very nature a social occasion in which everybody knew everybody and personalities and friendships and the dynamics these relationships engendered dictated the terms of discourse. For Southern Unitarians especially, attacks by evangelicals often turned sour, particularly when done directly or aggressively. According to Moltke-Hansen, "ideas often assumed the personalities of their propagators, and debates were conducted according to the rules of social intercourse." For the Charleston intelligentsia, "to criticize or disagree was permissible; to attack directly or disparage (though done often enough) was not." As Moltke-Hansen puts it:

In attacking ideas, it was understood, one could not help attacking their spokesmen—often one's friends or one's friends' friends. This being the case, decorum, grace, delicacy, and diplomacy often were valued more highly than directness, rigor, forcefulness, and cogency. While originality was permitted, it was not applauded.[40]

Although Southern orthodoxy did achieve a great degree of denominational consensus and conformity, there were internal divisions. While other denominations in the South faced theological and ecclesiastical controversies over wide-ranging issues such as infant baptism, clerical dress, and religion and science, Unitarianism, for the most part, was able to avoid internal discord. Through the "spirit of improvement," the search for the primitivist church, ecumenical reform, and intellectual cultivation, Southern Unitarianism remained active below the surface of organized religion in the South, oftentimes existing in the shadows of ecclesiastical controversies. With the establishment of denominational colleges and universities in the South and increased activity and visibility of clergy in secular activities like the lyceum movement, urban clergy frequently faced accusations that they had perverted their calling "from the great end of pleasing God to that of pleasing men merely—in the tendency to make the office of the ministry a theatre for human display."[41] Taking aim at voluntary societies and reform movements, opponents often accused town ministers of watering down Christianity in their appeal to the professional and educated classes. While Southern Unitarian clergy cultivated notions of gentility in their secular activities and in their sermons, articles, and tracts, they also shared a great degree of clerical power and authority with the professional classes in their own pews, a strategy that masked some of their "visibility" and made these kinds of charges less poignant than they might otherwise have been. While other denominations grappled over issues of reason and faith, Southern Unitarians had long formed a consensus for intellectual improvement, believing that every academic discipline was, at heart, theological. For Southern Unitarians, as long as Biblical revelation remained at the center of academic and theological activities, intellectual pursuits were to be encouraged, and in the end would only confirm the reasonableness of Christianity and affirm the purity of its truths.

Dr. Joseph Priestley
English Unitarian and founder of Unitarianism in America. His *An History of the Corruptions of Christianity* (1782) greatly influenced the religious views of Thomas Jefferson. Portrait by Rembrandt Peale, c. 1801. Courtesy of the American Philosophical Society, Philadelphia, Pennsylvania.

Reverend Samuel Gilman

Author, poet, and minister of the Unitarian Church of Charleston and the most influential Unitarian in the South. During his long ministry in Charleston, Gilman and members of his church established the Charleston Unitarian Book and Tract Society, the first organization in the United States for the circulation of Unitarian literature; established churches in Savannah and Augusta, Georgia; and initiated an "Association of Southern Unitarians." Portrait by Thomas Sully, oil on canvas. Collection of the Sargent House Museum, Gloucester, Massachusetts.

Caroline Howard Gilman

Author, editor, poet, reformer, devoted wife of Rev. Samuel Gilman. Although a New Englander by birth, Caroline Gilman adopted South Carolina as home, advocated the Southern way of life in both word and deed, and became a staunch defender of states' rights. During the Civil War, she moved to Greenville, South Carolina, where she volunteered as a nurse for convalescing Confederate soldiers. Miniature portrait, artist unknown, watercolor on ivory. Courtesy of the South Caroliniana Library, University of South Carolina, Columbia, South Carolina.

Reverend Charles Manson Taggart
Associate minister, Unitarian Church of Charleston. One colleague said of
Taggart, "His inclinations led him to the West, [but] his predilections were still
stronger for the South," a region he would at times defend with "chivalric
enthusiasm . . . worthy of Calhoun." Photograph taken from *Sermons by Charles
Manson Taggart, Late Colleague Pastor of the Unitarian Church in Charleston, S. C.,
With a Memoir by John H. Heywood* (Charleston: S. G. Courtenay, 1856). Courtesy
of the South Caroliniana Library, University of South Carolina, Columbia,
South Carolina.

James Moultrie, Jr., M.D.
Member, Unitarian Church of Charleston, president of the American Medical
Association, founder and president of the South Carolina Medical Association,
and one of the South's most prominent medical reformers. Courtesy of the
Waring Historical Library, Medical University of South Carolina, Charleston,
South Carolina.

Samuel Henry Dickson, M.D.
Member, Unitarian Church of Charleston, co-founder of the Medical College of
South Carolina, leading temperance advocate, author of numerous articles on
medicine, philosophy, history, and current events, and one of the South's most
prominent medical and educational reformers. Courtesy of the Waring Historical
Library, Medical University of South Carolina, Charleston, South Carolina.

Colonel Thomas Roper
Unitarian benefactor and founder of the Roper Fund and Roper Hospital,
Charleston. Courtesy of the Waring Historical Library, Medical University of
South Carolina, Charleston, South Carolina.

Roper Hospital
Sketch taken from *Ballou's Pictorial Drawing Room Companion* (August 8, 1857).
Courtesy of the Waring Historical Library, Medical University of South
Carolina, Charleston, South Carolina.

"Old" Unitarian Church, Charleston, South Carolina
Sketch taken from Samuel Gilman, *The Old and the New: Discourses and Proceedings at the Dedication of the Re-modeled Unitarian Church* (Charleston: Samuel G. Courtenay, 1854). Courtesy of the South Caroliniana Library, University of South Carolina, Columbia, South Carolina.

"New" Unitarian Church, Charleston, South Carolina
The congregation hired the young architect and church member Francis D. Lee to remodel the building in the popular Gothic Revival style. He was commissioned to incorporate the old walls and tower into his new design. Sketch taken from Samuel Gilman, *The Old and the New: Discourses and Proceedings at the Dedication of the Re-modeled Unitarian Church* (Charleston: Samuel G. Courtenay, 1854). Courtesy of the South Caroliniana Library, University of South Carolina, Columbia, South Carolina.

Interior of The Unitarian Church of Charleston
Architect Francis D. Lee was inspired by the Henry VII chapel at Westminster Abbey, especially the delicate and lacy fan tracery ceiling there. He duplicated that beautiful ceiling in this church, and it is considered to be some of the finest Gothic Revival work extant in America. Courtesy of The Unitarian Church of Charleston.

Richard Arnold, M.D.
Member, Unitarian Church, Savannah, editor of *The Georgian,* founder of the
Savannah Medical College, mayor of Savannah for six terms, and one of the
South's most prominent medical reformers. Courtesy of the Georgia Historical
Society, Savannah, Georgia.

Unitarian Church, Savannah
The Georgian described the Grecian Ionic exterior as "plain, but beautiful, and [it] does not suffer in comparison with any public building in the city. It is chaste and simple in its design." Courtesy of the Georgia Historical Society, Savannah, Georgia.

Reverend Theodore Clapp
President of the College of New Orleans and minister, Unitarian Church, New
Orleans. Clapp was just as much a landmark of New Orleans as the "Strangers'
Church" itself. The church was known for the engaging oratorical style of its
minister, and it was said for years that merchants, planters, and visitors would
not leave New Orleans without going to the "American theatre, the French
opera, and Parson Clapp's Church." Portrait from John Duffy, ed., *Parson
Clapp of the Strangers' Church of New Orleans* (Baton Rouge: Louisiana State
University Press, 1957).

The Church of the Messiah
After the First Congregational Unitarian Church of New Orleans burned when the St. Charles Hotel located next to it caught fire, New Orleans Unitarians built the new church on a lot given them by benefactor Judah Touro on the corner of Julia and St. Charles streets. Like the Charleston church, the new building reflected the new Gothic-style influence. With the approval of his congregation, Clapp chose the name, The Church of the Messiah, in an attempt to discard the trappings of sectarianism and erase the Unitarian name from its synonymity with abolitionism. Photograph from John Duffy, ed., *Parson Clapp of the Strangers' Church of New Orleans* (Baton Rouge: Louisiana State University Press, 1957).

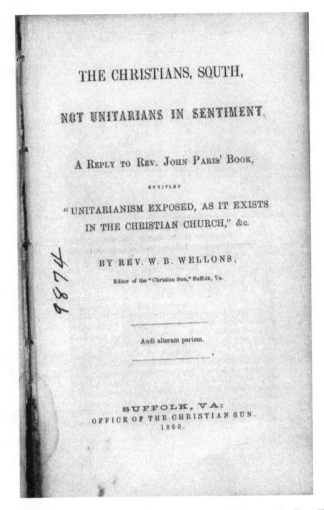

THE CHRISTIANS, SOUTH,

NOT UNITARIANS IN SENTIMENT.

A REPLY TO REV. JOHN PARIS' BOOK,

ENTITLED

"UNITARIANISM EXPOSED, AS IT EXISTS
IN THE CHRISTIAN CHURCH," &c.

BY REV. W. B. WELLONS,

Editor of the "Christian Sun," Suffolk, Va.

Audi alteram partem.

SUFFOLK, VA:
OFFICE OF THE CHRISTIAN SUN.
1860.

Title page, *The Christians, South, not Unitarians in Sentiment,* **by Rev. William Brock Wellons (1860)**
On the eve of the Civil War, Rev. John Paris, editor of the *North Carolina Christian Advocate,* charged that many Christians in North Carolina and Virginia, areas where there were no Unitarian churches, held Unitarian beliefs. In his rebuttal, *The Christians, South, not Unitarians in Sentiment,* Rev. William Brock Wellons, editor of the *Christian Sun* in Suffolk, Virginia, vehemently denied the assertion but finally conceded that it was absurd to classify "all Christians either with the Trinitarians or Unitarians." This debate, along with other accounts, suggests both the extent to which Arian Christology had infiltrated Southern orthodoxy and that Unitarian numbers in the South may very well have been much greater than historians have previously recognized. Generously loaned by the Elon College Library, Elon College, Elon, North Carolina.

FIVE • The Spirit of Improvement

At the dawn of the nineteenth century, religious leaders tried to reconcile the ideological expectations of the new nation with the more pragmatic realities of their everyday lives. Many looked upon the birth of the republic as indeed a New World, one that was far removed from the trappings of the Old World and free from the burdens of the past. They believed that the new nation represented a *novus ordo seclorum,* a new order of the ages, and that they stood at the threshold of millennialist expectation. As custodians of the new age, it was their responsibility to rid the universal church of the corruptions of history and the burdens of the past. But in addition to these ideological assumptions of the new age, religious groups were also faced with the difficult task of forging new responses to vast social and political changes brought on by the recent displacements of revolution, independence, debt, Anglican disestablishment, and federal direction. As churches reached a low ebb of activity and interest, the advent of the Second Great Awakening and readjustments of church and state relationship provided new opportunities for increased religious vitality and growth.

Spurred by the fear of past corruption and fed by the zeal of the Awakening, countless interdenominational groups bent on purity, reform, and benevolence sprang up across the new nation with high hopes for individual and collective progress and improvement and the pristine expectations of the new age. The American Board of Commissioners for Foreign Missions was founded in 1810, followed by the American Educational Society in 1815, the American Home Missionary Society and the American Society for the Promotion of Temperance in 1826, the American Peace Society in 1828, and the American Antislavery Society in 1833, just to name a few. These interdenominational societies and the individuals behind them carried the banner of a new purified, uncorrupted order, and they believed it their responsibility not only to redirect the moral path of the populace and deliver the nation from its collective sin, but also to provide stability along the way. Viewing their experience through the lenses of Scripture, religious leaders interpreted Scripture from the events that they witnessed. Many believed that sins such as public drunkenness, poverty, biblical illiteracy, and Sunday revelry were out of step with the new order and were, in large part, a direct result of various unprecedented forces unleashed on the new nation, forces such as rapid territorial expansion, new and challenging scientific discoveries, increased technology, growing industrialism, urban malaise, excessive greed, and heightened capitalism.

While reform societies did a good deal of work in the large rural areas of the nation, their presence and activity were more pronounced in America's growing number of cities and towns. Salvaging lost souls and implementing Christian principles appealed to citizens of seaport towns especially, where heightened activity and constant movement of people helped create feelings of instability and uncertainty. When sickness and disease exacerbated these forces and fueled feelings of instability, religious leaders knew they had their work cut out for them. Equating poverty with sin, nineteenth-century reformers found urban poverty different from the quiet and hidden poverty of the countryside. In towns, the visible and audible signs of poverty were more apparent to religious-minded reformers who sometimes confronted angry mobs, poor criminals, and hopeless unemployment.

Along with conscientious citizens of Boston and Philadelphia, Charlestonians eagerly joined local and national benevolent societies and enthusiastically entered into the circle of national reform. By 1826, Robert Mills believed that Charleston stood in the center of that circle of benevolence that extended across the entire nation. English traveler Captain Basil Hall included Charlestonians in his praise of zealous and liberal Americans who were "universally ready, not only with their money, but with their personal exertions to relieve the distress of their less fortunate fellow creatures."[1] Charleston claimed private and public relief systems dedicated to almost every human need. When Jeremiah Evarts, the head of the Boston-based American Board of Commissioners, visited the Southern coastal city fully expecting to bring lessons of charity to its citizens, he was surprised by Charlestonians' prosperity and generosity. "I was never in a place where so many people might give largely, without abridging any luxury, as here," he declared. "The mass of them give more liberally than the mass of people with the same wealth as New England." David Ramsay, historian and member of the Congregational church on Meeting Street, complained that citizens of Charleston carried charity "rather to excess."

But Southerners defined benevolence differently than did Northerners, and Unitarians in the South proved to be no exception. Northerners of Puritan heritage especially tended to see poverty in direct relation to degeneracy and used wealth to encourage virtue among the poor, assuming that a far-reaching reformation of society could be achieved through individual transformation. Southerners, on the other hand, retained an aristocratic view of duty, honor, and benevolence animated as much by noblesse oblige as Christian charity. They saw poverty as a product of God's ineffable world, and assigned charity to the ranks of duty within the existing hierarchical order. In Charleston, New Orleans, Augusta, Savannah, and other Southern cities, voluntary associations operated at full capacity. Empowered by a new sense of freedom, new notions of progress, and brighter views of the human will, individuals joined voluntary associations on their own terms, not as denominational representatives. The doctrine of free association had first provided the energy for disestablishment and later for separation of church and state in America. When coupled with the reform movement, voluntary associations allowed individuals to work for various causes with members of other denominations and to break out of once passive roles, becoming more active in expressing religious belief as well as reform interests. When Protestant ministers hesitated to leave the spiritual realm for worldly affairs to address social problems like intemperance, which they believed threatened the social and religious fabric of the Republic, lay activists took up the campaign against sin and immorality. In the process they began assuming much of the power of regulating public behavior that clergy once held. But as this power was distributed to the growing number of voluntary associations and reform movements, it also opened doors for problems. In many instances the individual and collective relations within and between these various groups were delicate: some individuals were consumed by missionary enthusiasm, some fed by religious zeal, and some interested in individual, family, and community betterment. The inherent tension existing among these various reform and voluntary impulses created some difficulties, but most were willing to put aside denominational and doctrinal differences and work toward a common good.

By fusing various notions of perfectibility with the optimistic mood of American "progress," and the growing belief in postmillennialism, religious leaders inextricably linked Arminian theology to the various reform movements of the nineteenth century. Compelled by an Arminian "democratic" theology without a democratic constituency, Unitarians in both the North and the South became pioneers of benevolent reform in the nineteenth century and sought social changes in many areas of American life. Along with evangelicals, many Southern Unitarians joined the vogue of voluntary associations that oftentimes served as bridges between religion and culture and religion and charity.

Through their reform work, the Gilmans and other Southern Unitarians worked side by side with evangelicals who were often members of the same organizations and who championed similar causes. Because of the voluntary nature of these groups and because individuals worked for reform through independent religious commitment and/or professional vocations, both groups, evangelicals and Unitarians, demonstrated remarkable degrees of toleration and acceptance in reform activities. Southern Unitarian reform many times penetrated the ground on which religion in the South was built without assuming ecclesiastical form. As part of the "spirit of improvement" it became intertwined with evangelical reform below the surface of organized religion in the South. There it continued to nurture a faith that had already begun developing "invisible" forms of expression alongside the visible rise of church steeples. As Unitarians became more active in reform, their faith took on a life of its own, independent of the church buildings they worshiped in, and unlike their theology, their reform efforts remained protected from institutional and denominational attacks.

Samuel Gilman's membership in benevolence organizations and Bible societies, including the Marine Bible Society in Charleston, bridged together other reform efforts, especially the ecumenical movement. Gilman praised Bible societies for their "simplicity . . . comprehensiveness . . . and adaptedness . . . [in] uniting together the worthy members of every sect, who might be otherwise repelled to an unapproachable distance from each other."[2] He encouraged religious reformers among Charleston's Jewish community. Members of the Charleston congregation declared, "Let us cultivate . . . love and affection . . . Christ teaches us that no peculiar forms of faith and articles of belief are necessary to constitute the tie of common brotherhood."[3] Theodore Clapp's work with other clergymen among New Orleans's poor personified the appeal of Southern Unitarian ecumenism (and reform in general). His unswerving ministry to the sick and bereaved endeared him to the hearts and minds of New Orleans's common citizens when numerous epidemics ravaged the city. Gilman, Clapp, and other Southern Unitarian clergy and laity not only believed in a core of Christianity, a central essence that sought to minimize denominational differences, but they also sought "to unite all persons who could possess and exhibit the true spirit of the Savior." Membership in Bible societies not only demonstrated the zeal of Southern Unitarians to purify the universal church of the taintedness of traditions by advocating the supremacy of Scripture, it also reflected their desire to do so outside of denominational categories.

It is perhaps their ecumenicism then that marked Southern Unitarians' most significant contribution to Southern orthodoxy. While other Protestant sects, in their quest to rid the church of the corruptions of the past, sought Protestant unity as part of the model of the primitive church of Jesus and the apostles, Southern Unitarians came closer to most, primarily because of their "invisible" status. Recent works by George Marsden, C. Leonard Allen, and Paul A. Baglyos shed new light on the primitivist quest and remind historians of the importance of the model and its concepts for antebellum Protestantism. Although concentrating primarily on Samuel Simon Schmucker and the Lutheran Church, Baglyos sees common characteristics of the movement within Protestantism as a whole. As Christians everywhere sought to plant in America a Christianity that thoroughly imitated the Christianity of the first century stripped of all later traditions, creeds, and other historical developments, Baglyos observes that religious groups shared three important features. One was a commitment to biblical supremacy ("no creed but the Bible"); the second was the tripartite division of history into a golden age, an era of decline, and an era of recovery; and the third, a tendency, not unlike that of Joseph Priestley, to denounce as "human invention" every aspect of church history not expressly warranted by Scripture.[4] But, as Baglyos concludes, as each sect sought to mirror the ancient apostolic order more closely than all others, the inherent competition "belied the rhetoric of Protestant unity that accompanied the quest for the primitive church: while biblicist Protestants agreed that conformity to the primitive model could eliminate the divisions between denominations, they disagreed about the details of the model and so perpetuated and even multiplied divisions."[5] The tendency of American primitivism to exacerbate sectarian division rather than promote genuine unity became the rule rather than the exception. But Southern Unitarians proved to be an exception despite the attacks by zealous evangelicals, not only by nourishing a faith underneath the surface of organized religion, but also through a fundamental commitment to the separation of church and state. One Northern Unitarian, writing of the importance of Dr. Clapp's church within the city of New Orleans, declared, "[T]here is less Sectarianism in this place than in any I was ever in. The prevailing spirit is liberal. Unitarians, Calvinists, Episcopalians, Catholics, and Nothingarians, contributed towards building the Methodist Church."[6] In Savannah, J. Allen Penniman declared, "[Our society] is made up of Unitarians, Presbyterians, Baptists, & Methodists, and has been from the beginning of my labors here."[7]

Southern Unitarians were able to move freely and oftentimes "invisibly" within and between those religious circles that for a long time had one foot in and one foot out of what was then deemed "orthodoxy." "Though we could not assent to all the doctrines of the Presbyterian, Episcopal or Baptist Churches," wrote Joseph Gales, "we scarcely ever failed to attend one or the other with our family during our residence in Raleigh. And as an evidence to my attachment to Christianity, I performed the duties of Corresponding Secretary of the Bible Society of the State for twenty years."[8] Likewise in Charleston by the early 1850s, Samuel Gilman could declare:

With the clergymen of this city, although not on terms of ecclesiastical interchange, it has ever been my good fortune to hold the most friendly relations. During a long season of illness, and absence from my charge, the pulpit was kindly supplied, in succession, by nearly twenty ministers.[9]

But as fellow custodians of the primitivist movement, Southern Unitarians had to reconcile ideological goals with everyday realities. In their ecumenical work and throughout all of their reform efforts, Southern Unitarians demonstrated a commitment to a divinely sanctioned, socially responsible, hierarchical world, and to its "peaceful occupations, privileges, and rights."[10] While Southern Unitarians were optimistic about the possibilities of human activity, their optimism was grounded and tempered by their belief that humanity was still very much dependent upon divine grace for any "worldly" accomplishments this side of heaven. This did not mean that one gave up on social improvements and progress. It did mean, however, that they worked for reform within existing parameters, respecting individual, familial, community, state, and constitutional obligations. The choices for Southern Unitarian reform, like the organizations they chose to work for reform in, reflected their fundamental commitment to the Southern way of life and the Southern world view. Southern Unitarians championed those reforms that strengthened the relationships of the family and cultivated intellectual and moral improvement. In addition to primitive and ecumenical reform, Southern Unitarians worked diligently alongside Presbyterians, Baptists, Methodists, and Catholics for the Bethel movement and maritime aid, Sabbatarianism, biblical literacy, temperance, medical improvements, increased opportunities for education, intellectual cultivation, women's rights, improvements in the health and living conditions of slaves, the inclusion of slaves and free blacks in worship services, and the education of slaves, just to name a few.[11]

The desire for reform among Southern Unitarians stemmed from their belief in an objective sense of religious conviction, personal, familial, and social obligations, and the Southern way of life. Heir to the latitudinarian/Jeffersonian ideal of separation of church, and propelled by disestablishment and voluntarism, Southern Unitarians avoided those reforms that were "isolationistic" in nature or that tended to cultivate "political feuds" and "public involvement." In his *Address to the South Carolina Society for the Promotion of Temperance*, Samuel Gilman, in characteristic ecumenical tone, spoke of the importance of the separation of church and state within the temperance movement. He declared, "The principle [of temperance] touches no jarring string of speculation. It involves no political feud. It is unconnected with theological divisions. It knows nothing of national distinctions."[12] The venue of choice for reform for Gilman and other Southern Unitarians, and for Southerners in general for that matter, came by way of benevolent societies, their own professional work, and social interaction with prominent Southerners in and out of their own ecclesiastical spheres. Because there were "no polished courts . . . to which the whole nation [could] look [for] the standard of approved manners," and because they wanted to keep the worlds of church and state separate, Gilman and other conscientious Southern Unitarians looked to benevolent societies as one of the best venues for reform. While the activities of benevolent societies often flirted with public involvement, they were done outside of the auspices of the church. For Gilman, benevolent societies were forums for "quiet, calm, reasonable" change. Membership in them was a *personal* statement of opinion and social preference, and not fiery demand for denominational approval based on moral self-righteousness. Gilman explained, "By uniting with [benevolent societies] I can reveal my opinion, without giving offence. I can share with others the obloquy of being a monitor. I can declare my conscientious testimony, which shall at once be silent and modest, yet public."[13]

Eugene Genovese and Elizabeth Fox-Genovese have argued that religion in the South "developed in large part as the world view of a modern slave society enmeshed in an increasingly capitalist Atlantic world." They suggest that the divine sanction of slavery led inexorably toward attacks on capitalism. For them, the Southern agrarian economy and the world view it encompassed assigned labor to the auspices of "household relationships." "Labor that escaped household governance," they argue, "could plausibly be viewed as anomalous and disruptive."[14] Samuel Gilman agreed. He lamented the dividing gulf between "lordly capital" and "panting labor," and cautioned that "wealth has no value except as being a means to higher ends." In support of Sabbath observance, he cited examples of industrial accidents that occurred when workers were denied a weekly day off. He claimed that medical reports indicated that the health of laborers and draft animals deteriorated without periodic time for recuperation.[15] Though many Unitarians in the South could claim New England heritage, they were part and parcel of the Southern landscape, and their reform efforts were very much a product of the regions' religious development and its political economy. In urban areas across the South, Unitarians saw excessive drinking, long hours, illiteracy, and poor working conditions as hazards of an encroaching industrial capitalism and believed something had to be done to turn the tide.

From roughly 1815 to 1830, Unitarians in both the North and South were leaders in a national conservative desire to ground the nation in Christian principles, forging what Barbara L. Bellows calls "one of the most enduring cultural ties between North and South."[16] In Charleston, many Unitarians became active members of the New England Society, an organization that sought to foster respect for and strengthen the various ties that bound their places of birth with their new homes in the South. Acting as both a social and benevolent organization, the New England Society often worked closely with the Charleston Port Society assisting sailors, many from Maine and Massachusetts, who sometimes found themselves in the "most destitute of circumstances."[17] In other river and seaport towns Southern Unitarians witnessed the same plight of sailors away from home and family. Bemoaning the disruptive isolation of maritime labor outside of "household governance," Unitarians throughout the South became active members in port societies and championed various maritime aid movements.

In Charleston, Augusta, and Savannah, Unitarian laity established a Sunday school for their children, a step that firmly placed them within the growing Sunday School movement then taking place in America and England, which sought religious and secular education for industrialism's uprooted populations. For nineteenth-century Southerners literacy was the first step toward biblical knowledge and Unitarians were quick to embrace the Sunday School movement as a solid step in that direction. Urban Sunday schools attracted teachers from a variety of churches who felt the need to do mission work. The editor of the *Southern Christian Advocate* argued that "a right principle in the heart, a simple hymn in the memory, or a pleasant little book in the hand, may be as a light to shine in a dark place." In the end, he asked, "is not this the true remedy for social evils, introduced at the right time and place and operating on the right class of persons?"[18] As members of the Female Domestic Missionary Society, women of the Circular Church, the Unitarian church, and other churches in Charleston often combed back alleyways and the poorer industrial sections of town, rounding up "vagrant and neglected children of our city" to enroll in these "nurseries of sacred learning."[19]

The temperance movement in Charleston and other port cities in the South was in many ways a reaction against one of the most obvious disruptive tendencies of industrial capitalism: excessive drinking. Dr. Samuel Dickson of Charleston delivered one of the first temperance addresses ever heard in the South and is said to have established the first temperance organization, the South Carolina Society for the Promotion of Temperance, of which Samuel Gilman was an active member. Targeting the medical and social harms of distilled liquors, Dickson, Gilman, and other Southern Unitarians championed a moderate approach, approving a temperate use of wines and fermented alcohol.

As a general movement, temperance was tied closely with other nineteenth-century reform efforts, especially the establishment of Bible societies, the ecumenical movement, and marine relief. The first Bible society was formed in England in 1780 and eventually became the British and Foreign Bible Society in 1804. The purpose of that organization was "to give to seamen in the British Navy, and soldiers in the army, the Bible." Other Bible societies dedicated to the "moral and religious improvement of seamen" were later formed in Boston and New York. In Charleston, the Marine Bible Society was formed on April 14, 1818, "to encourage the circulation of the Holy Scriptures, without note or comment, among seamen."[20]

In addition to their regular roundups in the streets of Charleston, members of the Female Domestic Missionary Society worked diligently to secure a minister for the Marine Society of Charleston. In 1819, the Rev. Jonas King arrived in Charleston as minister of the Marine Society. In 1822, the Bethel Union was formed to institute prayer meetings on board vessels, and the next year, 1823, the Charleston Port Society was organized for the purpose of promoting the Gospel among seamen. In 1826, the Ladies' Seamen's Friend Society was formed and in conjunction with the Bethel Union, originated for the world the idea of a "Temperance Boardinghouse" to accompany the world's first "Sailor's Home" already established in Charleston. For many Southern reformers, a Sailor's Home was merely one remedy for labor that "escaped household governance." As members of the board of managers, J. B. Whitridge, J. W. Harrison, and other prominent Southern Unitarians devoted themselves to the Charleston Port Society and maritime relief in general.[21] In Savannah, Jason Whitman and members of the Unitarian church devoted much of their time to the Savannah Bible Society, the temperance movement, and a local seaman's welfare group, as did Herbert C. Peabody and other Unitarians in Mobile.

The existence and impact of Unitarian reform efforts in New Orleans, including maritime relief, have been overlooked by overly simplistic portraits of "Parson Clapp's Church"—a church with "no donation party, no fairs, no organ recital, absolutely 'no nothing,' but Dr. Clapp and his weekly sermon."[22] But an 1839 contributor to the *Christian Register*, an "H.B.B.," discounts this notion, especially in regard to the Bethel movement in New Orleans. "Only let the proper efforts be made, by the proper authorities," H.B.B. declared, "and you will find the Southern people are not the wicked men in which some call them." The writer related that Clapp and members of the church raised more than twelve thousand dollars for a Seaman's Church, but the money fell into hands of those who "could do nothing for Christ" and was either mishandled or swindled by individuals or lost through extra-ecclesiastical factions and divisions.[23] The Unitarian church in New Orleans was also active on other fronts as well. Members channeled the proceeds from numerous educational and intellectual enterprises to various local social causes, including relief for "Destitute Orphan Boys." Clapp was also named one of the trustees of the Touro Free Library Society of New Orleans.

Thomas Adams, an active member of The Church of the Messiah and chairman of the board of trustees, worked assiduously for the establishment of a savings bank for the laboring poor in New Orleans. As an original trustee of the New Orleans Savings Institution, and its vice-president, Adams led the first institution of its kind in the South. In this and many other capacities, Adams's name became synonymous with charity in New Orleans. He also was vice-president of the Printing Institution for the Blind. His biographer described his quiet and reflective nature and his choice for a behind-the-scenes image:

Quiet and retired in his habits and tastes, he has uniformly declined any proposition of a political or public nature—shrinking always from attracting any kind of publicity. With a large and well selected library, a devotee to his profession, he may be said to seek happiness with his books, and in the refined domestic intercourse which awaits him, at his elegant mansion of Prytannia street. Here he is the earnest and sincere friend, the courtly host, and the frank, genial companion, fully informed on all subjects.[24]

Along with ecumenism, advances in literacy through the activities of Bible societies, the Sunday School movement, and the Printing Institute for the Blind, Southern Unitarians were leaders in various educational movements of the nineteenth century. In the field of medicine particularly, Southern Unitarians formed a formidable circle of doctors, administrators, surgeons, reformers, educators, and philanthropists. Dr. Richard Arnold in Savannah and Dr. Samuel Henry Dickson, Dr. James Moultrie, Jr., Dr. Joshua Barker Whitridge, Dr. Jacob Ford Prioleau, Dr. Albert G. Mackey, and Dr. Samuel Logan in Charleston were leaders of public and medical education throughout America and the South and founded many of the medical schools in states across the South.[25] By the bequest and funding from philanthropist Colonel Thomas Roper, a prominent Unitarian in Charleston and founder of the Roper Fund, the first community hospital of any size or distinction in South Carolina was opened in Charleston in 1856. According to Roper's will, certain parts of his estate were bequeathed to the Medical Society of South Carolina to act as trustees in erecting a hospital "for the permanent reception or occasional relief of all such sick, maimed and diseased paupers as need surgical or medical aid and whom without regard to complexion, religion or nation . . . should [be] admit[ted] therein." While the building itself was completed in 1852, it was not opened for regular use until 1856 though some rooms were used by the Medical Society for meetings and a library during the interval. During the summer of 1852, portions of the hospital were used to treat victims of the yellow fever epidemic.

Samuel Henry Dickson was among the relatively few vigorous and vocal proponents of reforms in American medical education during the early part of the nineteenth century and was largely responsible for the establishment of the Medical College of South Carolina. According to medical historian Joseph Ioor Waring, Dickson was an "able clinician, an advanced educator, a prolific writer, a capable orator, and a beloved citizen." He left a marked impression on his contemporaries and the many institutions with which he was associated in his earlier years in Charleston and later in New York and Philadelphia.[26]

Dickson was born in Charleston of Scotch-Irish parentage and received his undergraduate education at the College of Charleston and Yale College. He received his M.D. degree from the University of Pennsylvania in 1819 and returned to Charleston to develop a successful practice. In 1824, he left his practice to assist in establishing the Medical College of South Carolina. In 1833, he accepted a professorship in the newly created Medical College of the State of South Carolina. In 1847 he accepted a teaching position in the medical school of New York University, but returned to Charleston in 1849 to continue his previous work in medical and educational reform. In 1857, Dickson accepted a post at the Jefferson Medical College in Philadelphia. When the Civil War broke out, Dickson lost a great portion of his income when more than two hundred of his Southern students returned home to enlist in the Confederate cause. Dickson eventually fell into financial troubles and his health declined. He spent his remaining years in poverty in Philadelphia.[27]

Dickson is credited as the first doctor in the country to employ stimulants and anodynes in febrile diseases. He was also one of the early writers on racial anthropometry.[28] Dickson wrote many articles and monographs on medicine, philosophy, history, and current events. His most important medical works are *Manual of Pathology and Practice* (1839 with later editions); *Essays on Pathology and Therapeutics* (1845); *Essays on Life, Sleep, Pain, Intellection, and Hygiene* (1852); *Elements of Medicine* (1855); and *Studies of Pathology and Therapeutics* (1867).[29]

James Moultrie, Jr., was born in Charleston in 1793 and was the fourth successive doctor in his family. He was educated at Hammersmith, England, but was forced to return home when tensions between England and the United States began to escalate. He received his undergraduate degree from South Carolina College and then entered an apprenticeship under Dr. Alexander Baron and Dr. Robert Wilson. After receiving his medical degree from the University of Pennsylvania, Moultrie began his practice in Charleston. He worked with Dr. George Hall at the Marine Hospital and Drs. Hall and Thomas Akin at the hospital for slaves and free blacks.[30]

Early in his career he became interested in medical education and was largely responsible for the presentation of a memorial from the Medical Society of South Carolina to the state legislature requesting permission and funds for the establishment of a medical school. When the position of chair of the anatomy department was offered to him, Moultrie declined, feeling that the College could not succeed without the funding, which the legislature had refused. In 1833 when the funds were finally appropriated and the College organized, Moultrie accepted the chair of physiology, a position that he held for many years.

In 1827, Moultrie led a committee from the Medical Society to improve and expand medical education in South Carolina. In his *Memorial on the State of Medical Education in South Carolina delivered to the South Carolina Society for the Advancement of Learning* (1836), Moultrie explained that the content of current medical lectures was inadequate and professors were not properly selected and had no proven skills as teachers. Pointing to the schools of Paris, Vienna, and Edinburgh as examples, Moultrie cited the inadequacies of premedical education and medical examinations in America. He also sought improvements in clinical material, especially increased numbers of beds in the Marine Hospital, the Poor House, and the Maniac Department in Charleston. To address some of these problems, Moultrie advised that adequate salaries be paid in order to maintain a faculty properly prepared. He expressed his desire that the legislature of South Carolina survey the entire subject of medical education and take it under its care.

Moultrie was one of the delegates from the Medical Society of South Carolina to the organizational meeting of the American Medical Association in Philadelphia in 1847, and he became one of its first vice-presidents. In 1850 he was elected president of the Association. He was largely responsible for the organization of the South Carolina Medical Association in 1848 and served as its first president, a position he held for five years. He was also active in the organization of the Society for the Relief of the Families of Deceased and Disabled Indigent Members of the Medical Profession of the State of South Carolina. In addition, he was an active member of the Elliott Society of Natural History and the South Carolina Historical Society.

Dr. Richard Arnold's medical reforms in Savannah matched those of Dickson and Moultrie. Arnold was one-time editor of *The Georgian,* mayor of Savannah for six terms, founder of the Savannah Medical College and a member of its faculty, and the most influential member of the Unitarian society in Savannah. In addition to being an editor of the *Savannah Journal of Medicine,* Arnold was on the Board of Commissioners of the state Lunatic Asylum. According to one newspaper account, the Commissioners made "every effort . . . to render those edifices as unlike prison-houses as possible . . . it compares favorably . . . with any in our country."[31] Arnold's medical education reforms were similar to those of Moultrie in Charleston. In 1859, the *Georgia Telegraph* declared, "Dr. Arnold is . . . one of the most eminent medical men in the Union . . . he is for a higher standard of Medical Education . . . [he] recommends a [state] Board of Licensing Examiners . . . [which] would separate the Licensing power from the Teaching."[32]

Through her unswerving commitment to "household relationships," Caroline Gilman best personifies the diligent, interrelated, domestic qualities of Southern Unitarian reform. As a devoted wife, mother, and literary figure, and an intelligent, independent woman, Caroline Gilman worked consistently for various reforms within the familial, household, and community boundaries in which she lived and thrived. In addition to founding a number of women's aid societies, she sought improvements in education, literature, domestic affairs, women's rights, temperance, and reforms within the institution of slavery. As a Southern Unitarian woman dedicated to family and community she became one of the South's most dedicated defenders.

But Caroline Gilman was best known as a literary figure. In addition to her work with the *Southern Rose,* she published *Recollections of a Housekeeper* in 1834, which humorously described the "little vicissitudes" of the early years of married life. As she described the book, "it was the first attempt, in that particular mode, to enter into the recesses of American homes and hearths." Other books followed in quick succession: *Recollections of a Southern Matron* (1836); *The Letters of Eliza Wilkinson during the Invasion of Charleston* (1839), which she edited; *Ruth Raymond* (1840); *Oracles from the Poets* (1844); *Verses of a Life-time* (1849); *A Gift Book of Stories and Poems for Children* (1850); *Oracles for Youth* (1852); and in collaboration with her daughter, Mrs. Caroline Gilman Jervey, *Poems by Mother and Daughter* (1872). As a literary figure and proponent of family relationships, Gilman was not alone in Charleston.

Fellow member Mary Elizabeth Lee published numerous poems and prose works, including *Social evenings; or Historical tales for youth*. Upon Lee's death, Samuel Gilman eulogized her life as a devoted mother, wife, and literary figure, publishing *The poetical remains of the later Mary Elizabeth Lee* in 1851.

By providing lighthearted literature for youth, women, and family, Caroline Gilman, Mary Elizabeth Lee, and other Unitarian women consistently worked for improved education within the nurturing environment of "domestic affection" and care.[33] As a mother, Gilman devoted significant attention to the purpose and content of the education of her daughters, an education that would fit them for their futures. Unlike Northern educational reformers who often envisioned their daughters as teachers, Caroline Gilman envisioned educational reforms for her daughters as "members of a female community devoted to social and personal improvement."[34] Though not on the vanguard of educational reforms going on in the North, Caroline Gilman, like most Southern Unitarians, worked individually and quietly for social and personal educational improvement. With a strong devotion to God, husband, family, and community, a solid educational background, and a substantial number of literary publications to her credit, Caroline Gilman represented the ideal Southern Unitarian woman.

For women, educational reform in the South was tied closely with the idea of "women's rights." As strong, intelligent, independent Southern Unitarian women, Caroline Gilman and Winifred Gales had much in common. Both women never conformed to the romantic view of the "Southern lady," and when they spoke for women's rights at all, they grounded them within the family circle and around their social responsibilities. Although neither Gilman nor Gales was a native Southerner, both readily conformed to the ideals of "Southern principles." Accordingly, Gales and Gilman preferred to consider women's lot "from the objective perspective of society rather than the subjective perspective of their personal experience."[35] Both women stood far apart from the women's rights movement of the Grimké sisters going on just around the corner in Charleston, as well as those going on in New England. Clement Eaton explains that what set Winifred Gales apart from the Grimké sisters and the women's movement in the North was her "practice of tolerance." "In her letters," Eaton declares, "there is not a trace of a crusading spirit for women's rights, such as motivated her contemporaries, Sarah and Angelina Grimké of Charleston, South Carolina."[36]

That Southern Unitarian women were primarily devoted to the social welfare of family, households, church, and community was ably demonstrated by the activity of the women of the Unitarian church in Charleston, who worked quietly and steadily for women's rights within the relationships and structures Southern society then provided. As members of the Sunday School movement and the Female Domestic Missionary Society, Gilman and other Charleston Unitarian women were committed to strengthening the relationships of families weakened by less fortunate circumstances and the "evil" effects of poverty and industrialization. Women of the church helped raise money for an organ and new hymnals in 1825 and were introduced into the choir that same year. Caroline Gilman helped organize the Ladies Social Sewing Society in 1835 to supplement the finances of the church. In 1836 the Society organized the first fair ever given and conducted by women in Charleston, raising one thousand dollars. The women gave one hundred dollars to the Charleston Port Society and donated the rest to the church to meet the expenses of heavy repairs. The name of their organization was later changed to the Ladies Working Society and it provided money for supply pastors and church maintenance.

Prompted by the "spirit of improvement" and the idea of "progress" in an age of growing industrialization and constant change, Southern Unitarian reform represented an extra-ecclesiastical Unitarian presence in Southern society and exercised an influence not particularly linked to congregations or other denominational agencies. Its spirit took on a life of its own, independent of the church buildings Southern Unitarians worshiped in, and protected from institutional and denominational attacks. While the written word gave the invisible faith of Unitarianism its greatest voice in literary and religious journals, newspapers, and book and tract societies, the invisible spirit of reform found vitality out among the pews, the streets, the civic and professional organizations, and the quiet domestic households of the urban South.

SIX • "Our Old and Primitive Faith"
The Theology and
Influence of Southern Unitarianism

As a product of latitudinarianism, English Dissent, Scottish Common Sense Realism, Arminian theology, and the religious landscape in which it grew and evolved, Southern Unitarianism filtered out the excesses of both Enlightenment Deism and evangelical emotionalism, creating not only a synthesis between the two, but also a strong independent tradition as well. Southern Unitarians weathered the storm of theological attacks from evangelicals by insisting that their "old and primitive faith" was indeed very close to the primitive one, which rested on the teachings of Jesus and the apostolic order, and stressed the "purity" of Christianity, much as Priestly had argued. For Southern Unitarians and Deists alike this "purity" meant an uncorrupted interpretation of Scripture based on the tools of reason. However, there was an important and significant difference between Deists and Southern Unitarians. Deists believed in the sufficiency of natural religion, those principles of religion that can be established by reason alone, independent of any revelation from God. For Southern Unitarians, Deism was too radical. Conrad Wright calls Gilman's position "Supernatural Rationalism."

> It begins with the proposition of the deists that there is such a thing as Natural Religion, which can be established by the unassisted mind of man. But it denies the sufficiency of Natural Religion. On Natural Religion as a foundation there must be built a structure of Revealed Religion, to supply additional guidance, beyond what the unassisted reason could ever discover, as to the way by which salvation is to be attained.[1]

Even for the liberal minded of the nineteenth century, "unassisted reason" was a radical notion.

Gilman assured his fellow Southerners that "an immeasurable distance" separated him from the "disreputable" Thomas Paine. He declared that a Unitarian embraced revelation "with his whole heart" and believed "devoutly in the truth of the Bible."[2] Gilman and other Southern Unitarians sought an understanding of God through the tools of *both* revelation and reason. For them, reason was to be cultivated so as to better understand the will of God, but it was still to be held in check by the revelation of God's will in Scripture, the divine mission and message of Christ, and the miracles he and his apostles performed. In 1831, Stephen Bulfinch in Augusta's *The Unitarian Christian* declared, "We do not exalt reason above revelation!—but we believe that by reason we must find out what is revelation, and what revelation teaches."[3] Before coming to Charleston, in a letter to Caroline Howard, soon to be his wife, Samuel Gilman reiterated his disdain for Deism and expressed his belief in the "light of reason" within a sustained commitment to God's revelation.

> The age of speculative infidelity, Dear Caroline, is no more. The enemies of Christ have been driven from argument to argument, till every inch of the ground is won by his faithful and unwearied disciples. All the doubts and conjectures about the chronology of scripture, all the contradictions of the Mosaic history, all the disputes respecting miracles, all the objections to a revealed religion, and all the arguments against the revelation by Jesus Christ, are at length chased by the overwhelming light of reason. . . . There is now scarcely to be known a man of science and learning, who pretends to doubt the religion of Jesus.[4]

Throughout this letter and other letters and notes, Gilman reflected the level of optimism inherent in the early years of the Unitarian movement.

Because Gilman believed in the right balance of the "light of reason" and revelation, he along with other Unitarians welcomed the initial stirrings of biblical criticism as a discipline. Indeed, the most common complaint of first-generation Unitarians North and South was not that the orthodox clergy were too much bound by Scripture in their doctrinal formulations, but rather they were not biblical enough. The greatest attraction of biblical criticism to these early liberals was that they were convinced it would enable them to demonstrate that the orthodox views of the Trinity were unscriptural. Unlike orthodox clergy, Gilman believed that biblical interpretation, and not the nature of God or Christ, was the primary issue dividing liberal and orthodox theologians. "We only wish to understand and interpret that precious and sacred book on the principles of criticism," Gilman declared, "which, if stated, without any reference to previous doctrines or prejudices, every man would cheerfully allow."[5]

Much like the primitivist movement in general, such a position dictated a general suspicion, if not rejection, of dogmas, which tended to establish presuppositions about Scripture that maligned the "purity" and true meaning of Christianity. And yet, there were parameters to this enterprise that Southern Unitarians insisted must be maintained, especially in regard to particular texts that tended to cater to individual interpretation. On these questions, Southern Unitarians realized that some degree of conformity had to exist. They sought middle ground between the "conscientious Trinitarian" and the "thoughtless infidel": the former declaring, "Take it just as it stands, with all its mystery, all its difficulty, all its opposition . . . to reason, and inquire no farther," and the latter saying, "Not so. Reject the whole thing at once."[6]

> It is not to be expected or demanded that all Unitarians should precisely agree together in their explanations of every difficult Scriptural text. If their interpretations are not inconsistent with their own leading doctrine, nor with the general tone of Scripture, and come with clearness and satisfaction to their own minds, it is all they ever ask of God to give them— it is all they ever require of each other.[7]

While doctrinal consensus was not a requirement for Unitarians, they did share a desire for a "like-mindedness" that they believed was very much in step with Southern orthodoxy.

Through his expositions on biblical criticism, moral philosophy, and Scottish Realism, Gilman made significant contributions to the rationality of the Southern faith. Within the discipline of biblical criticism itself, the scholar who most impressed Gilman during his early years was the Scotsman Gilbert Gerard. Upon reading Gerard's *Institute of Biblical Criticism* (1806), Gilman wrote in 1813, "Biblical Criticism is not the dangerous weapon which I had once apprehended it. Instead of its having a tendency to overthrow any of the vital articles of our faith, it is on the contrary rather calculated to confirm and establish them. . . . It has excited a curiosity to know something more of these invaluable Sacred writings."[8] He was not alone. Gilman and Jasper Adams, Episcopalian minister and then president of the College of Charleston, decided to study the thirty volumes of Albert Eichhorn, the German biblical scholar, from five until six in the morning. Gilman recalled, "As he [Adams] lived in my neighborhood, I visited his house every morning at that hour, summer and winter, for about two years. I always found him at his post, awaiting my arrival, with his fire glowing and his candle burning, in the short and gloomy mornings."[9] In addition to Eichhorn, Gilman also admired Johann Griesbach's New Testament criticism from which he could learn to recognize and compare ancient manuscripts behind the biblical text and to understand the new literary analysis of the Gospels.[10]

But Gilman did not completely embrace the discipline. Although initially optimistic about the potential of biblical criticism, Gilman eventually began to distance himself from its more radical tendencies, especially those of German critics. While he continued to support the ability of criticism to "elucidate" Scripture and to diminish doctrinal differences, he believed that the radical German critics had done much to undermine the advances the discipline had made. For Gilman, German critics had reduced the gospel accounts to "impalpable myths." He believed that there were ethical and philosophical imperfections in the Bible that required occasional correction to be sure, but he continued to maintain that Scripture consisted of historical records, which included the miracles of Christ witnessed by multitudes, that offered a "plain" and "conclusive" revelation. For him, Scripture contained the "highest truths of absolute religion." Without the Bible there would be no Unitarian Christianity.[11]

Throughout his ministry in Charleston, Gilman continued to uphold the supremacy of revelation over reason in what Holifield describes as the liberal desire for "understanding." Gilman's Dudleian lecture at

Harvard in 1848 was a sustained defense of what he called a "special, supernatural revelation."[12] Other sermons throughout his ministry reiterated this theme as well. "The supernatural element in the character of Christ and his religion," Gilman declared, "mingled with, elevating, and strengthening that human reason to which it is addressed, seems to me to meet all the wants and capacities, the aspirations and the destiny of man. It is such a system that I wish to live and die by."[13]

While Gilman utilized and filtered the findings of biblical criticism, he found his major intellectual sustenance in Scottish Realism, and his commitment to Scottish thought remained strong throughout his career in Charleston. In addition to the names of Joseph Priestley and Thomas Bentham in the latitudinarian and English Unitarian tradition, Scottish authors such as George Campbell, Dugald Stewart, and Thomas Reid loomed large on Gilman's reading list.[14] But it was perhaps Thomas Brown who attracted Gilman's attention most consistently in the early years of his career. Early in his career, he referred to Brown as "the closest analytical reasoner of modern times."[15] In the 1820s, Gilman prepared lengthy assessments of Brown's works for publication in the *North American Review* and the *Southern Quarterly Review.*[16] As editor of the latter publication, James Thornwell reviewed Gilman's 1856 publication *Contributions to Literature,* and though lauding Gilman as one of the leading intellectuals of the Southern clergy, was disappointed with Gilman's early attraction to Brown, confessing "surprise" that Gilman admired a figure who followed "a purely sensual philosophy." While Thornwell discounted Brown for viewing the conscience as "a mere sanction belonging exclusively to the emotional department of our being," he was careful not to fall prey to guilt by association by reserving the same conclusions for Gilman.[17] Holifield has broken down the liberal tradition in the South into three main strands and associates them with leading Southerners: "sensual," with Thomas Jefferson, "understanding," with Samuel Gilman, and "reason," with Episcopal minister James Warley Miles. In typical fashion, Samuel Gilman chose the middle ground. He may have had an early attraction to "sensual" philosophy as Thornwell suggests, but that attraction soon changed. Both Gilman and other Southern Unitarians took Northern Unitarians to task for demonstrating affinities toward "sensual" philosophy, arguing that sensational philosophy always ended in "fanaticism." As a collection of writings over the span of his career, Gilman's *Contributions* constituted an early attraction to Brown that did not reflect later devotion. By the late 1850s, Gilman recognized that he had shifted to the right, closer to the rationality of Southern orthodoxy, declaring that while he admired Locke earlier, he felt more of an affinity to Reid's philosophy of the mind and to "the thorough scholarship of Dugald Stewart."[18]

For Gilman and other Southern Unitarians, Scottish philosophy provided an epistemology of "understanding" that could best support both reason and revelation. At its center was the conviction that the mind contained an innate "consciousness" that regulated sensory experience and allowed human beings to describe the world accurately. While Southern Unitarians believed that every individual doctrine was to be tested by the canons of reason, they did not insist that the unassisted powers of reason could have independently deduced the truths of the Christian revelation. For them, reason was "a sentinel at the entrance of the human mind, to determine what is true and what is false, what is to be admitted and what is to be kept out." It was "an understanding" that was an internal "faculty of the mind" with its own inherent laws.[19] According to Holifield, "Revelation did not impart the religious capabilities but simply invigorated ineradicable native instincts that were a part of human nature . . . Among the 'principles' that Scottish philosophers found underlying all concrete knowledge, Gilman included a 'religious appetency,' an instinctive impulse toward and receptivity to divine revelation."[20]

The notion of "relation" within moral philosophy provided Gilman with the perfect category to view Christianity, society, and the world. Moral science sought to exhibit man in his relations with others, the law, and God. Gilman admired *Elements of Moral Philosophy* (1837), written by his good friend Jasper Adams. Adams argued that the purpose of moral science was to form and cultivate the "sense" of duty and to determine the obligations implicit in the "various situations and relations of life."[21] For Gilman, man in his relation with God, with law, with others, and with nature provided harmony and gave order to the natural world. Gilman believed that the genteel notions of balance, harmony, and structure in the hierarchical world view of the South were completely congruent with the simplicity, symmetry, and purity of the Unitarian faith. Even James Thornwell saw this in Gilman. He described

Gilman's taste as "refined and delicate; he has an ear for every harmony, and an eye for every beauty of nature."[22]

For Arminians, Unitarian included, human beings, with their "native instincts," were free agents who could resist divine grace. God's grace was certainly needed, but because grace was *not* irresistible, human beings were responsible for their own salvation, and even for the sin that resistance engendered. Although Southern Unitarians like Gilman believed that humanity existed "in a sinful state," sin was not the final word.[23] There was hope and optimism about what human nature could accomplish. Samuel Gilman declared, "We feel our constant danger of becoming worldly-minded and earthward-tending. Come and remind us of our higher, better destinies."[24]

The idea of human perfectibility (though never fully embraced) within Southern Unitarianism translated into an optimistic attitude toward ecumenism within the primitivist movement. In this respect, Southern Unitarians were indebted to the supremacy of Scripture, biblical criticism, and Scottish Realism. Scottish philosophy was ubiquitous as an ethical system and reached beyond denominational and regional lines. It allowed Southern clergy of all denominations to put aside their divisions and "unite" in confidence that Realism itself "could solve the pressing dilemmas of both epistemology and ethics, and thereby . . . demonstrate the congruity between thought and behavior and prove the reasonableness of faith."[25] For Southern Unitarians, biblical criticism not only supported their concept of the nature of God and an Arminian view of the nature of man, but it also had given them an immediate advantage in the doctrinal controversies of the day. The longer they lived side by side with Southern orthodoxy, the more they believed it was "misunderstandings" and not "intolerance" that divided them. In 1849, the Charleston congregation declared:

Standing . . . as we do, separated from other denominations of Christians, sustained but by our Bibles and consciences, it is incumbent that our light so shine, that all should see, comprehend, and duly appreciate our religious platform. We are misunderstood, doubtless the result of misconception rather than intolerance; but not the less is it obligatory that the public mind be disinfected.[26]

The degree to which Southern Unitarians placed their hopes in the ecumenical possibilities of biblicism, biblical criticism, and Scottish Realism is reflected in the 1812 letter Samuel Gilman wrote to his wife, Caroline. Gilman believed that Christians everywhere were united "to promote the cause of Christianity" by the work of Bible societies and other institutions and the almost universal zeal to study Scripture "principally for the love of truth." For Gilman, this "peaceful spirit of Christianity" blunted the "sword of controversy" and "its cruel sharpness."[27]

Southern Unitarians believed that in the long run, a rigorous appeal to Scripture would heal theological disagreements, remove grounds for controversy, and promote unity in the Christian fold. As far as Unitarians in the South were concerned, they believed that they already had much in common with orthodoxy, for they all agreed on the chief doctrines of Christianity, though they differed on particular points of interpretation. Southern Unitarians believed that both groups affirmed the unity of God while they disagreed on the doctrine of the Trinity; both regarded humans as accountable beings under God's morality, while they disputed the natural state of man and his power to do the will of God; both agreed that human beings were in need of God's mercy and that Jesus Christ was the only instrument of salvation, even though they were divided over the terms of salvation. Samuel Gilman believed strongly in the "unity" of Christianity, declaring that "if we differ in one particular, we unite in a hundred." He saw no reason why different groups "impaired one anothers' good reputations." All this did was paralyze the good that each group tried to achieve. "If our speculative metaphysics are at war," he declared, "our practical morality, our evangelical spirit, may meet together and embrace each other. In all great topics of Christian exhortation, we are alike."[28]

Southern Unitarians preferred to emphasize what they saw as the commonality of the Christian message, not its doctrinal or ecclesiastical divisions. They chose not to promulgate the intricacies of Unitarianism in general, but rather to concentrate on the broad and liberal gospel on which it rested. In 1856, Samuel Gilman, addressing the possibility of Rev. Dr. Sheldon coming to Charleston to assist him, declared to the A.U.A., "If he came, it wouldn't be demanded that he should preach up-and-down Unitarianism, if he has not thoroughly embraced the system. Pure, broad, liberal gospel would satisfy my people. If he is an impressive speaker, and of genial presence, he would no doubt meet all requisitions."[29] For Gilman and other Southern Unitarians, the "genial presence" of both minister and laity was fundamental. Southern Unitarians believed that genteel notions of balance and structure in their hierarchical world view were completely congruent with the simplicity, symmetry, and purity of their faith. In his sermon *Unitarian Christianity free from Objectionable Extremes,* Samuel Gilman expounded the balance and symmetry of the Unitarian faith and advocated its place within the balanced paternalistic world view of the Southern landscape.

Indeed, a "pure, broad, liberal gospel" free from all imbalances was the theological ideal of nineteenth-century Southern Unitarianism. Throughout its long history, the members of the Second Independent Congregational Church, which eventually became the Unitarian Church of Charleston, had always acted "upon the freest and most liberal principles, as occasion may serve, and edification direct." Members of the church had insisted that they never would adopt any "platform or constitution" but rest on a "broad dissenting bottom, and leave themselves as free as possible from all foreign shackles."[30] Theologically, this oftentimes meant Unitarian "shackles" as well, particularly as demonstrated by their Northern coreligionists. By concentrating on "practical" and "pure" Christianity instead of "up-and-down Unitarianism," Southern Unitarians demonstrated their indebtedness to the various sources that helped produce, cultivate, and even prune their liberal faith over the years: Anglican latitudinarianism, English Dissent, Arminianism, Scottish Common Sense Realism, biblical criticism, evangelicalism, and Southern orthodoxy, just to name a few. In turn, whether those around them were willing to acknowledge it or not, Southern Unitarians influenced the rationality of Southern orthodoxy by establishing the *reasonableness,* if not of Unitarianism per se, at least of anti-Trinitarianism. To this extent, Southern Unitarians attracted many followers within orthodox ranks.

Throughout the entire antebellum period, Gilman and other Southern Unitarians insisted that what divided them from orthodoxy was not their views of the nature of God or Christ, but rather their views of biblical interpretation. For them, it was more an epistemological difference than an ontological one. Southern Unitarians believed that the right measure of the "light of reason" within a framework of "supernatural revelation" would help give them the critical insights needed to better understand the true ontological nature and spirit of God and his Son, Jesus Christ. Yet, they realized that their attempts to grasp ontological truths were inherently limited by the restraints of epistemology itself. Undaunted, however, Gilman and others forged ahead with the tools God and history had provided them. While Southern Unitarians chose to concentrate more on the practical instead of the speculative, many nevertheless did formulate what, to them, was a clearer picture of the truths of Christianity, a picture many Southern Christians found much like their own.

Samuel Gilman was more a strict Arian than Unitarian in his Christology. In the fourth century, while still seeing Jesus as the Messiah, the divine Logos, begotten before time and fully divine, Arius assumed a subordinationist view of Christ. In his sermon *Introduction to the Gospel of St. John*, Gilman utilized the same idea of the begotten or spoken Logos to delineate his arguments both for the divine Messiah and for the "unity" of God, mentioning Christ's admonition "The Father is greater than I," a key verse that Trinitarians had a difficult time explaining, only in the last sentence of the sermon.[31] In the course of arguing for the unity of God, Gilman refuted another text written by John that had "contributed most largely to the opinion [he had] been opposing in the discourse." His commentary on 1 John 5:7 ("There are three that bear record in heaven, the Father, the Word, and the Holy Ghost, and these three are one") demonstrated an acute indebtedness to works of Albert Eichhorn and Johann Griesbach. Citing eminent Calvinist and Trinitarian scholars who themselves had found the verse "indisputably spurious," Gilman declared that the verse "belongs not in the Bible." "It is found in no Greek manuscript, except one, which is of a very late date, and of no authority . . . though the words immediately contiguous, both before and after, are often cited," he continued. "Learned and good men are now for the most part agreed in the rejection of this controverted passage." In characteristic calm and equanimity, Gilman concluded, "I will not call it a gross slander, I will not call it an abusive falsehood, but I will call it an unhappy error, which induces our opponents to represent us as bringing down the Savior to the level of a mere man."[32] With an Arian Christology Gilman adamantly rejected the Socinian notion that Christ was a "mere man" and confirmed his belief in the Virgin Birth.[33]

For Gilman, the differences that existed between Southern Unitarians and orthodoxy concerning the nature of Christ were more questions of "arithmetic" than "true theology." Southern Unitarians emphasized a divine "union" between Father and Son while the latter stressed a divine "unity." Gilman declared, "The difference between the two parties, for which Unitarians are so bitterly and unsparingly denounced and excommunicated, is simply this; Unitarians believe in the closest *union* between the Father and the Son; Trinitarians, as far as we can comprehend them, contend for a *unity*, or *identity*."[34] In 1827, Charles Wentworth Upham told the Charleston community that "there was a mysterious and intimate connexion" between the Father and Son.[35]

Epistemologically, an ontological "unity" was incomprehensible to liberal Christians, who, nurtured in Scottish Realism, sought an "understanding" of God's revelation through their innate "consciences." "I think it to be impossible that any thinking being could suppose," Gilman declared, "that Jehovah himself resigned his existence for our sins." Christ's divine nature and existence on earth were best explained by him as "immeasurable degrees of power and wisdom . . . poured out upon and closely connected with his human nature, by the Spirit of God." For Gilman, the idea of divinity being "poured out" was inherent in John's invocation of the "Word" being "spoken" or begotten by God.[36]

In addition to confirming the Virgin Birth, and upholding the "immeasurable degrees of power and wisdom" in Christ's nature, Gilman argued for the necessity of the Resurrection. "His death you regard as the seal of his ministry, as a sacrifice called for on account of the sinful state of the world," Gilman declared, "and as a necessary forerunner of that glorious resurrection, which demonstrated him to be the Son of God, and on which you hang treasures of living hope."[37] Southern Unitarians believed that Christ was the Messiah, the Savior, and Redeemer of humanity and they never hesitated to address him as such. Gilman regularly addressed Christ as Savior from the pulpit as his *Introduction to the Gospel of St. John* confirms. Unitarian Joseph Lewis in Kabletown, Virginia, invoked the name and words of "our Savior" in a rebuking letter to the A.U.A. In New Orleans, after Clapp's death, M. J. Rice, secretary of the board of trustees, wanted a replacement who could "preach the gospel of Christ." Two years after her husband's death in 1858, Caroline Gilman spoke of her strong desire to hear "Christ preached" and to hear the "name of the Savior" during communion. She expressed her fear that the Rev. William A. Miller, a former Methodist, supplying the Unitarian pulpit in Charleston, had fallen into "mere rationalism." "I fear," she lamented, "that Mr. Miller will not supply my spiritual wants. While I profess Christianity, I must desire to hear Christ preached . . . This is the fifth service I have heard, and the name of the Savior has not been in a single hymn, even at Communion. . . . Sometimes I fear that he has made too wide a leap, and fallen over on mere rationalism. . . ."[38]

With Christ as the Messiah and Savior, Southern Unitarians believed that their faith, like that of other Christians, required equally compelling responses from its adherents. "Supposing now, that we went farther," Samuel Gilman postulated. "Supposing we took the single step more which our opponents demand us to take . . . supposing we actually allowed that Jesus were God and man at one and the same moment. . . . Should we have any greater motives to pass lives of holiness and piety . . . and to prepare for the eternal realities of another world? . . . I solemnly say to all this, No. Because in whatever degree we honour the Father, to that same degree it is clear we honour the Son and Messenger whom he has sent."[39]

Indeed, there is much credence in Unitarian claims that they were "misunderstood" by orthodoxy and that they were maligned by those ignorant of their faith and Christian principles. Gilman negated the idea that his faith brought "down the Savior to the level of a mere man" and elevated humanity to a level just a little less than God.[40] For Southern Unitarians, Christ was more than just a "mere man" and mankind itself was still very much in a state of sin.

THE INFLUENCE OF SOUTHERN UNITARIANISM

Throughout the antebellum period and up until the start of the War, many in the orthodox community continued to take Unitarianism seriously enough to publish pamphlets against it on a regular basis, as well as consistently misrepresent the faith. In 1859, Rev. W. B. Wellons, editor of the *Christian Sun,* in response to the Rev. John Paris's claim in the *North Carolina Christian Advocate* that many Christians in North Carolina and Virginia held Unitarian beliefs, erroneously declared:

> Unitarians do not believe in conversion as the Christians understand it and teach it; believing Jesus Christ a mere man, they do not pray to Him, nor do they think that they are required to have faith in Him, in order to win their salvation, consequently, an intelligent Unitarian in sentiment, would not apply, and could not be received in the Christian Church South with their present platform of principles.

In the end, Wellons, admitting the degree to which Arian Christology had infiltrated Southern orthodoxy, conceded the "absurdity of the effort to class all Christians either with the Trinitarians or Unitarians. This point is clear to my mind," he explained, "that a man may be an Anti-Trinitarian and yet not be a Unitarian, or an Anti-Unitarian and yet not be a Trinitarian."[41]

A glimpse into many orthodox churches in the South would have revealed the legitimacy of both Paris's claim and Wellons's concession. In Charleston, Presbyterian minister Rev. Thomas Smyth found it necessary to continue the struggle against Unitarians throughout the 1840s and 1850s, consistently preaching on the Trinity in hopes that his message would at least allay the influence that Gilman exerted on members of Smyth's congregation who church-hopped regularly between the Presbyterian and Unitarian church buildings. Similarly, Catholic Bishop John England worried that the Unitarian laity wielded considerable influence in intellectual circles throughout the United States and especially in Charleston.[42] In 1860 J. R. Blossom in Wilmington, North Carolina, described Unitarians in that North Carolina port city where there existed no such church and where religious liberals (Unitarians) freely moved within orthodox circles. "Our faith here is held avowedly by very few & we are absorbed within other denominations," he declared. "Yet I find here as well as elsewhere," he continued, "[those] who hold our simple ideas of United and Derived Authority who are in Trinitarian Communion & who strange to say not only do not deem their ideas heretical, but seem surprised to know that such views are not those held by their own churches. What a commentary upon the demanded necessity for holding orthodox doctrines of God's personality!"[43] In an 1858 letter, Herbert C. Peabody described the continued activity of some two hundred Southern Unitarians in and around Mobile, Alabama, eighteen years after the Mobile congregation supposedly folded when George Frederick Simmons, the minister there, fled (upon the urging of his friends) after preaching a sermon suggesting emancipation.[44] Peabody wrote, "My wife and our boys, Thomas and Henry, with a goodly number of the true blue Unitarians, went to Temperance Hall to hear [?] Karcher—they returned delighted—the congregation assembled were about 200, more or less, the Smith & Sampson family not included. but [sic] their places were made up by others quite as distinguished & with longer purses! & thicker Pocket *Books*."[45] Several weeks after the December 1858 letter, Peabody found out about the curious absence of his friends Smith and Sampson: "Henry Sampson has lost his wife[,] Sid Smith and others . . . will be attending the Episcopal in their faith."[46]

Eugene Genovese has recently argued that during the antebellum period mainstream churches of the North retreated "into rosier views of human nature" and won "astonishing doctrinal concessions even from northerners who claimed to be orthodox." According to Genovese, the "theological, ecclesiastical, and sociopolitical conservatives of the North were steadily retreating in the face of the rise of Unitarianism in New England and of assorted forms of liberalism in the principal denominations."[47] But there were major theological and philosophical differences between Northern and Southern Unitarians that Genovese fails to consider, differences that would prove pivotal not only in the split within the denomination, but also in those that would determine the divergent paths that each would take on the sectional compass of social theory and progress as well.

In addition to their core Realist assumptions and their common belief in the primacy of revelation, Samuel Gilman and other Southern Unitarians shared a great deal with Southern orthodoxy. They believed that their faith was grounded in the centrality of Christ's death and resurrection and its atoning sacrifice for a humanity still very much in the state of sin. In response to those above and below the Mason-Dixon line who charged Unitarians with an optimistic view of human nature, Gilman argued that it was Northern not Southern Unitarians who had begun to ground their faith in the inherent goodness of humanity. In his 1848 Dudleian lecture at Harvard, Gilman lamented that the "ancient endearing affinities and conventions" between North and South had been overwhelmed by the advancing tide of "changing attitudes and opinions."[48] In addition to speaking out against the "fundamental error of those who reject the idea of a special revelation," Gilman took the opportunity to directly address the threat of Transcendentalism within Northern Unitarianism. In 1842 Ralph Waldo Emerson had claimed that "the powers of the Soul are commensurate with its needs, all experience to the contrary notwithstanding." Gilman strongly disagreed. He rejected the notion that "the soul of man is naturally sufficient for its own religious necessities." Gilman argued that humanity was still grounded in sin and in need of salvation.[49] Gilman and other Southern Unitarians believed that Northern Unitarians formed the vanguard of what Barbara L. Bellows calls the "power elite" of the North who were turning Arminianism into the "romantic theology" of Transcendentalism. Unitarian Joseph B. Lewis in Kabletown, Virginia, declared that "a gradual change" had taken place in the denomination, one in which "sensational philosophy has usurped the place of rational philosophy." Lewis declared that "a philosophy based upon the feelings has always & always will end in fanaticism. . . . And I believe for this dereliction in faithfulness, God is withdrawing his countenance from the denomination."[50] Lewis and other Southern Unitarians believed that the subjective tendency within Northern Unitarianism threatened the harmony, balance, and purity of their "old and primitive" faith.

Conrad Wright has written perhaps the most in-depth intellectual and theological analysis of Southern Unitarianism heretofore published, but even he fails to appreciate the significance and implications of his findings. Wright explores Gilman's intellectual foundations without accurately assessing the overall nature of what Gilman represented.[51] He correctly places Gilman within the context of Supernatural Rationalism, the conventional theology of first-generation American Unitarians that was "accepted by many Calvinists as well as Arminians [and] was virtually the orthodox theology of the Age of Reason."[52] According to Wright, Supernatural Rationalism insisted that reason was still held in check by revelation and revelation was attested by the miracles of

Christ. But Wright emphasizes what he sees as a change in Gilman's theology in the late 1840s: a change that would "contribute to the earliest phases of one of the main lines of development" in what he deems the "prevailing motif" of "evolutionary optimism" within the denomination as a whole by century's end.[53] For Wright, this change suggests that the conservative, first-generation, "old Unitarianism" (as represented by Gilman) completely disappeared by mid-century. Wright argues that this departure was not solely the product of Transcendentalism, which swept through the moderate to radical schools of New England Unitarianism during the middle of the nineteenth century. Rather, Wright concludes, with this author's concurrence, that the divergence for conservative Unitarians like Gilman came by way of science, not romantic theology. For him, a pre-Darwinian "biological evolution," coupled with, among other things, "scientific work in geology and paleontology," accounted for much of the shift, however slight, within conservative Unitarian thought.

What Wright fails to consider is that such a shift was common and occurring on an increasing level among the Southern clergy as a whole. Dozens of ministers in the South, mostly from orthodox urban circles, were engaged in publishing articles on science and religion in many of the church journals—so much so that by 1851, as Holifield concludes, "it was possible to speak of a 'theology of natural science' that was supposedly in perfect harmony with the Bible." The primary motive behind this theology, Holifield reminds us, was not only "to demonstrate the compatibility between Genesis and geology," but also "to show that scientific investigation, properly conducted, provided a vast and grand extension of the traditional argument that design and order in nature demonstrated the existence of God."[54] Gilman's utilization of "theology of natural science" was less a sign of divergence within conservative *Northern* Unitarian thought toward "evolutionary optimism," as Wright would have us believe, than it was a convergence between Southern Unitarians and the orthodox clergy around them. While Southern divines, including Gilman, believed that scientific investigation would only confirm the truths of Scripture, the tools of reason were never to replace revelation. For Southern Unitarians, Scripture was not only the foundation for their primitivist mission and ecumenical zeal, it was also the cornerstone of their faith.

PROBLEMS OF ASSOCIATION

The success and originality of the Unitarian Book and Tract Society, the financial independence of the church itself, and the unique position the church had within Southern ecclesiology all contributed to the Second Independent Church of Charleston's serious consideration of a proposal they received from the American Unitarian Association in 1827. In May of that year, the congregation had published the Sixth Annual Report of the Charleston Unitarian Book Society and forwarded a copy to the newly formed A.U.A. A good portion of the report was the congregation's reflections upon the "proposition . . . received from the American Unitarian Association in Boston inviting this society to become an auxiliary to that institution." Raising numerous questions about the proposition, the Managers reflected on the "supposition" that if the A.U.A. met their criteria and the Charleston society "accede[d] to the proposal," they would still "not be bound for more than a year, but might at pleasure withdraw, and act again with our usual entire independence." Members of the church were concerned not only over questions of the equitableness of funds, but also over the fact that their society had been formed before the American Unitarian Association had even been organized and had enjoyed a long independent tradition free from "all shackles":

> In the first place, it seems highly desirable, that some mutual organiza-
> tion of sympathy should subsist between Unitarians in different parts of
> our country. Had our own society not been already in existence before the
> American Unitarian Association, there is no doubt that we should all

have cheerfully united to form an auxiliary of that institution, on the first intimation to such an effect. To comply with the recent proposition, therefore, would only be to carry into execution what we should gladly have done under other circumstances. The question now is, are our present circumstances a serious obstacle to the measure, and can we regularly spare one half of our subscriptions to contribute to the association's funds, consistently with the original nature & character of our Society? And if we do, shall we have received a fair equivalent?[1]

From the 1827 Annual Report it is clear that while the Charleston congregation believed that some "mutual organization" ought to be formed between Northern and Southern Unitarians, they were, as early as the late 1820s, seriously concerned that their initial and peculiar interests be protected and their independence secured. On the basis of the proposal they received from the A.U.A., the Charleston congregation believed that another auxiliary in Charleston instead of their own should be established, one that the A.U.A. itself would be responsible for founding and supporting, and one that would exist independently of the Archdale Street Unitarians. Because their origins, purposes, and outlook were different from and sometimes at odds with those of the A.U.A., Charleston Unitarians took this opportunity to dictate the reasons why they would retain a great degree of independence from the A.U.A. The congregation would withhold financial contributions from the A.U.A., censure their publications, and, in essence, declare that their primary responsibility as liberal Christians rested with their Southern, not Northern, constituency:

[S]ince our society was instituted for a single & simple object, there may be some weight in the objections that arise from identifying ourselves with another, whose remote purposes at least are more miscellaneous— than our society not [yet?] arrived at such maturity & magnitude, as will enable us to spare a portion of our proceeds for the missionary & other objects of the northern association? . . . If an auxiliary be wanted in Charleston on the terms of that Association's, would it not be better to establish one apart from our own Society? But is it really the case that an auxiliary is wanted in Charleston?—Are we not already to all intents and purposes, an auxiliary, a fellow labourer, and even so to speak, a *branch* of the American Association? We therefore do not see any impropriety in their formally recognizing us at once as an auxiliary & publishing as such in their reports.—We think that a sufficient aspect of mutual organization might be affected by our agreeing to take at least one hundred of all such of the Association tracts as we may think adapted for this region & paying for them their usual price.[2]

It is not exactly clear what terms of association the A.U.A. had in mind. From this Annual Report, however, it appears that the A.U.A. was interested in claiming the Charleston society "at once" and "publishing such in their reports," whether for propaganda, self-aggrandizement, or some other such end one can only speculate. Although the Charleston congregation assented to their inclusion in the A.U.A.'s publications, they expected a greater degree of clarity of the terms proposed by that organization, for they were then optimistic that some "mutual organization" could be established between the two. While the Charleston society hoped that their dictated petitions, hesitations, and concerns would be the grounds by which the two organizations could come to a greater understanding and compromise for future association, the Charleston society felt obliged to reject the offer as the terms then stood. "We . . . decline the proposition," they declared, "but respectfully submit the question to your consideration, together with the rest of our Report."[3]

Samuel Gilman and the members of his church waited throughout the summer for a response from the A.U.A., hoping that the petitions in their Report would receive the serious consideration and careful thought they believed they warranted. In August, Gilman wrote the general secretary of the A.U.A., "I have been anxiously looking for some notice, either public or private, of the proposals of our Society to yours, which I sent you two or three months ago. I hope they were favorably received."[4]

If they were Gilman would not hear it, for the A.U.A. did not respond. But they did move quickly to include the Charleston society as an auxiliary to that expanding organization, despite that congregation's hesitations and initial rejection of the proposition. After a year of silence, the Managers of the Charleston Unitarian Book and Tract Society wrote, "No answer has been received, and no report of the Association has been published during the last year. We have, however, seen it recorded in the *Christian Register*, a religious newspaper, indirectly connected with the American Unitarian Association, that the Charleston Society had become an auxiliary to it."[5] For years, Gilman continued to have reservations about the manner in which his society was "associated" with the A.U.A. By 1834, he realized that his location in Charleston, his congregation's missionary and financial activities in South Carolina and Georgia, and his own personal standing among Southern Unitarian ecclesiastics placed him in the center of what his adopted region and its own brand of liberal faith stood for.

THE SOUTHERN ASSOCIATION

Samuel Gilman knew that the Unitarian churches in Augusta and Savannah, Georgia, were started by his own "missionary" activity and the financial support of the Charleston congregation. From 1825 to 1827 Gilman, other members of his congregation, and Daniel Whitaker frequently traveled from Charleston to Augusta and Savannah, preaching to large and attentive audiences in both locations. Even as early as the 1820s, Gilman and other Charleston Unitarians believed that they could not readily allow this small Southern network of liberals to lose their unique heritage by accepting an offer to join a larger national association centered in Boston.

Daniel Whitaker was born in Sharon, Massachusetts, on April 13, 1801, to Rev. Jonathan and Mary (Kimball) Whitaker, the second of ten children. He was first educated by his father and then attended various academies in New England. At the age of sixteen he entered Harvard College, receiving his bachelor's and master's degrees in 1820 and 1823, respectively, and winning the Boylston Gold Medal for a dissertation entitled "The Literary Character of Dr. Samuel Johnson" and a Bowdoin Gold Medal for Oratory. After Harvard, he studied privately for the ministry and received a license to preach from the Bridgewater Association of Divines. When ill health compelled him to try a warmer climate, he made a successful preaching tour through the South, but not before his father had severed his ministerial connection with the congregation he had served in New Bedford, Massachusetts. From all accounts, Whitaker and his father were independent agents in this ministerial enterprise and were under no "missionary auspices" of any New England church.

Starting an itinerant ministry, Whitaker and his father preached to large audiences in New York City; Washington, D.C.; Baltimore, Maryland; Richmond and Petersburg, Virginia; Raleigh and Fayetteville, North Carolina; Cheraw, Camden, and Charleston, South Carolina; and Savannah, Milledgeville, and Augusta, Georgia. Samuel Gilman invited Daniel Whitaker to supply his pulpit in Charleston during the summer months and to accompany him on mission trips to Georgia.

By the winter of 1826–1827 Gilman and Daniel Whitaker preached to large audiences in Augusta, Georgia, had good prospects of a large society, and secured rents for nearly half of the fifty pews in the church.[6] That summer a church building was constructed in the center of town. On December 27, 1827, Samuel Gilman and Charles Briggs, a Unitarian minister from Lexington, Massachusetts, and later general secretary of the A.U.A., who happened to be in Augusta for his health, dedicated the new building. That day, Gilman preached a sermon not unlike William Ellery Channing's famous "Unitarian Christianity" delivered during the ordination service of Jared Sparks in Baltimore. For many Southern Unitarians Gilman's *Unitarian Christianity free from Objectionable Extremes* became the manifesto for their faith. It attempted to calm the alarm caused by the creation of a Unitarian congregation in Augusta and to espouse its place within the hierarchical and genteel landscape of the South. It was published both in Charleston and in the Unitarian publications, the *Christian Examiner* and the *Christian Register.*[7]

Daniel Whitaker was called as first pastor and had officiated there for nearly a year when sickness struck. This time, according to one biographer who was "intimately acquainted with [him and his] . . . entire career," Whitaker, "as a measure of duty and prudence, determined to abandon the ministry altogether . . . [after] constant and novel labors [had] . . . broken [him] down." Whitaker moved back to Charleston where his parents and family had recently settled and where he was able to recuperate and regain his strength. Shortly afterwards he met and married a widow of an eminent physician and planter and "devoted himself for about ten years to the culture of the great staples of the

South—rice and cotton."[8] Gilman came and preached at the Augusta church on several occasions, but without a minister the congregation had to rely on its own members to coordinate activities and to provide leadership. As one of their first steps they established a Sunday school for their children and started plans to begin a book and tract society similar to that of the Charleston church.

Largely through the efforts of Samuel Gilman, Stephen Greenleaf Bulfinch was called by the Augusta society as minister of the second-oldest Unitarian church in the South. Bulfinch, a recent graduate of Harvard Divinity School, was the twenty-one-year-old son of Charles Bulfinch, noted architect of the state house in Boston and the national Capitol in Washington (as well as a member of the First Unitarian Church in Washington, D.C.). On January 9, 1831, he was ordained before "a very crowded and highly respectable congregation." At the ordination service Gilman noted that in New England eight ministers usually participated in an ordination service, but in the South, he alone held the honors and solely represented the larger Unitarian cause. At the end of the ordination, the choir sang a hymn composed by Samuel Gilman's wife, Caroline, and after the service forty-two pews were sold or rented for the year.[9] Assessing the makeup of his congregation, Bulfinch wrote, "We have the great advantage over most Unitarian Societies of New England, of numbering a very fair proportion of *natives* [sic], and those too among the most attached members of our church and congregation."[10]

The beginning of the Unitarian church in Savannah closely mirrored that of the Augusta church, as Samuel Gilman and his Charleston congregation were responsible for both its origins and its continued support. On several occasions Gilman spent every night for a week lecturing and preaching in Savannah, gathering adherents and listeners among the city's professional and literary classes. In addition, Daniel Whitaker and Stephen Bulfinch made several trips into the area in the late 1820s and early 1830s, stirring up an already indigenous liberal flock. By 1830 a small group of professional and commercial men organized a Unitarian society and were granted a lot by the council of the city (then a common practice for the city of Savannah) for the purpose of erecting a church within five years. By the early part of 1832, services were conducted by laity in the congregation in a rented building on Court House Square until the church could be completed. By December of that year the society was incorporated as the Unitarian Association of Georgia. Stephen Bulfinch recalled the promising climate in the early 1830s, noting that "Rev. Messrs. Gilman, Ford, Bascom, and Huntoon" had already officiated there and that a "handsome place of worship is nearly completed." He declared, "The prospects of a Society are flattering." In addition, he noted that he himself had also preached in "Sparta, Milledgeville, Macon, Warrenton, Clarkesville, & Dabolenega . . . as well as at camp meetings of our friends the 'Christians' who harmonize fully with our sentiment, & number about 20 congregations."[11]

As Bulfinch mentioned, after a few months of searching, the services of Ezekial Lysander Bascom were secured and he began preaching in January 1833, exchanging pulpits with Bulfinch in March of that year. Serious illness prevented Bascom from preaching the following fall, however. Benjamin Huntoon, who was in the area and who also was recuperating from poor health, managed to fill in for the months of December and January. When Bascom's condition finally improved in the spring of 1834, he accepted the position on a permanent basis. With renewed vigor the congregation pushed forward with its building plans. It decided to sell the lot given to the society by the city and to buy a lot on the corner of Bull and York streets. By mid-December the ten-thousand-dollar building was completed and *The Georgian* described the results: "Its exterior is plain, but beautiful, and does not suffer in comparison with any public building in the city. It is chaste and simple in its design, being of the Grecian Ionic order. The interior is furnished in a style of neatness and simplicity corresponding with the exterior."[12] On December 21, the dedication service was held before a sizable and promising audience of merchants, professionals, and literary leaders of the city.

When Samuel Gilman wrote the A.U.A. in 1834, he communicated a "favorite idea" he had long nurtured of establishing an Association of Southern Unitarians with Charleston as its center. Although he had never heard back from the A.U.A. after it had readily adopted the Charleston church into its fold despite the congregation's initial rejection of the proposition, Gilman nevertheless tried to reopen negotiations:

I have long had a favorite idea in my mind . . . I wish the Tract Society would be replaced by an *Unitarian Association. . . .* We would be an auxiliary to the A.U.A. But I think we should be more efficient, if our resources, and activity were not merged into the doings of the larger Society. We might affiliate other Southern societies. But I do not know of any great objections of our being entirely tributary to A.U.A. If we could expect of it in return substantial assistance.[13]

Gilman was not alone. Months before he died and a few months after Gilman's request, J. B. Pitkin of the Unitarian church in Richmond had the same idea for a Southern Association: "Do you Sir intend visiting the South?" he asked. "A Southern Association of Unitarians extending from Washington to Georgia ought to be formed."[14]

The idea of a state or regional association within the A.U.A. was not new to Northern Unitarians. Indeed, *The Unitarian Congregational Register* of 1854 lists state "Associations" of Maine and New York within the larger A.U.A. organization and there were many other associations within the New England area itself. From 1842 to 1863, the Autumnal Convention of Unitarian ministers met every year in the northeastern United States in order to "awake mutual sympathy and consider the wants of the Unitarian body." In 1853, Samuel Gilman attended a meeting of the Convention at Worcester, Massachusetts. The Convention cited him for the long distance he traveled to attend and even elected him a vice-president. But this was the only meeting he attended, and he was able to attend it only because he was traveling in New England to recuperate from a serious illness.[15]

What is new and curious, however, is that Gilman's idea of a Southern Association, like the rejection of the A.U.A.'s original proposition, was never accepted or recognized by that organization. But not to be outdone, Gilman, Bulfinch, and others continued their missionary activities throughout the South unabated. Stephen Bulfinch confirmed the activities of the Southern Association. In 1836 he wrote, "Mr. Bascom & I were then together in Augusta, & I compared notes with him, with my parishioners, & last with Mr. Gilman, whom we have met here in a sort of Association Service on a small scale."[16] In September 1835, Henry Bright wrote from Mobile, Alabama, "I've heard it mentioned that the Unitarian clergymen of Charleston, Savannah, & Augusta have been talking of each one passing a month in this city next winter with the views of forming a society, that might be useful in doing so."[17]

MOBILE

While historian Clarence Gohdes claims that the Unitarian society in Mobile "seems to have been due entirely to the efforts of missionaries and agents of the American Unitarian Association," there is ample evidence, and even some suggestions within his own history, that this was not the case. Apparently, well before James Freeman Clarke, the minister in Louisville and an agent of the A.U.A., first came to Mobile in December 1835, a sizable group of individual Unitarians was already in existence and had already been placed within the scope of the Charleston-centered Association. Henry Bright wrote to the A.U.A. that the Unitarians in Mobile had been worshiping alongside a liberal faction of Episcopalians and in fact for a while had shared a clergyman, Rev. Norman Pinney, "who was a gentleman, scholar, writer," and a "pious liberal & rational Christian" who was "most popular." "The Unitarians," Bright declared, "feel very little desire for a change." But when Pinney decided to withdraw from the ministry to establish a seminary in Mobile, Unitarians began talking about the possibility of forming a Unitarian society. It was Bright's hope that clergymen from Charleston, Savannah, and Augusta would help "form the society" after the Episcopal minister withdrew. It was clear to Bright and the Rev. Pinney that Unitarians in Mobile shared a great degree of comfort with other Southerners and wanted a Southern society.[18] In December 1835, before James Freeman Clarke visited Mobile, Stephen Bulfinch from Augusta had written the A.U.A. to relay a message he had received from Pinney. Pinney described his desire for a *gradual* establishment of a Unitarian society within the existing ecclesiastical establishment. His suggestion was that it would be best for such a church to be organized by native liberals in due time. Bulfinch quoted Pinney's message to the A.U.A. verbatim.

Nothing decisive I believe has been written to Mr. Briggs as yet on account of the absence of some of the most prominent Unitarians. I have no doubt that a good Unitarian society can be built up here. So far as I alone am concerned however, I would prefer leaving the establishment of such a church to another year, when the fever of the public mind for my change of sentiment would be somewhat allayed.[19]

Apparently the message was received too late, for Clarke was either already there or was well on his way. Before coming to Mobile, Clarke first preached on the riverboats of the Mississippi and in Clapp's church in New Orleans. His narrative of his visit to Mobile reflected the pervasive "colonizing" spirit of the A.U.A. in its ongoing effort to establish "what was true and right." While he described those in Mobile as mixed, Southerners and transplanted New Englanders, he did not recognize the group's earlier desire to align with the Charleston-centered group or their efforts at organizing gradually along their own lines. In the end, Clarke, like Briggs in Richmond, claimed Mobile for the A.U.A. despite the initial hesitations put forth by Bulfinch and Pinney:

> I have formed a society at Mobile, and have persuaded the members to subscribe a number of thousands of dollars to build a church; have made some good friends and acquaintances, and have induced some of them to think better of Christianity than before. . . . I was touched with the generosity of the Mobile people to myself, and the enthusiasm with which they entered into church matters. . . . There were half-a-dozen men in Mobile who put aside all regard to the plausible and expedient, and asked only what was true and right.[20]

In the winter of 1837, after preaching in Tennessee and Louisiana, Charles Briggs and W. G. Eliot came to Mobile, where they found the society "prosperous." The church building that the members had financed themselves was nearly complete by the time of their arrival. After Briggs and Eliot left, Ephraim Peabody, a Unitarian missionary in the West, and Henry W. Bellows, then a student at Harvard, preached in Mobile on several occasions. On October 9, 1938, George Frederick Simmons, a recent graduate of Harvard Divinity School, was ordained in Boston, and he immediately set out for Mobile as their permanent minister. He was received in Mobile with accolades. "We are delighted," wrote Herbert C. Peabody. Samuel St. John, Jr., declared, "He has won the whole society." Indeed the congregation grew rapidly as more and more people expressed interest in renting pews to hear the minister who delivered such "splendid discourses."[21]

By the mid-1840s the A.U.A. decided that its efforts would be more productive in the West, and from that point on virtually ignored the South.[22] Efforts to use New Orleans and Mobile as springboards to the West became equally frustrating and problematic as Unitarians in these areas thwarted the missionary activities of the A.U.A. In 1855, the A.U.A. divided the country into districts "for the collection of annual contributions." The A.U.A. resolved:

> That there are other Unitarian Societies in this country beside those em-
> braced in the foregoing Districts, but which, from their position, cannot
> conveniently be arranged in any District,—such as the Societies in Bur-
> lington, Vt., Lancaster, N. H., Montreal, Philadelphia, Baltimore, Wash-
> ington, Charleston, Savannah, New Orleans, and San Francisco,—we
> hereby invite them to co-operate fraternally with us in an annual contri-
> bution in behalf of the Association.[23]

Even so, Samuel Gilman and Charleston Unitarians realized that if Unitarianism were to be nurtured and supported in the South, it would ultimately be up to them to do so.[24] That they took on the task with zeal, determination, consistency, and patience endeared them to Southern liberals and placed them in the center of Southern Unitarianism. The Augusta Book and Tract Association had been conceived primarily as an auxiliary to the Charleston Book and Tract Association, not the A.U.A. It filtered and censured many of its publications as it saw fit and circulated them throughout the community. Frederick J. Gray, a mem-ber of the Augusta society, wrote the A.U.A. in August 1830 to report the status of the book association:

> The members are all anxious to pay $2 per year—& connect themselves
> with Mr. Gilman's Book Society by way of an auxiliary to that, though I
> am desiring they should become an auxiliary to the A.U.A. In all events,
> let it be which way it may, much, very much will be gained by the forma-

tion of a society in this place & in the end the A.U.A. will gain as much, as if directly connected with them."[25]

When the A.U.A. sent Charles Briggs and W. G. Eliot of St. Louis to visit New Orleans, hoping to establish a second Unitarian church there, they met with little to no success. Clapp welcomed them, however, and expressed an interest in helping them, but reserved doubts about their intentions. He and other Southerners had come to see Northerners in general as "traducers" who carried an obnoxious sense of moral superiority, and Clapp believed those in his own denomination were no exception. In an article in the *Christian Register*, one commentator noted that "the spirit of [the] southern country . . . is impatient and impetuous. The style of preaching common in Boston, that of Dr. Channing or Dr. Ware for instance, would not be popular here. It is too quiet. Rashness is much more excusable here than tameness."[26]

Clapp loathed such gross distortions and stereotypes and the condescending and self-righteous tone Northern ministers took when speaking of Southern Christians. "I am often pained by hearing Louisiana spoken of in terms of disparagement and vituperation," Clapp declared. When a Massachusetts minister told him that he could hardly "conceive of a greater calamity" than for a "pious and enlightened minister" to live in Louisiana, where "Christianity was encumbered by the corruption of the Roman Catholic church," Clapp took exception. He charged that "the inhabitants of Louisiana have quite as much religion as those of Massachusetts, New York, or any other northern state." "If gospel benevolence proves the existence of Christian principles," Clapp concluded, "it is certain that true religion reigns and flourishes as vigorously in Louisiana as on the banks of the Hudson or Connecticut."[27]

Clapp was not alone. Undoubtedly many in New Orleans, including Briggs and Eliot themselves, knew that a New England seed would not last long in the warmer semitropical climate of the Mississippi Delta, especially when a Southern one grew so strongly and vibrantly there already. While Clapp was cordial to his Northern guests, he maintained serious doubts about their intentions, especially given the different stance both parties had taken on Universalism. Though entertaining great expectations for a warm reception in New Orleans, Eliot and

Briggs left with bitter disappointment. Briggs lamented, "I can find no place to preach in for the purpose of starting it [a second Unitarian society]. And Mr. C does not want his church used for that purpose, though he says he should like to have another society. . . . [Clapp] will let Mr. Eliot & myself preach in his church in afternoons (when nobody goes to church) if we will preach practical sermons & not Unitarianism as such . . . His people feel a delicacy about recording my movements. I have set all my wits to work to accomplish the object but my impression is that it cannot be done immediately."[28] Several weeks later, Eliot recalled a meeting he had with "Brother Clapp." If he was not aware of the independent nature of this congregation before his tour of the Mississippi Valley, his meeting with Clapp certainly gave him the hint he needed. "After sitting an hour, and talking about the propriety of his having a new Church built for himself, I told him that I meant to raise money to buy a lot if possible. 'Well' said he, 'I hope you will succeed—but I can tell you one thing, Mr. Eliot—that the best thing for you to do is to do *nothing*: we can do it better a month hence, and as well without you as with you.'"[29]

The exact date is not clear, but sometime before 1854, when their charter expired, the new First Congregational Unitarian Church was absorbed into the fold of the A.U.A., despite the real and present differences between the two that had been ably expressed over the years. But even after the entrance of the New Orleans congregation into the A.U.A., Boston clergy continued to demonstrate that they wanted the benefits of a large and vibrant church in the South without its responsibilities.

THE MOTTE AND SIMMONS AFFAIRS

In 1841, Jason Whitman agreed to assume ministerial responsibilities for a year in Savannah. After leaving a Unitarian church in Portland, Maine, Whitman found the group in Savannah more serious and spiritual than he expected. While in Savannah he preached twice on Sunday and organized a Bible class. He devoted much of his time to the Savannah Bible Society, the temperance movement, and a local seaman's welfare group. In 1842, Whitman wrote to the *Christian Register* and explained that an indebtedness of three thousand dollars remained on the church building and requested that the A.U.A. fulfill its promise of financial assistance. The Charleston church contributed $165. The A.U.A. did not make a contribution though a few small individual contributions were sent.[30] According to his agreement, Whitman left Savannah in the fall of 1842.

In December 1842, after receiving a request from the Unitarian society, the A.U.A. sent the Rev. Mellish Irving Motte to Savannah. Motte was a former Southern Episcopal minister who had recently converted to Unitarianism. But before Motte even arrived in Savannah, the Unitarian society there had found him unacceptable and refused to allow him to preach in their pulpit. Members of the society explained to the A.U.A., "Unfortunately, [his] reputation had preceded him and although he may have been born a Southern Man, it was but too evident that he abjured Southern principles . . . [he] was known as an open and avowed Abolitionist."[31]

The Northern reaction was explosive. The general secretary of the A.U.A. declared, "Our Association declines having anything further to do with the supply of your pulpit." Angry letters from Unitarian laymen and clergy were printed in the *Christian Register*. An editorial protest appeared in the conservative *Monthly Miscellany*. In Dover, New Hampshire, Garrisonian Unitarian John Parkman began formulating a protest for the A.U.A. annual meeting on May 24, 1843, only a few weeks away.[32] At the meeting, Parkman invoked the name of Channing. He told his fellow Unitarians to rally public sentiment against slavery and argued that because there were few churches in the South, and because the denomination did not practice excommunication, it should send to Southern congregations a "solemn protest against the sin of slavery." Afterwards, William Henry Channing, nephew of Dr. Channing, took the stage and declared that if the denomination could not condemn slavery, then Unitarianism was an "empty profession."[33]

For Southern Unitarians, such a statement was "untruthful," "uncharitable," and "fanatical." For them, not only did it go beyond the idea of separation of church and state that lay at the very foundation of the "pure" and "uncorrupted" religion that Unitarianism espoused, but it also claimed for Unitarian Christianity a theological "necessity" that was never there. In September 1843, only a few months after Motte's dismissal, Samuel Gilman refused copies of the *Eighteenth Annual Re-*

port of the A.U.A., which carried Parkman's "fanatical" charges and William Henry Channing's statement of the "emptiness" of Unitarianism's silence regarding abolition. Gilman reminded the A.U.A. that his church had, ever since its inception, censured and returned those items that were incongruent with the Southern liberal faith. And this occasion would be no different. "I am directed by the Book Committee to return you the entire number of copies of the last Annual Report of the American Unitarian Association," Gilman declared. "The Committee finds that portions of the Tract, if distributed in this community, would injure the interests of Unitarian Christianity, and along with them those of truth and charity," Gilman continued. "You will please deduct the amount charged for the returned tracts, from my current account."[34]

But the "affair" was not over. Parkman's protest was taken up for consideration the next year at the nineteenth annual meeting of the A.U.A. After three long days of intense discussion, the A.U.A. finally accepted and passed by a vote of 40–14 a series of six resolutions and a preamble offered by Stephen C. Phillips of Salem, Massachusetts. The preamble merely retold the story of the "Motte Affair." The resolutions that passed were (1) the affair required deliberation by the A.U.A. on slavery; (2) the A.U.A. had to "speak the truth in love" to the Savannah congregation; (3) the Association perceived that slavery subverted the "fundamental principle of Christian Brotherhood"; (4) everyone should work to end slavery; (5) no clergyman should be rejected because of his antislavery views; and (6) the Association commended these resolutions to the Savannah society.[35]

While Southern Unitarians had always thought of themselves as inherently "independent," incidences like the "Motte Affair" in Savannah, and actions and statements they engendered from Northern Unitarians, increasingly precipitated acts of independence from Southern congregations and individuals, especially from Unitarians in Mobile, Alabama. Unitarians there were immediately impressed by the talents of its new minister, George Frederick Simmons. But things quickly changed on Sunday, May 17, 1840.

Simmons preached a sermon to the Mobile congregation on the emancipation of slaves and declared that if laws prevented emancipation, a slaveholder should hold his slaves as freemen, pay them, secure their domestic rights, protect them from wrong, and provide them with religious instruction. With the exception of paying their slaves, many in the congregation, if not Southerners in general, believed that they had been doing these things all along. What was upsetting to those in and out of the Unitarian church in Mobile was that their pulpit had been used for political purposes. While Simmons was advocating a kind of "freedom within bondage," a plan that would "eat out the heart of Slavery even while Slavery continues," and not immediate emancipation itself, many felt the sermon was inappropriate, especially since it came from a liberal faith that advocated separation of church and state, and calm, reasoned debate over excited oratory. Though it did not advocate emancipation, many believed the thrust of Simmons's message was political. During the course of the sermon, while members listened attentively, only one person walked out.

Two days later, on the evening of May 19, 1840, four black slaves rowed Simmons out into Mobile Bay to place him upon the brig *Emily* for passage to New England. Though the main opposition to Simmons came from those outside the congregation—rumors had spread that some citizens were plotting to harm Simmons—members of the church urged him to leave. It was this event that led James Freeman Clarke to declare that a Christian clergyman in a slaveholding state ought not to preach on the subject of slavery, a policy Samuel Gilman in Charleston had been committed to for years.[36]

EIGHT • Oil and Vinegar
The Politics of "Puritan Fanaticism"

On December 22, 1850, the editor of the New Orleans *Daily Picayune* rebuked the "pulpit treason" of the Unitarian minister Theodore Parker and other abolitionist fanatics who had, he believed, put their own individual consciences above scriptural authority and the laws of the Constitution and had violated their clerical "duty of non-interference." The editor recommended the "Thanksgiving Sermon" of the Unitarian minister Theodore Clapp, which the *Picayune* carried on the front page. In his sermon, Clapp called the abolitionists the "aggressors" and the "authors" of the "late agitation in our political world." He declared, "I hope most sincerely that our clerical brethren at the North will see the folly of again disturbing the peace of this Union by preaching absurd, impracticable theories on the subject of slavery . . . [and by casting] . . . a deliberate, conscientious judgment of their most enlightened fellow-citizens residing in the slave States."[1]

Throughout the sermon, Clapp cited the name of the Unitarian divine William Ellery Channing. He was particularly bothered by Channing's recent remarks on slavery. Clapp asserted that Channing had put his own individual conscience above scriptural authority. He, along with other abolitionist clergy, had "unhesitatingly . . . nullif[ied] the instructions of Moses, whenever they did not happen to suit their peculiar, distinguishing views," said Clapp. "Either Moses or the learned doctor [Channing] is in the wrong," Clapp declared. "When [Moses] speaks agreeable to them he is treated with reverence; but when [Moses] is opposed to their dogmas, he is the object of their utter disregard and even contumely."[2]

Dr. Richard D. Arnold repeated Clapp's concerns. As the most prominent Unitarian in Savannah, Arnold remembered the actions and statements of John Parkman and other Northern Unitarians after the "Motte Affair" had revealed the growing sectional difference between Northern and Southern Unitarians. Twenty years after the "Motte Affair," on September 28, 1861, Dr. Arnold scribbled the following line in his scrapbook: "We are now in the midst of a war waged against us by our quondam Brethren of the North in order to subjugate us to make us bow supplicating for mercy at their feet." To support this claim, Arnold glued to the pages of his scrapbook a newspaper article of February 3, 1861, entitled "The Reaction Against the Abolitionists—American Civilization Versus Puritan Fanaticism." For Arnold and other Southern Unitarians, their own Unitarian coreligionists in the North formed the vanguard of the abolitionists. They believed that through their greater confidence in human perfectibility, lapse into religious emotionalism, and heightened political agitations, Northern Unitarians had shown their true colors and their true blood, "Puritan fanaticism."

> The fearful consequences of the abolition propaganda in breaking up the Union and inaugurating civil war are coming home to every man's business, if not to his bosom. . . . The fertile source of the ever-recurring mischief is the Puritan idea of the superiority of their sect over other men, and a mysterious divine right which they claim to possess of dictating to all mankind—a right which they held to be higher than the authority of the Bible and the constitution, and which ought to be maintained at all hazards, even with Sharp's, rifles, bayonets and cannon balls.[3]

For Arnold and other Southern Unitarians, it was inevitable that the "Puritan idea of superiority" would soon become tantamount to war.

During the first half of the antebellum period, Arnold and other Southern Unitarians had formed strong cultural ties with Northern Unitarians, many of whom led national benevolent societies, voluntary associations, and other venues for "progress" and reform. In Charleston and other port cities in the South, Unitarians not only became actively involved in reform, but they also had formed and joined local New England Societies attempting to forge closer bonds between places of birth and their new homes. Barbara L. Bellows has recently argued that as long as "reform remained unpolitical and focused upon personal morality, southerners enthusiastically supported the Home Mission movement, Bible and tract societies, and temperance unions." Southern Unitarians were no exception. In Charleston, though asserting a great degree of independence from the A.U.A., the Unitarian congregation nevertheless tried diligently to maintain close ties not only with their Northern coreligionists but also with other national reform groups as well. But as Bellows contends, "by the time of Andrew Jackson's election . . . a romantic revolution engineered by a New England 'power elite' rocked American theology."[4] For Southern Unitarians, the theological attacks they had endured earlier from Southern orthodoxy did not compare to what they deemed the "Puritan fanaticism" of Northern Unitarians. While attacks by evangelicals prompted Southern Unitarians to develop "invisible" outlets for their faith, alongside the visible institution of the church, Southern Unitarians blamed their institutional decline and close of their church buildings, not on evangelicals, but on their Northern coreligionists.

Southern Unitarians were proud of their reform efforts and their work in the national "benevolent empire." Even when centrifugal forces in the North and the South split other Protestant denominations in the 1840s, Unitarians in the South through their own denominational ties, and especially volunteer organizations like the American Sunday School Union, worked diligently to mediate sectional differences. Hopeful partisans saw the ASSU as both a soul-saving and "Union saving" institution that forced South Carolina and Massachusetts to "exchange the kiss of peace and to work shoulder to shoulder in the great cause of Christian love."[5]

But along with other Southerners, Unitarians in the South were enraged when they realized that representatives from national benevolent organizations, many of whom belonged to Northern Unitarian churches, frequently engaged in what John Wells Kuykendall has called blatant "spiritual swindling" by siphoning off the hard-earned donations from earnest Southerners and diverting them to projects in the North.[6] When this news was coupled with accounts of heightened abolitionist activity among Northern Unitarians, Southern Unitarians saw the writing on the wall.

Southern Unitarians were angered that Unitarians in the North were making abolitionism the ultimate expression of national reform, and that they were using pulpits to make it a political issue and revival meetings to gather emotional zeal and ferment. Through their written expositions of liberal faith and their involvement in benevolent reform, Southern Unitarians believed that they had "kept the faith" and done much to forge visible and invisible spaces for themselves within Southern orthodoxy. Enduring earlier attacks by zealous evangelicals, Southern Unitarians had worked ardently for the "purity" and "rationality" of primitive Christianity, insisted on a "broad and liberal" faith that minimized doctrinal and denominational differences, worked tirelessly for ecumenical accord, and sought to "render unto Caesar" by keeping politics out of the pulpit. While they believed that they had remained steadfast to the truths of Christianity, Southern Unitarians were most disheartened in the belief that the perversion of their faith and their loss of ecclesiastical strength was caused by the political agitations from Northern Unitarian ranks.

William Ellery Channing had once declared that if nothing but political action could remove slavery, "then slavery must continue." As the most influential Unitarian in the North, Channing knew well that the idea of separation of church and state lay at the very foundation of the "pure" and "uncorrupted" religion that Unitarianism espoused. He declared, "If we faithfully do our part as Christians, we are not responsible for its continuance. We are not to feel as if we were bound to put it down by any and every means. We do not speak as Christians when we say that slavery *must* and *shall* fall. Who are we, to dictate thus to Omnipotence?"[7]

Even so, such a statement proved ominous for many Northern Unitarians, including Channing, who eventually proved powerless to the magnetic attraction that "Puritan fanaticism" had over its own wayward grandchildren. For Southern Unitarians, not only had their Northern coreligionists used the pulpit as a political tree stump, but they also had felt it their duty to "dictate thus to Omnipotence." Joseph Lewis in Kabletown, Virginia, lamented the "destruction" of Northern Unitarianism by both the encroachment of the state upon the denomination and the increasing willingness of its ministers to taint the pulpit with political agendas and self-aggrandizement. Admonishing Unitarians in the North to "cast not your pearls before swine," Lewis declared:

The number of ministers that fall—your vitiated literature which is thrown broadcast over the country—misrepresentations, exaggerations, the ignoble appeals of certain politicians to the masses to excite their passions & their prejudices for the sole object of gaining political power. Such is the aspect of northern society as it presents itself to me, & what is to save it from destruction, but the ministers of the Gospel returning to the faithful and earnest discharge of their duties by preaching the Kingdom of heaven & leave the affairs of Caesar to statesmen. Who ever heard of a minister of the Gospel being a statesman? . . . A true statesman understands the proverb uttered by our Savior, "cast not your pearls before swine"—but it appears a large portion of the North has not the slightest conception of the truth conveyed by it.[8]

Lewis was not alone. In New Orleans, former New Englander Thomas Adams argued that the A.U.A. might have sustained a greater missionary presence in the West and South with money flowing in freely from both regions to support the effort, if not for the political deviations of its ministers.

Had the clergy of that denomination confined their preaching to the truths of Christianity and to the abolition of sins prevailing among their own people—and leave political matters—and the institutions of other states and people—to be governed by those interested—quite an important sum of money might annually flow into your treasury.[9]

For Adams and Lewis, the return and restoration of the "truths of Christianity," the original goal of the Unitarian movement itself, had been sacrificed on the altar of "Puritan fanaticism" and Unitarian abolitionism.

Douglas C. Stange has recently assessed the change within and the nature of Northern Unitarian political activism in his important work *Patterns of Antislavery among American Unitarians*. Tracing the progression of political activism from "Antislavery as Religion" (1831–1840), "Antislavery as Philosophy" (1831–1842), and "Antislavery as Politics" (1840–1850), Stange accounts for the early divisions within the denomination and the forces that ultimately triumphed in enabling the Northern ranks to articulate an antislavery political position within its national convention platform in 1860. Stange chronicles the activity and careers of Northern Unitarian ministers who often found it their duty to wear political hats along with their clerical robes. While some ministers used the pulpit to encourage parishioners to use the vote to "say no to slavery," other ministers ran for elected office themselves. Throughout New England one could find a Unitarian minister who was also an attorney, a governor, a state legislator, a political party activist, a congressman, and a United States senator. Stange labels James Freeman Clarke "The Practical Abolitionist," John Pierpont "The Moralist of Political Action," Theodore Parker "The American Revolutionary Reborn," and Thomas Wentworth Higginson "The Political Abolitionist of Newburyport."[10] What is of particular interest is that within Northern Unitarian ranks the largest and most consistent opposition to this type of political activism came from members of King's Chapel, like that of many Southern churches, a congregation born out of English Unitarianism and one of the first Unitarian churches in the United States. Though initially state supported, the congregation, through the influence of latitudinarianism, produced many prominent individuals firmly committed both to the Constitution and to the principles of separation of church and state: Samuel A. Eliot, Judge R. Curtis, George Ticknor Curtis, Edward G. Loring, and Nathan Hale.[11]

John Pierpont, Jr., minister of the Savannah church, chose to calmly disagree with the radical individualism, abolitionist sentiment, and political "pulpit treason" of his father. In 1842, John Pierpont, Sr., had declared to his congregation that if the Constitution of the United States stood in the way of his own "heaven-bound journey . . . It shall not hinder—it shall help me on my way; for I will mount upward by treading it under my feet." For Pierpont, when the work of "our forefathers" became incompatible with God's commands, then Christians could not obey both "our dead fathers" and the "Living God."[12] Pierpont Sr. detested the fact that his son had accepted the ministerial position in Savannah and rebuked him for living with slavery. But Pierpont Jr. believed that emancipation would prove a blessing neither to the slaves nor to others.[13]

Though he once declared that a Christian clergyman in the Southern states should not preach on the subject of slavery, within a few years of leaving the South, James Freeman Clarke lauded the virtues of po-

litical participation and declared that political activity was an obliga-
tion of both citizenship and religion—for the clergy as well as for the
laity. "Why have we separated what in the Bible are so closely united—
Politics and religion?" he asked. "Why does it seem to us a desecration
of the Sabbath and the Church, to speak of such things . . . ? We have
treated politics as though God had nothing to do with them. We have
been Atheists in our Politics."[14] But Samuel Gilman was determined
that such "pulpit treason" and political agitations would never enter his
Archdale Street church. He stopped Russell Lant Carpenter, a guest
clergyman from England, from offering a prayer from the Charleston
pulpit that included the words "we would remember those in bonds as
bound with them."[15] In an 1856 letter to the A.U.A., he declared, "I enter
into no discussion of these everywhere agitated themes."[16] In New Orleans after Theodore Clapp's death, M. J. Rice, secretary of the board of
trustees, expressed the church's desire to secure a minister with "good
judgement" who could preach the Gospel without introducing any personal or political "crusade" into the congregation or the community.

> It has been apprehended that the slavery question would be a stumbling
> block in the way of our getting a pastor. We do not expect any man that
> comes here from the North, to be an advocate for slavery. . . . Neither do
> we wish an abolitionist, or a man that would think it his duty to lead a
> crusade against slavery here, but we require a man of prudence and good
> judgement, who can preach the gospel of Christ, without introducing the
> subject of slavery.[17]

Gilman and members of his congregation felt that the theological attacks they had endured earlier from "those around them," from Southern evangelicals, did not compare to the attacks of Northern Unitarians,
many of whom formed the political vanguard of the abolitionist movement. Members of the Charleston Book and Tract Society loathed the
"insane" interference into their "peaceful occupations, privileges, and
rights."

> At the present time, the Northern States of our common country may be
> said to be suffering under the infliction of an epidemic insanity, or rather
> an epidemic monomania of a peculiar kind. The predominant idea which

tyrannizes over the minds of all victims, is that of self-righteousness; and the derangement makes itself known by a violent and insane attempt to interfere with the peaceful occupations, privileges, and rights, and (as they wildly imagine) to correct the morals of those towards whom the demagogues of their communities have thought it politic to direct their attention.[18]

While Samuel Gilman insisted that "pulpit treason" would never enter the Archdale Street church, his earlier experience with theological attacks from Southern orthodox circles had taught him that a defense was sometimes necessary, particularly when attacks and "agitations" were unwarranted, obnoxious, and intrusive. In an 1849 letter to Henry W. Bellows, a conservative Unitarian minister in New York, who for a while had preached in Mobile, Gilman expressed his belief that Southerners had a perfect right to a "vehement *defence* of slavery."[19] Leonidas W. Spratt, editor of the *Charleston Standard* and a member of the Unitarian congregation in that city, declared, "These things being so, it is time that slavery should be roused to a consciousness of responsibility for its own preservation; that it should become an actor in the drama of its own fate; that it should speak for itself upon this great question."[20]

Southern Unitarians advocated the legitimacy and purpose of slavery for the South within the "distinct principles of [its] nationality . . . according to the ordinances of nature,"[21] not for its spread over the "national aegis" as Orville Dewey had contended in his Elm Tree Oration in Sheffield, Massachusetts.[22] They believed that if the moral responsibility between slave and master were intact, then Christians should strive for the improvement of slavery, while the state worked for its *protection* (unless the state decided to abolish slavery, as Massachusetts and each Northern state had done earlier). But this was becoming an increasingly difficult task as Northern Unitarian ministers took to the pulpit and their own denominational platforms to intrude politically and morally into institutions and households outside of their own "peaceful occupations, privileges, and rights."

Theodore Clapp believed that "the Southern States are able to take care of themselves," and that ministers in the North had enough to keep them occupied without turning their gaze and fingers southward. He warned, "*Physician heal thyself.* Let the clergymen of the free States . . .

pay a due attention to their own affairs." Clapp believed that industrial capitalism in the North provided ardent reformers and Puritan fanatics more than sufficient material for meddling, handiwork, and pity. "Let them direct their united and vigorous efforts towards meliorating the condition of the suffering, impoverished and immoral thousands at home," he declared, "instead of wasting their declamation and resources upon visionary projects that relate to remote parts, over which it is not possible for them to exert the slightest salutary influence."[23] For Clapp and other Southern Unitarians, moral self-righteousness had placed a plank in the Northerners' eyes large enough to blind them with acute farsightedness, a case so severe that the only things they could see were distorted images just south of the Mason-Dixon line.

During the revolutionary and early antebellum years, Unitarians North and South were united in their opposition to revivalistic enthusiasm and what many deemed a religion of the heart. During the First Great Awakening of the 1740s, Charles Chauncy warned his New England constituency that "an *enlightened* Mind, and *not raised Affections,* ought always to be the Guide of those who call themselves men; and this, in the Affairs of Religion as well as other things."[24] But it was not so much that Chauncy and other eighteenth-century liberals disliked emotionalism in general, it was more its usurpation of the role of reason in religion that they disdained. After all, the Enlightenment was an era not only of reason, but also of sentimentalism, and both left their mark on liberal religion. Though Chauncy is remembered more for his stance against emotionalism, religious liberals of the eighteenth century tried to foster what they considered legitimate evangelicalism even while deploring emotional "enthusiasm."

But over the course of the antebellum period, Southern Unitarians believed that Northern Unitarians had fallen victim to the "fanaticism" they themselves had originally disdained, particularly the fanaticism associated with "revivalistic" evangelicalism. Unlike the Harvard Moralists, who sought to establish what Daniel Walker Howe calls "evangelical Unitarianism," through the "spoken word" and "sacred music," Southern Unitarians preferred to counter theological attacks and (in the process) demonstrate their indebtedness to evangelicalism through the "written word," through tracts and pamphlets. For them, the individual conscience could best be enlightened by one's reading and understanding the "reasonableness" of Unitarian faith through study, through biblical criticism, and through the tools of Scottish Realism. When Northern Unitarian clergy engaged in the "spoken word" in Southern pulpits, many Southerners immediately noticed the stark difference. One Unitarian in Richmond, commenting on the preaching style of a Northern Unitarian clergyman, wrote, "his manners are not well adapted to *Southern* people, and he is vastly deficient in the tact necessary to retain that respect from the community *generally,* so very necessary for every clergyman."[25]

However disdainfully Northern Unitarians initially viewed evangelical revivals and the "excited" flames its flamboyant ministers fanned throughout the North, recent scholarship has outlined how they eventually succumbed to the power of the evangelical presence and allowed emotions to usurp the role of reason. Unlike Unitarians in the South who shared with Southern urban orthodoxy the "pietistic" strand of evangelicalism reminiscent of the Jeffersonian enlightenment, Northern Unitarians were eventually enveloped by an "emotional" revivalism that was anathema to precursors and founders of Northern Unitarianism. In describing the emotional pull of the Civil War, Douglas C. Stange has concluded, "To describe and to interpret the intense excitement of this war for sovereignty, liberation, and civilization, the calm, 'reasonable' theological language of the Unitarian tradition was found insufficient." Indeed, many prominent Unitarians were responsible for wrapping the war in the cloak of religion thereby justifying the almost universal abandonment of an otherwise pacifist position.

> In any event, Unitarians almost universally conceived the war as a holy war, and it is most significant that a Unitarian, Julia Ward Howe, gave to the war one of the most awe-aspiring battle hymns of all time. She had set her poem, the "Battle Hymn of the Republic," to the tune of "John Brown's Body," at the suggestion of James Freeman Clarke.[26]

Before, during, and after the war, in addition to their significant contributions to the abolitionist movement, Southern Unitarians believed that their Northern coreligionists were responsible for fueling the emotional elements of a civil religion, which gained momentum with every battle fought and every soldier buried.

That Orville Dewey himself was once one of the most effective spokesmen in the nineteenth century against the "excitement" and emotionalism that revivals engendered endeared him to Southern and Northern Unitarians alike. His emphasis on individual pietism and rationality appealed to Southern liberals, while Northern Unitarians appreciated the passion of his Calvinistic heritage that allowed him to hit the revivalists on all their most vulnerable and exposed points.[27] In a loftily condescending tone, Dewey had earlier spoken out against the emotionalism revivalists used to sway and influence the rural and middle- to lower-class masses, groups his denomination was perhaps theologically best equipped to help but who were not a part of its ranks. With a hint of pity, Dewey declared, "[those in country villages] meet with but little to arouse and quicken the mind, where a general stagnation and stupor of mind is the thing most to be feared, it is not so much amiss that religion should come in the form of excitement."[28]

Perry Miller has chronicled the changes resulting from revivals in the nineteenth century and given the Third Great Awakening of 1858, which was concentrated primarily in cities and urban areas of the Northeast and Midwest, the prominent title of "The Event of the Century." According to Miller, the Revival of 1858 carried the "assertion of the unity of Christians and the expectation of an immediate attainment through a national religion of the millennium so long and so ardently sought in America."[29] For Northern Unitarians the emotional attraction of unity was too strong and, in the words of Miller, "even [they] came around." Daniel Walker Howe declares that "to maintain their moral influence in the community, they turned to quasi-evangelical preaching techniques, to music and ritual, and most important, to sentimental literature."[30] Unitarians in the North held weekly revival meetings in Boston and New York, and Frederic Dan Huntington conducted Wednesday services at Harvard. Theodore Tebbetts, Richard Pike, and James Freeman Clarke scolded other Unitarians for too much disregarding "the mysterious and spontaneous power of the union of hearts for the accomplishment of spiritual purposes."[31]

Southern Unitarians could not help but notice the change that their

Northern coreligionists had undergone. While they themselves were used to and had long advocated a minimization of denominational differences with other Southern clergy and laity, they had worked for it through a rational approach of "understanding" and "shared assumptions" with Southern orthodoxy: through the tools of biblical criticism and Scottish Realism. Accordingly, the venue of choice for Southern Unitarians was published tracts and sermons that articulated the "reasonableness" of their faith, never an emotionally heightened, feel-good revival meeting. Gilman sought the middle road and prayed:

> Come and remind us of our higher, better destinies. Kindle, but not inflame, our imaginations. Warm, but not distract and agitate, our affections. Preserve our thoughts and feelings at a blessed medium between every extravagance.[32]

OIL AND VINEGAR

As pacifists in general, Unitarians in both the North and the South had to come to terms with the situation in which they found themselves. Southern Unitarians in general tended to be Unionists during the early years of the antebellum period, but soon changed their minds as they saw abolitionist attacks as attacks upon the Union they supported. As the Northern Unitarian abolitionist "monomania" forced Unitarian churches in the South to close their doors, support for the Unitarian denomination, New England, and the Union dwindled. Samuel Henry Dickson declared that the "noisy throng of fanatical abolitionists" had united the South, and that the South in turn assailed the "misnamed reformers" for making the slaves' condition worse, for thrusting in the slaves' hands "dangerous and improper primers and picture books," for preaching insurrection to the slaves, for expounding "trashy" and "empty" arguments against slavery, for extolling private conscience above the law of the land, and leading the country into "horrors of anarchy."[33] Richard Arnold declared that abolitionists threatened the South's "very household" with their "unholy meddling."

For Southern Unitarians, abolition was neither a denominational nor federal issue, only a state one. If abolition were to come at all, it had to be done as it had been done in the North, gradually, by the sover-

eignty of each individual state, and when the time was best for its implementation. Southern Unitarians believed that the federal government should remain true to the original political structures and compro-
mises that created it when the states ratified the Constitution of the
United States in 1789. In his scrapbook Richard Arnold pasted the remaining portion of the article on "Puritan fanaticism." The author alleged that the state of Massachusetts conveniently discovered that slavery was a sin only after it was economically disadvantageous.

> The truth of history is, that at the time of the Declaration of Indepen-
> dence all New England including Massachusetts, was slave, and one of
> the grounds of revolution alleged in that manifesto was that the mother
> country excited insurrection of the negroes, as Puritan emissaries from
> New England have lately done in the South. Massachusetts was the only
> State of the whole thirteen that was not a slave State at the time of the
> Union. She never discovered that slavery was a sin till it had ceased to be
> profitable in her cold, barren climate, adapted only to the white emi-
> grant of Europe. . . . she made slaves of the Indians and sold them into
> captivity. All Northern States, like Massachusetts, have found out that
> white labor is more profitable, and the Puritan clergy have now discov-
> ered that negro slavery is a sin.[34]

Richard Arnold and most Southern Unitarians approved the Compromise of 1850 and felt that the South could accept it without "degradation or dishonor." But when the North failed to honor the compromise, Southern Unitarians quickly saw their hopes dashed. Arnold
declared that when Northerners shot down Southerners in pursuit of
their "just rights," and assisted "black pilferers and colored runaways
to escape, then the South could offer the prayer for these "misguided
brethren": "Father forgive them for they know not what they do!"[35]
Southern Unitarians believed that when the federal government
did not remain true to the Constitution, secession not Unionism was
the best option for a peaceful settlement. In a series of articles in the
Charleston Standard, editor Leonidas W. Spratt, a member of Gilman's
church, argued that there was little to no economic advantage of the
South staying in the Union.[36] While Samuel Gilman opposed nullifica-
tion in 1832, his support of his native Massachusetts and the Union di-

minished with each passing year.[37] With his own denomination blazing a path with "forky, fiery tongue[s]," Gilman realized in 1856 that secession was the most peaceful option and, overall, the best solution. Short of the "interposing hand of God," Gilman believed that only two separate commonwealths would bring peace to a country so embittered by distrust and disdain.

How the South and the North can continue as one people, I cannot comprehend. Was it ever intended that oil and vinegar should form one liquid compound? It appears to me that if we became two separate commonwealths, there will be more peace and satisfaction between us. . . . At present, how can there be peace? . . . God grant us some way of removing a little farther off from each other, in order that we may be a little more near. . . . I see no clear way through this fast gathering cloud and darkness, save the interposing hand and Providence of God.[38]

NINE • The Fork in the Road

While Southern Unitarians upheld the sanctity of individual conscience, they spoke from a tradition of individualism that was as socially
and realistically responsible as it was Southern. While Southern Unitarians believed strongly in individual conscience and sought to uphold
its primacy, they believed that such a position was not "isolationistic" in
nature, but rather was grounded both in the balance and symmetry of
their faith and in their strong sense of family and social responsibilities
as well. According to Richard M. Weaver, there existed "two types of
American individualism" during the antebellum period: one Northern
and "anarchic," epitomized in the Transcendentalism and isolationistic
tendencies of Henry David Thoreau; and the other Southern and "social" bound, epitomized by the life and writings of John Randolph.
Weaver declares,

> Anarchic individualism is revolutionary and subversive from the very
> start; it shows a complete despite for all that civilization or the social
> order has painfully created, and this out of self-righteousness or egocen-
> tric attachment to an idea. . . . When Randolph wrote out the emanci-
> pation of his slaves, he made economic provision for them. In Thoreau's
> anti-slavery papers one looks in vain for a single syllable about how or on
> what the freedmen were to live. The matter for him began and ended
> with taking a moral stance.[1]

While Southern Unitarians retained serious doubts about human
perfectibility, this did not mean that they gave up on reform or progress.
It did mean, however, that they worked for reform within existing parameters, respecting individual, familial, community, state, and constitu-

tional obligations. Southern Unitarians sought reform in their own communities, not beyond, and seldom used the pulpit as a political tree stump. In addition to gaining social interaction with prominent Southerners outside of their own ecclesiastical spheres, Southern Unitarians avoided the encroachment of church upon state through their work in voluntary and benevolent societies, and never sought to put the stamp of denominational approval on any of their reforms. Their choices for reform, like the organizations they chose to work for reform in, reflected their fundamental commitment to the Southern way of life, and the Southern world view. Compelled by an objective sense of morality and their commitment to social responsibility, Southern Unitarians worked for many reforms throughout the antebellum period.[2] But this commitment and the definitions of "progress" and "freedom" it sustained proved incompatible with those of Northern Protestantism in general, many sects of which were following the lead of Northern Unitarians who were already well down the path of the other fork in the road.

"Making Ladies and Gentlemen of Them"

For many Northern Unitarians, abolition, and eventually immediate abolition, became the ultimate social reform. Samuel Joseph May, one of the denomination's most radical abolitionist leaders, declared that Unitarianism possessed "the most fertile soil for a steadfast and unqualified protest against slavery . . . and [had] given to the antislavery cause more preachers, writers, lecturers, agents, poets, than any other denomination in proportion to [its] numbers, if not more without that comparison."[3] Yet, not all Unitarians agreed that their belief system dictated emancipation, protest, or immediate abolition, nor did they agree with the Northern capitalistic impulse and its notions of progress, which some believed fiercely and almost vengefully sought to assign free labor to every inch of American soil. Southern Unitarians rejected the "anarchic" qualities of Northern Unitarian theology and reform, which formed the front arsenals of what Genovese describes as a massive assault "against Christianity and the social order." For Genovese the root of this offensive was the "system of free labor that breeds egotism and extols personal license at the expense of all God-ordained authority."[4] The great majority of Southern Unitarians along with other Christians in the South believed that slavery, through the venue of gradual reform, would eventually give way to a milder form of personal servitude and racial dictatorship while still retaining a fundamental commitment to the Southern household.

Despite twenty-first-century standards concerning slavery, which see the institution as intolerable and inhumane, nineteenth-century, and in this case, Southern Unitarian, views were very different. They deserve to be heard and understood on their own terms, in their own words, and through the lens of an agrarian system many then believed was in fact humane, tolerable, progressive, and "Christian." While Southern Unitarians believed that slavery would soon give way to a milder form of servitude, they believed firmly in the agrarian system that supported slavery, especially when it was contrasted with the "evils" of an industrial capitalist society that took little or no interest in its labor.

Southern Unitarians placed slavery on a paternalistic foundation that required accepted notions of place and status, as well as the proper moral responsibilities incumbent on each "family member."[5] To the extent that Southern Unitarians supported slavery in relational terms and saw its usefulness in its ability to confine labor to "household relationships," Southern Unitarians advocated the institution as a proper social system and alternative to the Northern fork of "free labor." While some Northern Christians, Unitarians included, supported the rhetoric of family values in their reform efforts, there was an important and fundamental difference. Southerners believed that family meant the extended family, servants and slaves included, and as such, was the proper social system on which their civilization and their way of life was based. Southern Unitarians were no exceptions. At the advent of the Civil War, Richard D. Arnold declared that "we inaugurated our revolution to save [slavery], because it was the corner stone of our Social institutions."[6] Arnold and other Southern Unitarians believed that personal servitude *was* conducive to a Christian social order and was an integral part of a divinely sanctioned, socially responsible, hierarchical world. Eugene Genovese has even concluded that "Theodore Clapp . . . an extreme theological liberal, joined Thornwell, Armstrong, Ross, Stringfellow, Smith, William G. Brownlow, and others in sounding like George Fitzhugh." But there were many others as well. Southern Unitarians believed that Scripture was the primary foundation for truth and it was the first source they utilized in their support of slavery as a proper social system. Genovese declares that the "Southern divines, both Arminians and Calvinists, supported by leading secular theorists, grounded their defense of social stratification and political order in Scripture and theology, and they identified the free-labor system itself as the source of Northern spiritual and moral degradation."[7] As legitimate heirs of the Arminian tradition in the South, Southern Unitarian clergy deserve greater notice and recognition.

Like other Southerners, Unitarians in the South could not help but notice the differences between slaves and free laborers in other parts of the country and the world, freedmen and working women included. Charles Taggart declared that, in sharp contrast to the "lazy, discontented, and disappointed freedman" of the North, the condition of Southern slaves was advancing remarkably in physical comforts, religious instruction, and moral and mental improvement.[8] Theodore Clapp praised the American slave's "salubrious" existence over the sad plight of the European working woman. When he traveled abroad, Clapp was shocked by the "animal-like" existence of the female peasantry and the laboring classes in England and France.[9] He believed that slaves were as free and undisturbed in their "domestic relations" as white women in the North:

> The slaves in Louisiana are, in all essential respects, as free as the female population of Massachusetts. In common with our fair sisters, at the North, they are cut off from the exercise of the political franchise, and the employments of public life. But in the private sphere marked out for them, they may taste the purest bliss of earth, and be an ornament, a light and blessing to all within their influence.[10]

In Charleston, Samuel Dickson concluded that the physical comfort of the black slave was "infinitely above that of the wretched white slave of the British manufactory, or worse still, of the coal mine, trained from infancy to push with their forehead a loaded wagon."[11] Samuel Gilman agreed and believed that "moderate and regulated labour, such as interposed on the vast majority of the slave population at the South, is conducive both to their bodily and mental happiness."[12] Caroline Gilman charged that "Northerners do not take [slaves] home, and make ladies and gentlemen of them, but put them in a freezing climate, to labor for their own living, good and bad together."[13] She believed that slaves were happier in the South than in the "frost bitten colony" in Canada. In *Recollections of a Southern Matron,* she portrayed a poignant encounter between a master and a free black man whose "only wish on earth was to live and die in his master's service."[14] She was not alone. Charles Taggart argued that there were numerous cases in which fugitive slaves voluntarily returned to slavery in order to "spend the remainder of their lives in comfort."[15]

Southern Unitarians believed that slaves benefited from oral instruction and that a majority of them were not only better educated than the laboring classes of the "higher races" in other countries, but also better provided for medically. They argued that the self-interest of the slave-holder necessitated proper medical care for slaves and advocated high standards for working health and retirement. Samuel Henry Dickson recommended proper medical care as the "soundest policy and the wisest self interest." Caroline Gilman assured readers that slaves received proper medical attention and that when they grew old they were withdrawn into a contented retirement.[16]

As both slaveholders and churchgoers, Southern Unitarians worked diligently for reform of the institution. They educated their slaves, provided them with medical care, included them in family and congregational worship, worked to restrict the slave trade, sought reforms to keep slave families intact, and in the long run, worked toward gradual emancipation and a milder form of personal servitude within the confines of the household.[17] Theodore Clapp declared that "to protect, feed, and clothe" slaves was not a sin, but a duty.[18] Samuel Dickson believed that in addition to education and keeping slave families intact, slaves should have the "privilege of owning certain property and of purchasing [their] freedom under definite regulations."[19]

The desire for slavery reform among Southern Unitarians stemmed from an objective sense of self and society: from personal religious conviction, familial and social obligations, and a divinely sanctioned, socially responsible, hierarchical world view. In every congregation in the South, Unitarians owned slaves. Dexter Clapp in Savannah wrote that in some Unitarian churches, nearly every member was a slaveholder.[20] Along with other Southern clergy and laity, Southern Unitarians held a view of slavery that recognized the humanity of the slave and the moral responsibility incumbent on both master and servant. For Southern Unitarians, to improve the institution of slavery was a family matter, a moral duty, and an economic necessity. Southern Unitarians worked for the improved health and education of slaves, the inclusion of free blacks and slaves in worship, and improved living conditions for slaves.

Dr. Richard Arnold himself owned at least seven slaves and was at the beginning of his medical career physician to slaves on plantations near Savannah. Although he later withdrew from this work, he continued his interest in the health of free blacks and slaves and studied "racial" aspects of disease. He accepted the role of guardian for a number of free blacks and exercised that role with care and patience. On several occasions Arnold had to intervene in order to assure his "wards" of proper treatment and their due legal rights. He even sold slaves on occasion, but did so only so as not to divide the slaves' families. In one instance he was placed in a situation of being the beneficiary of slaves in a will of one of his wards—a free Negro woman.[21]

For Southern Unitarians, the economic and personal interest of the slaveholder necessitated proper medical care for his or her slaves. Arnold declared that a "Cotton Lord" in the North could easily fill the place of a dead worker by hiring another laborer, but the slaveholder was forced to provide care and attention for his slaves.[22]

As a native Southerner and as a Unitarian, Samuel Dickson recognized that humanity demanded reform of both the slave trade and the "wanton" breaking up of slave families. Believing that the institution of marriage was sacred, he advocated that slave families remain together and be sold as units. His solution was the placement of district commissioners throughout the South who would oversee the sale of slave families. "Humanity . . . demands from us some restriction upon the traffic in slaves among ourselves," Dickson declared. "The wanton or capricious, resentful or penal sale of the negro,—the disruption of all ties of affection or consanguinity at the will of the thoughtless, unfeeling, or angry owner, should be put an end to."[23]

In addition to seeking improvements in health, medicine, and the slave trade, Southern Unitarians sought to educate their slaves. While actually illegal in many states in the South,[24] the education of slaves was not incompatible with accepted Southern religious norms, provided it was done discreetly and within appropriate boundaries. Samuel Dickson expressed his desire that all legal impediments for the education of free blacks and slaves in South Carolina be removed.[25] In 1844, Samuel Gilman wrote to his sister, Louisa Loring, "I am teaching . . . our little James . . . arithmetic . . . he has picked out for himself a very good knowledge of geography from Annie's old Maps and School Books."[26] Gilman and other Southern Unitarians were concerned about the spiritual enrichment of both slaves and free blacks.[27] While Gilman distributed Bibles to his own slaves, Dexter Clapp in Savannah wrote that almost every Unitarian congregation in the South included slaves and free blacks in worship and communion services.[28] In Augusta, Unitarians included slaves in the Sabbath School they had started for their own children.[29]

On the basis of scanty evidence, some historians have asserted that Samuel Gilman bought and educated his slaves for "ultimate freedom." Daniel Walker Howe has declared, "The emancipated individuals seem . . . to have been sent North where the Gilman connections helped them obtain 'situations.' It is impossible to tell how many slaves Samuel Gilman freed in this way; since his financial resources were limited and his actions attracted no unfavorable notice, presumably not more than a handful."[30] The lone reference to this activity in Gilman's own hand concerned the education of a slave, James. In the 1844 letter quoted above, Gilman spoke of educating "little James" in preparation for "ultimate freedom." But as Douglas C. Stange has argued, "by the time of the Civil War, James was still a slave of the Gilmans and very likely was over twenty-one years of age. In sixteen years, James had not earned his . . . freedom."[31] But even after the war, as late as December 1865, James was still a servant within the Gilman household. Having just returned to Charleston after working at the Confederate Refugee Camp in Greenville, South Carolina, Caroline Gilman wrote to her children, "James came a fortnight ahead of us, laid the carpets and prepared the bedding, and we had every reason, when placing our heads on our pillows, to thank God for a home."[32]

And James was still with the Gilmans six months after he had every legal right to leave. He stayed with the Gilmans on his own free will and out of personal desire. On the basis of the current record alone, James was educated and spiritually nurtured by the Gilmans, and by every indication was as fond of them as they were of him. It is not clear when, if ever, James left the Gilman household. Apparently, he believed that his individual freedom meant nothing outside of the balanced social relationships of the home he had grown up in and the economic provisions that household provided. Before the war, Caroline Gilman called James aside to reassert the dependency both had on each other. "James," she said, "I hope and trust there will be no fighting, but if there is, you must take good care of me, and I will take care of you." "Yes ma'am," said James.[33]

A Sanction for Slavery

Larry Tise's formidable work on proslavery ideology has seen its fair share of fans and critics alike.[34] Most recently, Eugene Genovese has taken Tise to task on many fronts. Not only does he criticize Tise's failure to confront the Southern critique of Northern conservatism, but he also scolds Tise for rejecting the "'final formulation held in common with others' that the threat of abolitionism provided the occasion for the full revelation of an already well developed southern proslavery ideology."[35] Along with Lewis Simpson, Drew Faust, and Elizabeth Fox-Genovese, Eugene Genovese argues that a "defense of slavery had been implicit in the specific type of republicanism that had long since taken root in the South but could not emerge explicitly until external challenge compelled a confrontation with the contrary ideological tendencies inherited from Enlightenment liberalism and crystallized in the defense of the American Revolution."[36] But such a stance distorts the historical realities of Enlightenment liberalism in general and Unitarianism in particular by discounting the proslavery and republican ideologies of Southern Unitarians. When Enlightenment liberalism turned on itself within Northern Unitarian ranks, Southern Unitarians joined the proslavery movement on various fronts and appealed to the republican qualities of Jefferson by advocating a strict separation of church and state.

While Samuel Gilman privately defended slavery in his actions, and in his own notes and in conversations with family and friends, he believed that a defense of slavery did not mean that the pulpit should be taken prisoner and used as a weapon in the fight. Always the purist,

Gilman believed that the pulpit was to be used only to preach the gospel and relay the Christian message of hope. Theodore Clapp did not always maintain this ideal himself. He did use the pulpit on two known occasions to defend slavery and his sermons were published by his congregation and by the New Orleans *Daily Picayune*. And yet, when seeking to fill his vacancy, New Orleans Unitarians, like Unitarians in Richmond, Savannah, and Mobile, expressed their strong conviction *not* to have their church used for "pulpit treason." When Southern Unitarians like Clapp defended slavery, they did so out of the belief that just as their religious beliefs demanded a response earlier when so vehemently attacked by "those around them," so did their institutions and their way of life. The sanction of slavery by Southern Unitarians was by nature "defensive," and came in direct reaction to the agitation of Northern Unitarian abolitionist attacks. Former New Englander Daniel K. Whitaker wrote in the inaugural issue of his *Southern Quarterly Review*, "The North . . . has acted as the North" so it behooves the South to contribute to "our country's literature . . . as the South." Whitaker, Taggart, and other Southern Unitarians took to the written word to defend the institution, filling pages of magazines, journals, and newspapers with a defense of the institution and Southern civilization. And yet so great was the desire for separation of church and state with their theology, that when abolitionist attacks did come, they were still able to pull only two ministers, Theodore Clapp and Charles Taggart, into the pulpit to defend the institution of slavery. Charles Farley, a visiting Unitarian minister, had been rebuked by the Richmond congregation for doing so.

Theodore Clapp and Charles Taggart, like most Southern clergymen, sanctioned slavery on three intellectual foundations: the Bible, moral philosophy (especially Scottish Common Sense Realism), and natural law. For Clapp, both the Old and New Testaments offered "conclusive evidence" of the divine sanction of slavery. In Genesis, God had given bond servants to Abraham. Clapp declared, "Here we see God dealing in slaves; giving them [to Abraham] as a reward for his eminent goodness." Clapp also concluded that there was "nothing . . . in the New Testament on slavery contrary to the spirit and the words of the texts already quoted from the Hebrew Scriptures" (those cited above).

Clapp argued that Christ himself had established duties governing the master-servant relationship. If slavery were abolished, Clapp argued, "the laws of Christ" would be abolished in the process.[37]

Clapp took William Ellery Channing to task for "unhesitatingly nullifying" the letter of the New Testament in favor of its spirit. Rather than substituting the literal with the virtual, taking Christ's command "Thou shalt love thy neighbor as thyself" as a "virtual condemnation of slavery," as Channing and others had done, Clapp grounded his biblical justification of slavery on both the spirit and the letter of God's revelation. Like other Southern Unitarians, while he believed strongly in reason, he thought that Northern Unitarians had taken it too far, relying solely on the "virtuality" of the spirit of Scripture based on human reason alone. For Clapp, Channing and others had neglected the letter of divine revelation. He posed this question to his audience: "If the institution were only evil—a scandalous sin—a daring outrage upon the first principles of right and freedom—an object of Divine abhorrence [as Channing had alleged] could Jesus have remained in silence on such a momentous subject[?]"[38]

> Jesus Christ . . . Our Saviour . . . was born, lived, labored and died in the midst of slaveholders. If it had been, in his opinion, a monstrous evil— the greatest of wrongs—a thing utterly criminal and irreligious—must he not have condemned it without qualification or reserve? If the modern doctrine be sound, Jesus should have said to the master, "Your slave is your equal; you cannot justly hold property in man; it is wicked in the sight of God for you to do so; it is an infringement of the natural rights of a fellow-being; you must immediately set him at liberty." Not a syllable analogous to this was uttered by our Lord . . . Let it be remembered that Jesus Christ, instead of reprobating the slavery of his time, most explicitly commanded his disciples to obey the civil constitution of government by which it was ordained.[39]

In his recent assessment of Southern clergy and the sanctification of slavery, Mitchell Snay explains that ministers in the South found moral philosophy, especially Scottish Common Sense Realism, appealing because its categories of analysis, namely those of "rights, duties, and relations," were analogous to the relationship between master and servant. According to Snay, because Southern clergymen "portrayed slavery as a relationship between morally responsible beings," they insisted "that the just treatment of slaves was a natural moral law dictated by the conscience . . . and if violated, punishable by God."[40]

Facing the "insanity" of Northern Unitarian abolitionism, the Charleston congregation appealed to the "relational" categories of Scottish Common Sense Realism when they accused their "quondam Brethren of the North" of taking it upon themselves to wage a "violent and insane . . . [interference] with the peaceful occupations, privileges, and rights" of their way of life.[41] Both Gilman and Clapp believed that the emphasis moral philosophy placed on "rights, duties, and relations," especially those involving family and household, provided the best categories for a defense of slavery. Clapp declared, "Christianity attempts to remove the evils of slavery—not by destroying the relation, but by enforcing the duties. Obedience to parents cannot exist, if you abolish the relation of parent and child."[42] In *Recollections of a Southern Matron*, Caroline Gilman wrote that the slaveholder was a man who "controlled the happiness of a large family, of his fellow-creatures" and sought to reign over his "little kingdom . . . in wisdom and love."[43] Privately, Samuel Gilman invoked the relational qualities of husbands to wives and fathers to children when he explained the "occasional" manifestations of cruelty within the institution. "I believe that occasional acts of private cruelty and oppression do not arise from the nature of the institution," Gilman reflected in his notes, "but from the imperfection of man; that husbands, fathers, masters, everywhere, are occasionally guilty of cruelty and oppression to their wives, children, and apprentices; and that oppression would still be exercised by the whites over the blacks if the latter were set free."[44]

Charles Taggart utilized many of the ideas inherent in natural law, especially the notion of inequality, in his defense of slavery. He and other Southern Unitarians argued that in the state of nature, human beings were dependent on other humans, and were thus social creatures. Because there were varying degrees of dependence existing between human beings, the resulting inequality was inherently natural. The natural law of inequality was the starting point of Taggart's argument for polygenesis (the concept that God created a diversity of races rather than a unity of mankind) in an article printed in the *Southern Quarterly Review*. Taggart declared, "No argument or fact can be adduced, to prove any thing as regards the original unity of the human family."

> The supposition [of] a diversity of original creations by the Supreme Father appears to . . . harmonize perfectly with all the known operations of the gracious author of nature, in adapting all living beings to the admirable and perfect, though to us, wonderful and incomprehensible laws by which he governs the universe.[45]

Eugene Genovese has argued that by invoking "scientific racism" to affirm polygenesis, ministers like Charles Taggart and James Warley Miles in Charleston stood outside of the norm established by Southern divines like James Henley Thornwell, who adamantly rejected both the concept and the reasoning behind it. But Thornwell and other Southern divines increasingly utilized science to reaffirm revelation and scriptural authority. Dozens of ministers in the South, mostly from orthodox urban circles, were engaged in publishing articles on science and religion in many of the religious journals: so much so that by 1851, as E. Brooks Holifield concludes, "it was possible to speak of a 'theology of natural science' that was supposedly in perfect harmony with the Bible." The primary motive behind this theology, Holifield argues, was not only "to demonstrate the compatibility between Genesis and geology," but also "to show that scientific investigation, properly conducted, provided a vast and grand extension of the traditional argument that design and order in nature demonstrated the existence of God."[46]

Though Samuel Gilman never embraced polygenesis and never took to the pulpit to defend slavery, he did quietly reflect notions of differences in the races in his private papers. "I believe," he wrote, "that their natural indolence and improvidence, would reduce them, if left to themselves, to vastly greater misery than the occasional privations they are now called to sustain." Continuing, Gilman reflected, "I believe that the vices of the blacks are not necessarily caused by slavery, but are characteristic of the race, as is proved by the testimony of all intelligent travellers to Africa."[47]

Most Northern Unitarians, if they were not supporters of polygenesis, agreed with Gilman and other Southern divines on a natural inequality of the races. Channing himself declared:

> I should expect from the African race, if civilized, less energy, less courage, less intellectual originality, than in our race, but more amiableness, tranquility, gentleness, and content. They might not rise to an equality in outward condition, but would probably be a much happier race. There is no reason for holding such a race in chains; they need no chain to make them harmless.[48]

Throughout his career, Orville Dewey, like many conservative Northern Unitarians, was a proponent, not of integration of the races, but of colonization. "If I were to propose a plan to meet the duties and perils of this tremendous emergency that presses upon us," Dewey declared, "I would engage the whole power of this nation, the willing cooperation of the North and the South . . . to prepare this people for freedom." Compelled not by any sense of equality between the races, but rather by what appeared to be an inherent sense of Puritanical and "ennobling" self-righteousness, Dewey's plan for freedom and colonization was to be an example for the world to follow. "I would give them a country beyond the mountains—say the Californias," he stated, "where they might be a nation by themselves. Ah! . . . What a purifying and ennobling ministration for ourselves!"[49]

For Clapp, slavery existed among other institutions that were part and parcel of human nature and the human experience. It existed along with "weakness, mortality, pain, ignorance and many other things . . . which are inseparable from the allotments of man on earth."[50] For Taggart, because slavery existed within the balanced category of social relations in the South and revolved around a parent-child relationship, slavery could not be sinful.[51] Theodore Clapp declared that "if I were persuaded of [slavery's] sinfulness, no fear of man should deter me from asserting my convictions of truth and duty on this subject."[52] That Orville Dewey once argued that slavery was not sinful and was a *moral* not a political question only endeared him that much more to Southern Unitarians.[53] But the Elm Tree Oration in Sheffield in 1856 ended any semblance of that former endearment.

TEN • Institutional Decline and the Ghost of Southern Unitarianism

By the 1850s, Southern Unitarians believed that Northern Unitarians had shunned their responsibilities under the weight of the "prevailing monomania." They argued that their Northern coreligionists had violated the ideal of individual conscience by using the pulpit as a political tree stump, in their "romantic theology" had substituted the "fatherhood of God" with the "brotherhood of man," had tainted the religious duties of ministers by their political shenanigans, and had made abolition a politically and an emotionally charged issue. By turning their backs on reasonableness, antirevivalism, and political purity, Southern Unitarians believed, Northern Unitarians had grossly perverted the "old and primitive faith." In an attempt to turn the tide, Unitarians throughout the South, whether in churches or not, gradually declared their independence. But by the time Southern Unitarians realized the extent of the damage, it was too late. The orthodox "association" of Southern Unitarians with the "perversions" of their Northern coreligionists spelled doom for many ecclesiastical organizations in the South. In Richmond, Charles A. Farley complained, "The Abolitionists at the North, are doing every thing to prejudice Virginians against us—I hope it will not injure us, and look confidently to a proper expression of feeling from our community in Boston." In Savannah, E. L. Bascom declared, "Dr. Channing & *The Christian Register* have done much to ruin the cause of liberal Christianity—I mean—Christianity in its purity—by leading *man* to believe & the orthodox to *say*—that Unitarianism & Abolitionism are identified. I have a burden on my shoulders that I need many helps to sustain." In Mobile, Samuel St. John, Jr., explained that "there exists among the Southern members of our society—Who are natives of the Southern States—an idea that there is little fellowship—or true Christian feeling among the Unitarians of the North for us here ... The North is so excited against the South on the subject of abolition that our church & society could not expect much sympathy from you of the North."[1]

AUGUSTA AND SAVANNAH

Throughout the South, Unitarian churches eventually closed their doors. In Augusta, Stephen Bulfinch's ministry lasted only about seven years. Thereafter members of the congregation kept the Unitarian society alive for the next twenty years, with little if any funding from the American Unitarian Association: certainly no small feat. Although unwilling to support the church financially, the A.U.A. still desired to claim it for propaganda. The Unitarian yearbook continued to keep the Augusta church on its list, always without a pastor, until 1856, coincidentally the year of Orville Dewey's Elm Tree Oration, even though the church building itself was occupied by a Jewish congregation by 1850. The known historical record contains no further clues as to the theological course of the members. On the basis of the record of other Southern Unitarians, however, many in the Augusta church undoubtedly were absorbed into orthodoxy while continuing to hold their liberal views.

In one of its last issues, the *Unitarian Christian* reminded the Augusta congregation of its roots and obligations to its old friends in Charleston: "To that city we have long been used to look for kindness and support, with the certainty of not being disappointed. Indeed, but for the prompt and efficient encouragement of our Charleston friends, our present undertaking, slight as it is, could never have commenced."[2]

In Savannah, early in 1842, Dexter Clapp, a recent graduate of Harvard Divinity School, was engaged as a supply for the Savannah church and was soon asked to become its permanent minister. On November 26, 1843, Clapp was ordained into the ministry in the Savannah church. Henry W. Bellows of the First Congregational Church of New York City delivered the ordination sermon, and Samuel Gilman delivered the charge. Clapp served the Savannah congregation faithfully until the summer of 1846 when he succeeded Theodore Parker as minister of the Second Parish Church in West Roxbury, Massachusetts.[3]

Without a minister, the congregation, though not disbanded, was eventually forced to sell its church property to settle its debts. The building was sold to a Baptist congregation who met there until February 1859. The building was then used as a Confederate armory. In the winter of 1864–1865, while General William T. Sherman was using it as a guardhouse, the building caught fire.

In 1835, Stephen Bulfinch had written the A.U.A. to communicate how "incomprehensible" it was to him how that organization could refuse to send money to help the struggling church. "As to Savannah," he declared, "I yesterday received a letter from Mr. Bascom, in a tone of deep mortification at the utter failure of their application in Boston, a failure which I must acknowledge is utterly incomprehensible to me." In the end, however, despite their lack of help, he reminded the A.U.A. of the tenacity of the church's members to survive the struggle. "I have no doubt," he concluded, "that they will eventually weather their difficulties."[4]

But help continued to come from the Charleston congregation and from a dedicated and wealthy member of the Savannah congregation itself. Moses Eastman, a longtime member of the congregation, bought a lot in Ogelthorpe Square for the construction of a church. In April 1851, the *Daily Morning News* described the building under construction as a "little gem": "It is built of brick to be stuccoed, and it is a very pretty specimen of Gothic Architecture. Its roof forms a cross; and its buttresses and pediments have a very pleasing effect . . . It will accommodate without reference to its gallery, about two hundred and sixty persons."[5]

J. Allen Penniman had been the minister of the congregation since October 1848 while the church building was under construction. During this time, Penniman held services for members in the Armory Hall of the Chatham Artillery Company. In August 1849, he wrote a report of his society who had long struggled against what often seemed insurmountable odds. His report reflected the increased fluidity between orthodox Christians and Southern Unitarians, for many in his flock moved freely between both groups: "Our Society is small but yet hold together. Many members are absent from the city for business & health, still the audience at our hall on the Sabbath, in number exceeds my most daring expectations. It is made up of Unitarians, Presbyterians, Baptists, & Methodists, and has been from the beginning of my labors here."[6]

But Penniman did not last long in Savannah. The congregation dedicated the new church building on November 21, 1851, with both Gilman and his new associate minster, Charles Manson Taggart, assisting. After Penniman left, the Reverend Mr. Larned of Mobile took over and preached during the winter of 1852, but he became seriously ill and went to Charleston to recuperate at the Gilmans' home. Unfortunately, like the short stays of Thacher and Bascom before him, the illness of Larned interrupted what seemed to be another promising start for Savannah. Later that spring, Samuel Gilman wrote the A.U.A. to inquire about the possibility of securing ministerial nominees for the Savannah congregation. While he asked the A.U.A. for names of any possible candidates, he also made clear the fact that the Savannah congregation had bestowed upon himself and Mr. Larned the ultimate responsibility of finding a pastor.[7]

John Pierpont, Jr., the son of the Rev. John Pierpont, Sr., the avid abolitionist and also the grandfather of the famous industrialist J. P. Morgan, answered the call. Savannah was attractive to Pierpont in many respects. He wanted a change of pace from New England after the death of his wife, and he also wanted to assert his own individualism in the face of the heightened expectations of having as a father a famous Unitarian minister and a "dogmatic believer in abolition, total abstinence, and phrenology."[8] After less than six weeks in Savannah, Pierpont accepted the invitation to be the permanent minister even though he had often faced "obloquy and misrepresentation" by the orthodox establishment during the six-week period. In 1854, his father begged him to return to the North, but he knew that if he left Savannah, the church would probably break up for good. His father rebuked him for living with slavery, but Pierpont Jr. believed that emancipation would prove a blessing neither to the slaves nor to others.[9] But even with his avowed Southern sympathies, Pierpont was pessimistic about his prospects. In an attempt to turn the tide, Pierpont preached on "The Zest of Christian Discipleship" in February 1855 and in April he began a series of historical lectures under the auspices of the Georgia Historical Society. In December 1856, Pierpont got a temporary psychological boost from the arrival of Charles Farley in Savannah. Farley had recently retired from the Unitarian ministry and had come to Savannah to start a private school. Farley preached a number of times at the church and Pierpont taught in his school. But the numbers were growing smaller and by January 1859 there was no money to pay Pierpont's salary. To support himself, he joined his brother James in the factorial business in Macon, Georgia. In May 1861, he moved to New York City to enter the insurance business. With no minister, no money, and few numbers, the trustees of the Unitarian Association sold the property in August 1859.

RICHMOND

For several years after the ministry of Edwin Hubbell Chapin, the First Independent Church of Richmond had a succession of ministers. Daniel D. Smith, a Universalist minister, preached there in 1840 and appears to have been well received within the orthodox community, especially among the Episcopalians.[10] John H. Gihon, editor of the *Nazarene* in Philadelphia from 1840 to 1843, preached in Richmond during 1845 and "diligently expound[ed] his doctrine." But here as among other Southern Unitarians who preferred a broad and liberal base instead of dogmatic doctrines, his expositions were "not marked with success."[11]

In 1848, after the success of Chapin years before, and after the disappointing succession of ministers since, John M. Daniel, a religious radical who apparently did not have any church affiliation during the antebellum period (after the war he did become a pewholder in Dr. Moses D. Hoge's Second Presbyterian Church) attempted to stir up the liberalism of the city by delivering a sermon himself in what was increasingly seen by the community as the "long-silent Universalist Church." His preaching efforts were not successful, but Daniel was able to create a favorable intellectual climate for liberal religious thought, especially among local New School Presbyterians, through newspaper articles. As the "leading editor of the South," Daniel pushed the *Richmond Examiner* in directions no other Southerner would. His was the "first southern newspaper to review and applaud the works of Transcendentalist Ralph Waldo Emerson and to review the works of the [liberal] Unitarian minister Theodore Parker."[12] Five years later his cousin, Moncure Daniel Conway, a Methodist-turned-Unitarian minister who also flirted with Transcendentalism and who was soon to become the minister of the Washington D.C. society, delivered two sermons to the Richmond congregation.[13]

Even though by all evidence it appears that Daniel and his cousin Conway were the only Southern Unitarians to seriously entertain Transcendentalist notions (with the possible exception of James Warley Miles, an Episcopal minister in Charleston), their efforts may indeed have helped to raise the name "Unitarian" out of the trenches and keep the church afloat, at least for a while (Conway himself would not last long at the Washington church because of his avowed antislavery beliefs). In September 1858, the Richmond congregation was able to secure a permanent minister, James Shrigley, of Reading, Pennsylvania. He accepted the position and remained at the church for almost two and a half years. While in Richmond Shrigley received a salary of fifteen hundred dollars a year, which the congregation raised by itself through annual pledges.[14] A week after South Carolina seceded from the Union, Shrigley left Richmond. The timing and the fact that the congregation hastily borrowed money to pay Shrigley suggest that he left Richmond because of the political situation.

Almost immediately, however, the congregation was able to secure another minister. Alden Bosserman, originally from Maine but who had recently relocated to Baltimore, began his duties on January 1, 1860. By outward appearance at least, Bosserman must have seemed to be acceptable to the church and the city not only theologically, but also socially, politically, and economically as well, for he brought his slave with him to Richmond. A little over a year later, however, in March 1862, he was arrested as a Union sympathizer and crossed through Union lines under a flag of truce.[15]

Though small in number, the First Independent Church of Richmond continued to exist throughout the antebellum period, demonstrating a remarkable degree of survival in the face of intimidating odds. During the war, the congregation broke up and individual members dispersed throughout the orthodox community. The church building in essence became a hall for hire and the building gradually fell into disrepair and decay. In 1903, a Virginia court ordered the Mayo Street property sold and the proceeds distributed. The Unitarian and the Universalist denominations each received one thousand dollars from the sale.[16]

NEW ORLEANS

In 1851, the church in New Orleans burned after the St. Charles Hotel located next to it caught fire. When the time came to build another church, Jewish philanthropist Judah Touro again came to the church's rescue. He offered them a lot on the corner of Julia and St. Charles and the congregation immediately began to erect a new Gothic-style church there. With members and Touro contributing seventy-one thousand dollars, the church was completed in 1855. Sparked by the heightened tensions between himself and Northern Unitarians and the increasing synonymity of Unitarianism with abolitionism, Theodore Clapp desired to discard the trappings of sectarianism and align his church closer to Southern orthodoxy. With the approval of his congregation, Clapp changed the name of the new building to The Church of the Messiah.

In 1856, Clapp resigned his charge in New Orleans because of ill health and moved to Louisville, Kentucky, away from the summer "epidemics." He remained there until his death in 1866. In his final letter to his congregation he expressed his desire to spend his closing days with them and to be buried among those with whom he had spent the greater part of his life. However, when he died on May 17, 1866, he was quietly buried in Louisville. Nonetheless his congregation voted unanimously to return his body for burial in New Orleans. With the consent of his wife, his remains were brought from Louisville on March 22, 1867. Notices were carried in all the city newspapers announcing that the final services for Clapp would be held on March 24. On Sunday, March 24, the funeral procession, described as "longer than is often witnessed," extended over a half dozen blocks along Canal Street from St. Charles to Rampart Street.

Orville Dewey supplied the New Orleans pulpit in the spring of 1856 (the last year he preached in Charleston also) and delivered his lectures to crowds of more than six hundred people. The next full-time minister was Edwin C. Bolles, a Universalist, who came to New Orleans in February 1857, but he remained for only two years. The next pastor was Charles B. Thomas, a Unitarian, who began preaching in the fall of 1859. In May 1861, Thomas suddenly resigned, ostensibly so that he might not be separated from his parents during the ensuing "Crisis." Before Thomas left, however, Thomas A. Adams, president of the board of trustees and himself a native New Englander, requested that the congregation's annual fees to the A.U.A. be returned.

CHARLESTON

On Sunday, April 2, 1852, the congregation in Charleston dedicated its newly remodeled church. The church had hired the young architect and church member Francis D. Lee to remodel the building in the popular Gothic Revival style and he was commissioned to incorporate the old walls and tower into his new design. Lee had been inspired by the Henry VII chapel at Westminster Abbey, particularly the delicate fan-like intricacies of the ceiling, and when the church was completed it was considered (and it still is today) to be some of the finest Gothic Revival work extant in America.

In addition to Gilman, Charles J. Bowen (son-in-law of Gilman) of New Bedford, Massachusetts, George Washington Burnap of Baltimore, John Healy Heywood of Louisville, John Pierpont, Jr., of Savannah, and Charles Manson Taggart, who would soon join the Charleston congregation as assistant minister, officiated at the dedication. At the beginning of the service, Gilman recalled the climate and conditions that he and his wife, Caroline, had first encountered in Charleston, and some of the changes that occurred over the course of the years. Though experiencing hostility from the orthodox churches early on, by mid-century Gilman could claim not only an "orthodox reputation," but also both an active, charitable, and "reform-minded" constituency and a "reasonable flourishing" of numbers despite circulating reports of declining numbers. "I have frequently heard of our declining and dying away," he remembered, "when the church was as flourishing as we could reasonably desire . . . [that was] a favorite mode of depreciating and discouraging us for many years." Gilman looked back in wonder at the steadfastness and perseverance of members in the face of so much opposition. "There was often everything to overwhelm timid and sensitive minds," he recalled, "and yet timid and sensitive minds held on." Such perseverance reinstated Gilman's "confident assurance" in the "redeeming power" of Unitarian Christianity: that if allowed a full and fair field, "it would at length be felt by many at heart to be the power of God unto salvation."[17]

During the service, Gilman also took the opportunity to recount his ministerial activities among a four-hundred-member congregation. In addition to his move to initiate the establishment of the Book and Tract Society and the congregational purchase of Anthony Forster's theological and literary library, Gilman recalled that he had performed 148 marriages, 484 child baptisms, 37 adult baptisms, and 300 funerals. Gilman also mentioned his ministerial activities among the "colored portion" of his congregation. "Owing to the absence of efficient leaders," Gilman explained, "the colored portion of the communicants has generally been in a state of decline, in spite of my constant and earnest efforts to prevent it."[18]

Because of the age and illness of Samuel Gilman, the congregation called Charles Taggart as co-pastor in 1853. Taggart was born in Montreal, Canada, on October 31, 1821. He was raised a Presbyterian and spent most of his youth near Pittsburgh, Pennsylvania. In the early 1840s Taggart taught in Owensboro, Kentucky, where he came under the influence of John Heywood, minister of the Unitarian church. In 1845 Heywood persuaded Taggart to study at the Unitarian Theological School, which had recently opened in Meadville, Pennsylvania. Taggart graduated in the spring of 1849 and was ordained on July 31 in Albany, New York. After ordination Taggart's "inclinations led him to the West, and his predilections were still stronger for the South," a region he would at times defend with "chivalric enthusiasm . . . worthy of Calhoun."[19]

Without a church in which to settle, Taggart traveled throughout the South and West, preaching in Buffalo, Detroit, Chicago, St. Louis, Louisville, Cannelton (Indiana), New Orleans, Mobile, Wheeling, Washington, D.C., Charleston, and Augusta. In Nashville, Tennessee, Taggart preached to audiences that ranged from "eight to one hundred and fifty." Determined to settle permanently in the South, Taggart began preaching in Charleston on June 19, 1853, and became co-pastor on October 23. A month later, Taggart had a hemorrhage and took some time off to recuperate. He returned to Charleston in a weakened condition, caught yellow fever, and died on October 22, 1854.

In January 1858, Gilman exchanged pulpits with G. W. Burnap in Baltimore. From there he went on to the home of his son-in-law, Charles J. Bowen, in Kingston, Massachusetts, where he suffered a heart attack and died on February 9, 1858. The funeral service and interment in Charleston was conducted by Bowen and Burnap on February 17. According to the Charleston *Courier*, it was "the most solemn occasion since Calhoun's death":

> He lived the life, and illustrated the example of a Christian pastor, and in all respects and relations so meek and gentle, and lovable, so disinterestedly alive to the calls of courtesy and charity, so actively and efficiently identified with the literary culture and social amenities of our city, that his decease will cast a shadow far beyond the pale of the congregation which has grown up under his teachings.[20]

Burnap was ordained on April 23, 1828, and for nearly thirty years had a successful ministry in Baltimore. Sharing similar theological and ministerial opinions, Gilman and Burnap were sympathetic with the other's plight within Southern ecclesiology. They exchanged pulpits and corresponded on a regular basis. After his Baltimore congregation split in 1858, Burnap died suddenly the next year, apparently crushed by the ruin of his life's ministry.[21]

Through the assistance of Burnap, the Charleston congregation was able to engage James R. McFarland as a temporary supply. McFarland had graduated from Harvard Divinity School in 1852 and had been supplying the Unitarian church in Peoria, Illinois. He began preaching in Charleston on March 27, 1858, and the congregation soon requested McFarland to become its permanent minister. He readily accepted the offer and went home to Virginia to tell his family of his decision. Just before returning in November to be installed, McFarland became seriously ill. He died of tuberculosis on April 4, 1859.[22]

During the winter of 1859–1860, George Goldthwait Ingersoll, a sixty-four-year-old retired Unitarian minister, supplied the Charleston pulpit. The church was without a minister until November 1860 when William A. Miller, a former Methodist minister, supplied the pulpit through April 1861. At the beginning of the Civil War, the records of the church were moved to Columbia for safekeeping, where unfortunately, they were burned in the destruction of the city. The church building in Charleston itself, however, sustained little damage.[23]

During the war, most of the members of the church were scattered. At the end of the war, in 1865, without congregational approval and in their absence, Thaddeus Street, warden of the church at the outbreak of hostilities, applied to the A.U.A. for a minister. Unlike the case of Gilman's request in 1834 for organizational approval of a Southern Association, the A.U.A. promptly responded this time by sending Rev. Calvin Stebbins as minister to the Charleston congregation. Charles Lowe, chairman of the newly formed committee on Southern states, accompanied him. Stebbins was to be an agent of the A.U.A. and paid by that organization. After a few weeks, Lowe wisely returned to the North.[24]

Upon learning of these activities, returning members of the congregation elected a new warden by a wide margin and decided to refuse the services of Stebbins. Undaunted by these developments, Stebbins decided to obtain an order from the military officer in charge of the city, who gave him complete possession of the building as the agent for the A.U.A. After several unsuccessful attempts by the majority of the pew-holders to regain possession of their church, the A.U.A. decided to have the military order revoked and to return the church building to the members of the church.[25]

Through the assistance of John Gibbon, a member of the congregation then living in Paris, and also that of the celebrated minister James Martineau of London, an English minister was chosen for the Charleston society. Rev. Thomas Hirst Smith came to Charleston in November 1866 and made a "permanent and valuable record." In 1867, he married Alice Walker, the daughter of Joseph Walker, an active member and officer of the church. But in February 1868, the sudden death of Smith's father recalled him to England. While there, he accepted a successful ministry in Halifax. Five years later in May 1873, he died leaving a widow, a son, and two daughters.[26]

Even though many churches were forced to close their doors in the late antebellum period, Unitarianism continued to exist in both visible and invisible forms in the South. In New Orleans and Charleston beautiful Gothic churches reminded passersby that Unitarianism still had an impressive visible presence on the religious landscape of the South's two largest cities. Their ministers also, Theodore Clapp and Samuel Gilman, had been very influential in their communities, and upon their deaths, the South was reminded just how great a visibility Unitarians still enjoyed. And yet, with these two exceptions, many believed Unitarianism was long dead in the antebellum South, killed off by the choke of evangelicalism. But the ghost of Unitarianism continued to rattle the chains and creak the steps of many of the South's churches on the eve of the Civil War. At the end of the antebellum period, charges of Unitarianism were still thrown even after Southern evangelicalism had supposedly killed off any semblance of the "deviant" faith years ago. Detailed accounts surfaced of Unitarians existing within orthodox churches where there had never been any Unitarian churches and sightings were reported of over two hundred Unitarian laity still active, meeting regularly eighteen years after their church doors supposedly closed. In Charleston, Presbyterian minister Rev. Thomas Smyth remained threatened by Unitarianism as many members of his congregation church-hopped regularly between the Presbyterian and Unitarian church buildings. Catholic Bishop John England was worried about the influence that Unitarian laity had on the intellectual circles in Charleston. In 1859, on the eve of the Civil War, Rev. John Paris, editor of the *North Carolina Christian Advocate,* charged that many Christians in North Carolina and Virginia, areas where there were no Unitarian churches, held Unitarian beliefs. J. R. Blossom in Wilmington, North Carolina, and Herbert C. Peabody, in Mobile, Alabama, described Unitarian activity in these areas where, according to official record, there was none.[27]

By the end of the antebellum period, without their own church buildings in which to worship, Unitarians in the South had infiltrated other churches and had gradually influenced the thoughts, creeds, and beliefs of Southern orthodoxy. As members of the urban professional classes, Southern Unitarians contributed to the rationality of Southern

orthodoxy and promoted ecumenical zeal within Southern denominations. Southern Unitarian laity kept their faith alive under the surface
of organized religion, rattling the chains of their beliefs, breaking
through the transparency of their apparitions, and turning false doors
on evangelicalism. On the eve of the Civil War, Southern Unitarianism
represented a significant and continued strand of Enlightenment religious rationalism alongside, within, and underneath an increasingly
evangelical culture. John Butler was right. The intoxicating panacea of
dissenting evangelicalism as "the single most common explanatory device in contemporary American history" has "obscured the historical realities of eighteenth and nineteenth century America," distorted "the
substance of religious experience," and eclipsed the "dynamics of
American religious development and change."[28]

Notes

INTRODUCTION

1. Jon Butler, "Coercion, Miracle, Reason: Rethinking the American Religious Experience in the Revolutionary Age," in *Religion in a Revolutionary Age*, edited by Ronald Hoffman and Peter J. Albert (Charlottesville: University of Virginia Press, 1994), pp. 1–30.

2. E. Brooks Holifield, *The Gentlemen Theologians: American Theology in Southern Culture, 1795–1860* (Durham: Duke University Press, 1978), p. 3. Holifield cites the following works in this synthesis: Clement Eaton, *Freedom of Thought Struggle in the Old South* (New York: Harper & Row, 1964; 1st ed., Durham, N.C., 1940), p. 233; R. M. Weaver, "The Older Religiousness in the South," *Sewanee Review* 51(1943): 248–49; John B. Boles, *The Great Revival 1787–1805* (Lexington, 1972), p. 195; Henry Adams, *The Education of Henry Adams* (New York, 1931), p. 57; W. J. Cash, *The Mind of the South* (New York, 1941), p. 99.

3. See Francis J. Bremer, *Increase Mather's Friends: The Trans-Atlantic Congregational Network of the Seventeenth Century* (Worcester, American Antiquarian Society, 1984); also Bremer, *Congregational Communion: Clerical Friendship in the Anglo-American Puritan Community, 1610–1692* (Boston: Northeastern University Press, 1994). See also Elizabeth Ann Clark, *The Origenist Controversy: The Cultural Construction of an Early Christian Debate* (Princeton: Princeton University Press, 1992).

4. J. Clyde Mitchell, "The Concept and Use of Social Networks," in *Social Networks in Urban Situations*, J. Clyde Mitchell, ed. (Manchester, 1969), p. 46. The conceptual model implicit in this study is based on a variety of studies in social anthropology and psychology, including Jeremy Boissevain, *Friends of Friends: Networks, Manipulators and Coalitions* (New York, 1974); Jeremy Boissevain and J. Clyde Mitchell, eds., *Network Analysis: Studies in Human Interaction* (The Hague, 1973); J. C. Mitchell, "Social Networks," *American Review of Anthropology* 3(1974): 279–99; and J. Clyde Mitchell, ed., *Social Networks in Urban Situations*.

5. Clark, *Origenist Controversy*, p. 18.

6. Bremer, *Increase Mather*, p. 61.

7. Holifield, *Gentlemen Theologians*, pp. 6, 28.

8. Ibid., p. 4.

9. Richard Rankin, *Ambivalent Churchmen and Evangelical Churchwomen: The Re-*

ligion of the Episcopal Elite in North Carolina, 1800–1860 (Columbia: University of South Carolina Press, 1993), p. 10.

10. See John Duffy, ed., *Parson Clapp of the Strangers' Church of New Orleans* (Baton Rouge: Louisiana State University Press, 1957), p. 36. *Southern Quarterly Review,* n.s. (3d), 1(1856):430; *Louisa S. McCord: Poems, Drama, Biography, Letters,* edited by Richard C. Lounsbury (Charlottesville: University of Virginia Press, 1996), pp. 446–47; John Edwin Windrow, *John Berrich Lindsley, Educator, Physician, Social Philosopher* (Chapel Hill: University of North Carolina Press, 1938), p. 183; Stephen Franks Miller, *The Bench and Bar of Georgia: Memoirs and Sketches* (Philadelphia: J. B. Lippincott & Co., 1858), vol. 2, p. 217.

11. Holifield, *Gentlemen Theologians,* p. 57.

12. Frank Bell Lewis, "Robert Lewis Dabney: Southern Presbyterian Apologist" (Ph.D. dissertation, Duke University, 1946), p. 214.

13. James Henley Thornwell to Samuel Gilman, 12 February, 9 September 1856, Timothy Dwight II Papers, Massachusetts Historical Society, Boston. For a discussion of the influence of Scottish Realism on Northern Unitarianism see Daniel W. Howe, *The Unitarian Conscience: Harvard Moral Philosophy, 1805–1865* (Cambridge: Harvard University Press, 1970).

14. Samuel Gilman, *The Old and the New: Discourses and Proceedings at the Dedication of the Re-Modeled Unitarian Church* (Charleston: Samuel G. Courtenay, 1854), p. 66.

15. Paul K. Conkin, *American Originals: Homemade Varieties of Christianity* (Chapel Hill: University of North Carolina Press, 1997), p. 68.

16. For an elaboration of the Southern world view, see Elizabeth Fox-Genovese and Eugene D. Genovese, "The Divine Sanction of Social Order: Religious Foundations of the Southern Slaveholders' World View," in *Journal of the American Academy of Religion* 55(1987): 211–29.

17. Butler, "Coercion," pp. 23–24.

18. For an extended discussion on the relationship between "conservatives" and "evangelicals," see Robert M. Calhoon, *Evangelicals and Conservatives in the Early South, 1740–1861* (Columbia: University of South Carolina Press, 1988), pp. 9–10.

19. Herbert C. Peabody to Stephen St. John, Jr., 15 January 1859, Herbert C. Peabody Papers, Southern Historical Collection, University of North Carolina, Chapel Hill.

CHAPTER 1. A DECLARATION OF INDEPENDENCE

1. Orville Dewey, *An Address, Delivered Under The Old Elm Tree in Sheffield, With Some Remarks On the Great Political Question of the Day* (New York: C. S. Francis & Co., 1856), pp. 1–2.

2. Orville Dewey, *Autobiography and Letters of Orville Dewey, D.D.,* Mary E. Dewey, ed. (Boston: Roberts Brothers, 1883), p. 115.

3. William J. Grayson, *Reply to Dr. Dewey's Address, Delivered at the Elm Tree, Sheffield, Massachusetts* (Charleston: Walker, Evans & Co., 1856), pp. 1, 21.

4. Dewey, *Autobiography and Letters,* p. 115–16. Conrad Wright mentions Dewey's recollection of this event but apparently did not have access to or did not look at Charleston's response to Dewey's Elm Tree Oration. The focus of his essay is decidedly on Northern Unitarians and the different "schools" of thought among them regarding the abolition question. See Conrad Wright, "The Minister as Reformer: Profiles of Uni-

tarian Ministers in the Antislavery Reform," in *The Liberal Christians: Essays on American Unitarian History* (Boston: Beacon Press, 1970), pp. 62–80.

5. George W. Logan, et al., *Annual Reports Rendered by the Managers of the Charleston Unitarian Book and Tract Society On the Occasion of Its Thirty-Sixth Anniversary, Sunday, August 9, 1857* (Charleston: Walker, Evans & Co., 1857). Hereafter cited as *Annual Reports*.

6. Dewey, *Autobiography and Letters*, p. 117.

7. *Annual Reports*, pp. 9–10.

8. Ibid., pp. 7–8.

9. *Report of the National Conference of Unitarian Churches* (Boston, 1866).

10. Orville Dewey, *Discourses on Human Nature, Human Life and the Nature of Religion* (New York: Charles S. Francis, 1868), vol. 2, p. 366.

11. Orville Dewey, *An Address, Delivered Under The Old Elm Tree*, p. 24.

12. *Annual Reports*, p. 10.

13. The first attempt to look at Unitarianism collectively in the South was made in 1911 by Rev. Arthur A. Brooks. In this twenty-five-page account, *The History of Unitarianism in the Southern Churches: Charleston, New Orleans, Louisville, Richmond* (Boston: American Unitarian Association, n.d.), Brooks deals very briefly with the general histories of these churches, but fails to address those issues that made them "Southern" in the first place. In similar fashion, Earl Wallace Cory, Jr., in his 1970 University of Georgia dissertation, "The Unitarians and Universalists of the Southeastern United States during the Nineteenth Century," while offering one of the most extensive surveys of the topic, merely chronicles the historical markers of the individual churches of liberal faith in the South as they manifested themselves as either Unitarians or Universalists. He does offer a moderate analysis of nineteenth-century liberal theology, but he tends to lose focus as he parallels the chronology of these two denominations in anticipation of their eventual merger. Like Brooks, he fails to adequately describe and even recognize the evolution of the fundamental theological and philosophical differences between Northern and Southern Unitarianism. Clement Eaton's important *Freedom of Thought Struggle in the Old South*, while certainly formidable in regard to context and climate, tends to accept too readily the lenses of "decline" and "defense." He typecasts these Southern liberals as unfortunate victims in the growing wave of fundamentalist aggrandizement. Clarence Gohdes offers a good analytical treatise of Southern Unitarianism, particularly as he posits the origin of liberal faith in the South. Chastising the assumption that "Unitarianism in the South was spread entirely by New Englanders for New Englanders resident in that section," Gohdes offers a detailed account of each church that seriously questions that popular myth that has continued to plague Southern religious and American Unitarian historiography alike. See Clarence Gohdes, "Some Notes on the Unitarian Church in the Ante-Bellum South: A Contribution to the History of Southern Liberalism," in *American Studies in Honor of William Kenneth Boyd by Members of The Americana Club of Duke University*, David Kelly Jackson, ed. (Durham: Duke University Press, 1968; reprint), pp. 327–66. Similarly, George H. Gibson's two general histories of the Richmond and Georgia (Augusta and Savannah) congregations provide detailed accounts of their struggles and eventual demises. He concludes that these particular churches failed "because of the northern connections of its members, their unorthodox beliefs, and a lack of support by their fellow denominationalists." See George H. Gibson, "The Unitarian-Universalist Church of Richmond," in the *Virginia Magazine*

of History and Biography 74(1966): 321–35, hereafter cited as "Richmond," and "Unitarian Congregations in Ante-Bellum Georgia," in *Georgia Historical Quarterly* 54(1970): 147–68, hereafter cited as "Georgia."

14. Sydney E. Ahlstrom, *A Religious History of the American People* (New Haven: Yale University Press, 1972), p. 666.

15. Because many churches in the late eighteenth century were fearful of ascribing the name "Unitarian" to their cause or inscribing it on their buildings for fear of being labeled "Socinians," scholars have disagreed over where the first Unitarian church in America was located, though most do acknowledge the precipitative influence of English Unitarianism in the process. Earl Morse Wilbur (*A History of Unitarianism in Transylvania, England and America,* Boston: Harvard University Press, 1952, p. 396–97) declares, "[T]he first permanent Unitarian church in America . . . was gathered in Philadelphia." He goes on to clarify: " . . . that is the first to be permanently established, and openly avowing the Unitarian name. This is not forgetting the ephemeral case in Portland [Maine]." In March 1792, a former Episcopal minister, Thomas Oxnard, influenced by the writings of Joseph Priestley, formed a Unitarian church in Philadelphia that apparently did not last for long. Wilbur notes similar stirrings in Salem, Massachusetts, and New York. Sydney Ahlstrom, on the other hand, reverberating the often quoted line from F. W. P. Greenwood's *History of King's Chapel,* declares that "the first Episcopal church in New England [Boston's King's Chapel in 1787] became the first Unitarian Church in America." Ahlstrom, *Religious History,* p. 389.

16. Raymond Adams, "The Charleston Unitarianism Gilman Began With," Samuel Gilman Papers, Harvard University Archives, Cambridge, pp. 4–5.

CHAPTER 2. THE ENLIGHTENED JOURNEY

1. Because this project concentrates only on those states that would become the Confederate States of America, places like Washington, D.C.; Baltimore, Maryland; Louisville, Kentucky; St. Louis, Missouri; and Wheeling, Virginia, are purposefully omitted. Most of these churches would split over the many issues that divided North and South. Ministers and laity associated with these churches will be mentioned throughout this work, though no extended narrative of the congregations themselves will be provided. For a more complete history of Washington, D.C., see Jennie W. Scudder, *A Century of Unitarianism in the National Capital, 1821–1921* (Boston: Beacon Press, 1922). See also Gohdes, "Some Notes on the Unitarian Church," pp. 344–49. For Baltimore, see Jared Sparks, *The Life and Writings of Jared Sparks,* vol. 1 (Boston and New York, 1893); *Seventy-Fifth Anniversary and Reconsecration of the First Independent Christ's Church, Franklin and Charles Streets, Baltimore, Maryland, Sunday, October 29, 1893* (Baltimore, n.d.), pp. 3–6; and J. Thomas Scharf, *The Chronicles of Baltimore* (Baltimore, 1874), pp. 387–89. For Louisville, see Edith F. Bodley, *An Historical Sketch of the First Unitarian Church of Louisville* (Louisville, 1930); James Freeman Clarke, *Autobiography, Diary and Correspondence,* Edward Everett Hale, ed. (1891; reprint, New York: Negro Universities Press, 1968); and *In Memoriam, Reverend John Healey Heywood Minister to the Church of the Messiah of Louisville, Kentucky 1840 to 1880* (Louisville, 1903).

2. Paul K. Conkin, "Priestley and Jefferson: Unitarianism as a Religion for a New Revolutionary Age," in *Religion in a Revolutionary Age,* edited by Ronald Hoffman and Peter J. Albert, p. 294. See also *Dictionary of American Biography,* vol. 8, p. 223. For an

in-depth biography, particularly of Priestley's years in England, see Wilbur, *History of Unitarianism*, pp. 291–313.

3. F. W. Gibbs, *Joseph Priestley: Revolutions of the Eighteenth Century* (1967; reprint, Garden City, New York: Doubleday, 1995), pp. 18–20; Conkin, "Priestley and Jefferson," p. 294.

4. *Dictionary of American Biography*, vol. 8, pp. 224–25. With the exception of three very important works written in England, most of Priestley's theological treatises were written in America. In England: *Disquisition Relating to Matter and Spirit*, 1777; *A Free Discussion of the Doctrines of Materialism*, 1778; *An History of the Corruptions of Christianity*, 1782. In America: *A General History of the Christian Church* (4 vols.), 1790–1802; *Unitarianism Explained and Defended*, 1796; *A Comparison of the Institutions of Moses with Those of the Hindoos and Other Ancient Nations*, 1799; *Socrates and Jesus Compared*, 1803; *Notes on All the Books of Scripture* (4 vols.), 1803–1804; *The Doctrines of Heathen Philosophy Compared with Those of Revelation*, 1804 (written at the insistence of his friend Thomas Jefferson); *A General View of the Arguments for the Unity of God; and against the Divinity and Preexistence of Christ*, 1793.

5. Wilbur, *History of Unitarianism*, pp. 396–98.

6. Conkin, "Priestley and Jefferson," pp. 295–96.

7. Ibid., pp. 296–99.

8. Thomas Jefferson, *The Writings of Thomas Jefferson*, A. A. Lipscomb and A. E. Bergh, eds. (Washington, 1904), vol. 15, p. 392.

9. Jefferson to Moses Robinson, 23 March 1801, in Jefferson, *Writings*, vol. 15, p. 320.

10. Jefferson, *Writings*, vol. 16, p. 281.

11. Jefferson to Jared Sparks, 4 November 1820, in Jefferson, *Writings*, vol. 19, p. 245.

12. Clement Eaton, "Winifred and Joseph Gales, Liberals in the Old South," *Journal of Southern History* 10(November 1944): 461–74. Here Eaton cites the work of Niels H. Sonne, *Liberal Kentucky, 1780–1825* (New York, 1939).

13. Ahlstrom, *Religious History*, p. 389.

14. For a more complete discussion see Carl Bangs, *Arminius: A Study in the Dutch Reformation* (Nashville: Abingdon Press, 1971).

15. See Henry Petersen, *The Canons of Dort* (Grand Rapids, Michigan: Baker Press, 1968).

16. Holifield, *Gentlemen Theologians*, p. 188.

17. Ibid., p. 369.

18. Ibid., p. 111.

19. Howe, *Unitarian Conscience*, p. 302.

20. Ibid.

21. Holifield, *Gentlemen Theologians*, pp. 111–12.

22. Ibid., pp. 118–19. See also Robert B. Come, "The Influence of Princeton on Higher Education in the South before 1825," *William and Mary Quarterly*, 2d ser., 2(October 1945): 362–94.

23. F. A. Farley, "Congregational Unitarianism in the United States of America," in *Unitarianism Exhibited in Its Actual Condition . . . ,* J. R. Beard, ed. (London, 1846).

24. James Freeman Clark to William Henry Channing, 4 October 1833, Clarke Papers, Massachusetts Historical Society, Boston. Clarke to the editor of the *Western Messenger*, New Orleans, 22 December 1835, *Western Messenger* 1(February 1836).

25. Charles Briggs to the American Unitarian Association (hereafter A.U.A.), 17

February 1837, American Unitarian Association Letters, Andover-Harvard Theological Library, Harvard University, Cambridge. (This manuscript collection is hereafter cited as A.U.A. Letters).

26. See Gohdes, "Some Notes on the Unitarian Church," pp. 355–56, 363–64.

27. "Sixth Annual Report of the Charleston Unitarian Book Society," Charleston, 20 May 1827, A.U.A. Letters. Also Samuel Gilman to Jason Whitman, Charleston, 17 June 1834, A.U.A. Letters.

28. Cited in Gilman, *The Old and the New*, p. 18.

29. Sydney E. Ahlstrom, "The Scottish Philosophy and American Theology," in *Church History* 24(September 1955): 261–62.

30. Gilman, *The Old and the New*, p. 18.

31. George N. Edwards, *A History of the Independent or Congregational Church of Charleston, South Carolina* (Boston: Pilgrim Press, 1947), p. 59.

32. Ibid., pp. 38–39.

33. "Historical Sketch of the Unitarian Church," in *City of Charleston Yearbook* (Charleston, 1882), p. 411. Hereafter cited as *Yearbook*. Edwards, *A History of the Independent or Congregational Church of Charleston*.

34. Ernest Trice Thompson, *Presbyterians in the South, 1607–1861* (Richmond: John Knox Press, 1963), vol. 1, pp. 252–53.

35. Anthony Forster, *Sermons, Chiefly of a Practical Nature*, Foreword by M. L. Hurlbut (Raleigh: J. Gales, 1821), p. x.

36. Gilman, *The Old and the New*, p. 15.

37. *Yearbook*, pp. 415–16.

38. A more extensive profile of Caroline Gilman, including her literary accomplishments and reform efforts, appears in Chapter 5.

39. Samuel Gilman to the General Secretary of the A.U.A., 17 June 1834, A.U.A. Archives, Harvard Divinity School, Cambridge. Also Frederick J. Gray to the General Secretary of the A.U.A., 9 August 1830, A.U.A. Archives.

CHAPTER 3. THE UNI-UNI CONNECTION

1. Conkin, *American Originals*, p. 101.

2. *Christian Register*, 4 August 1849, p. 2

3. Meg Dachowski, "A Short History of the First Unitarian Church, New Orleans, Louisiana" (ms. in possession of the author). Ms. Dachowski was gracious in extending a good deal of her research and writing for the New Orleans segment of this project.

4. Theodore Clapp, *Autobiographical Sketches and Recollections during a Thirty-five Year's Residence in New Orleans* (Boston, 1857), p. 160.

5. Duffy, *Parson Clapp*, p. 15.

6. Clapp, *Autobiographical Sketches*, p. 8. Clapp to the editor of *The Christian Register*, 28 August 1849, in *The Christian Register*, 15 September 1849, p. 2.

7. Duffy, *Parson Clapp*, pp. 18–19.

8. Dachowski, "A Short History," p. 2.

9. G. W. Hosmer to the A.U.A., 28 March 1836, A.U.A. Letters.

10. Charles Briggs to the A.U.A., 17 February 1837, 18 June 1837, A.U.A. Letters.

11. *Christian Register*, 22 September 1849.

12. *The Unitarian Congregational Register for the Year 1846, Printed for the American Unitarian Association* (Boston: Crosby, Nichols and Co., 1846). The same holds true for the 1854 *Register*. For various reasons the church is listed here in our survey. First of all, it has been included in other histories of Southern Unitarian churches. See Gohdes, "Some Notes on the Unitarian Church," pp. 357–59; Brooks, *History of Unitarianism*, pp. 1–21; Gibson, "Richmond," pp. 321–25. It is, however, curiously absent in Cory, "Unitarians and Universalists," a dissertation devoted to the histories of the Unitarian and Universalist churches in the Southeastern United States. Also, members of the Richmond church itself communicated with the A.U.A. during the 1830s, but after that, correspondence between the two broke off. Finally, the First Independent Church of Richmond is cited in an unpublished work by Frederick Lewis Weis, Th.D., entitled "List of the Unitarian Churches and Their Ministers in the United States and Canada" (n.d. 1950s?), deposited in the Library of Meadville Theological School, Pennsylvania (later becoming Meadville-Lombard Divinity School of the University of Chicago). John Hurley, archivist of the Unitarian-Universalist Association, Boston, was helpful in locating Weis's work.

13. See Brooks, *History of Unitarianism*.

14. *Richmond, City of Churches: A Short History of Richmond's Denominations and Faiths* (Richmond, 1957).

15. Richard Eddy, *Universalism in America* (Boston, 1886), vol. 2, pp. 400–401.

16. Gibson, "Richmond," pp. 324–25.

17. Ibid., p. 325.

18. *Unitarian* 1(March 1834): 156–57.

19. J. B. Pitkin to the Editor of the A.U.A., 7 November 1834, A.U.A. Letters.

20. Charles Briggs to Samuel Gilman, Richmond, 4 March 1835, Timothy Dwight Papers.

21. Charles Briggs to the A.U.A., 23 February 1835, A.U.A. Letters.

22. Charles Briggs to Samuel Gilman, Richmond, 4 March 1835, Timothy Dwight Papers.

23. See Gibson, "Georgia," p. 165.

CHAPTER 4. URBAN UNITARIANISM AND THE INVISIBLE TRADITION

1. J. Allen Penniman to the A.U.A., 13 August 1849, A.U.A. Letters.

2. *De Bow's Review* 29(1860): 613–14.

3. Ibid.

4. Dexter Clapp, "Letter on the Religious Condition of Slaves," *Monthly Religious Magazine* 3(May 1846): 207.

5. Edmund L. Drago, ed., *Broke by the War: Letters of a Slave Trader* (Columbia: University of South Carolina Press, 1991).

6. David Moltke-Hansen, "The Expansion of Intellectual Life: A Prospectus," in *Intellectual Life in Antebellum Charleston*, Michael O'Brien and David Moltke-Hansen, eds. (Knoxville: University of Tennessee Press, 1986), p. 20.

7. *Christian Register*, 22 April 1837, p. 3.

8. Ibid.

9. Gilman, *The Old and the New,* p. 29.

10. Samuel Miller, D.D., *Letters on Unitarianism; Addressed to the Members of the First Presbyterian Church in the City of Baltimore* (Trenton, N.J.: George Sherman, 1821), p. 9.

11. David Henkel, *Against the Unitarians: A Treatise on the Person and Incarnation of Jesus Christ, In Which Some of the Principal Arguments of the Unitarians are Examined* (New Market, Va., 1830).

12. Printed in J. B. Whitridge, *Calling Things by Their Right Names: A Brief Reply To An Article Under That Title, In the Southern Watchman of May 19, 1837. By a Layman* (Charleston: Walker and James, 1837), p. 4.

13. Gilman, *The Old and the New,* p. 20.

14. See Ruth Rouse and Stephen Charles Neill, eds., *A History of the Ecumenical Movement, 1517–1948* (Philadelphia: Westminster Press, 1954), pp. 237–38.

15. *Unitarian Miscellany,* 1821. Also cited in Gohdes, "Some Notes on the Unitarian Church," p. 330.

16. Gohdes, "Some Notes on the Unitarian Church," pp. 328–29.

17. Joseph Gales to Sparks, 2 August 1822, Joseph Gales Papers, Southern Historical Collection, University of North Carolina, Chapel Hill. Printed in Joseph Gales, "Recollections," Gales Papers, p. 468.

18. Joseph Gales to C. H. Appleton, 20 June 1821, Gales Papers.

19. Samuel Gilman and the Charleston Unitarian Book & Tract Society to the A.U.A., 15 May 1831, A.U.A. Letters.

20. Stephen Bulfinch to the A.U.A., 20 September 1830, A.U.A. Letters.

21. Ibid., 13 September 1830.

22. Samuel Gilman and the Charleston Unitarian Book & Tract Society to the A.U.A., 15 May 1831, A.U.A. Letters.

23. Edwin H. Chapin, *Duties of Young Men, Exhibited in Six Lectures; with an Anniversary Address, Delivered before the Richmond Lyceum* (Boston, 1840); *Southern Literary Messenger* 5:725–33. *An Oration Delivered Fourth of July, 1840, At the Invitation of the Richmond Light Dragoons, the Washington Grenadiers and the Scarlett Guard* (Richmond, 1840); *Southern Literary Messenger* 4:2; 5:43, 615, 838–39.

24. Daniel Walker Howe, "A Massachusetts Yankee in Senator Calhoun's Court: Samuel Gilman in South Carolina," *New England Quarterly* 44(1971): 202, 214.

25. Ibid., pp. 197–220.

26. Samuel Gilman, Notes from "Essays delivered at the Charleston, South Carolina Private Club, 1850–1858," Samuel Gilman Papers, Harvard University Archives.

27. Holifield, *Gentlemen Theologians,* pp. 36–49.

28. Gilman, Notes from "Private Club."

29. Committee of the First Independent Christian Church, *The Faith of the Universalists: Being a defense of this denomination of Christians and their views, against an abusive article published against them by Rev. Wm. S. Plumer, in a paper edited by him, entitled, the "Watchman of the South," of the 28th of December, who declined publishing a reply or correcting the gross misrepresentation* (Richmond, 1838).

30. J. B. Whitridge, *Calling Things by Their Right Names.*

31. J. B. Whitridge, *Letters, advice, &c., from a father to his son, preparing for college* (Charleston: Walker, Burke, 1845).

32. Holifield, *Gentlemen Theologians,* p. 40.

33. Samuel Gilman, D.D., Pastor of the Church and Chaplain of the Washington Light Infantry, *Semi-Centennial Sermon, Delivered in the Unitarian Church, Charleston, S.C., 22 February, 1857, before the Washington Light Infantry, In Commemoration of the 125th Anniversary of the Birth of George Washington, And of the Semi-Centenary of the Corps* (Charleston: Walker, Evans, and Co., 1857).

34. George Eustis, Theodore Howard McCaleb, and Christian Roselius, *A history of the proceedings in the city of New Orleans on the occasion of the funeral ceremonies in honor of Calhoun, Clay and Webster* (New Orleans, 1853).

35. John Moncure Daniel, *The life of Stonewall Jackson. From official papers, contemporary narratives, and personal acquaintance. By Hon. J. M. Daniells [i.e., Daniel], a Virginian* (London, Sampson Low [and] Bacon; New York, Charles B. Richardson, 1863).

36. J. R. McFarland, *Julian, Emperor of Rome, commonly called Apostate: A discourse* (Charleston: Steam Power Presses of Walker, Evans, 1859).

37. Samuel Gilman, *A discourse on the life and character of the Honorable Thomas Lee, late judge in the District court of the United States, Pronounced in the Unitarian Church, Charleston, S.C., Nov. 3, 1839* (Charleston: Burgess and James, 1839). Joshua B. Whitridge, *A Tribute of respect to the memory of Mrs. Eliza Crocker* (Charleston: B. B. Hussey, 1842). Samuel Gilman, *The poetical remains of the late Mary Elizabeth Lee, With a Biographical memoir* (Charleston: Walker and Richards, 1851). Forster, *Sermons, Chiefly of a Practical Nature.* Charles Manson Taggart, *Sermons by Charles Manson Taggart, Late Colleague Pastor of the Unitarian Church in Charleston, S.C., With a Memoir by John H. Heywood* (Charleston: S. G. Courtenay, 1856). John Budd Pitkin, *Sermons by Rev. J. B. Pitkin with a Memoir of the Author by Rev. S. G. Bulfinch* (Boston, 1837). Herbert C. Peabody to Samuel St. John, Jr., 26 September 1858, Mobile, Peabody Papers. [Charleston] *Courier*, 11 February 1858; 18 February 1858. [New Orleans] *Daily Picayune*, 24 March 1867.

38. *Louisiana Advertiser,* 28 February 1832, 6 June 1832.

39. [Charleston] *Courier*, 8 April 1835.

40. Moltke-Hansen, "Expansion of Intellectual Life," p. 21.

41. William Winans to D.D. Venne, 15 March 1848, Winans Papers, William Winans Collection, Special Collections, University of Mississippi Library, Oxford.

Chapter 5. The Spirit of Improvement

1. Basil Hall, *Travels in North America* (1829; reprint Graz, Austria, 1964), vol. 3, pp. 166–67.

2. Samuel Gilman, *Address Delivered at the Anniversary Meeting of the South Carolina Society for the Promotion of Temperance* (Charleston, 1831), p. 8.

3. *Annual Reports*, p. 7.

4. Paul A. Baglyos, "Samuel Simon Schmucker and the Primitive Church," *Concordia Historical Institute Quarterly* 71, no. 4(1998): 168–83. See also C. Leonard Allen, "Roger Williams and the Restoration of Zion," in *The American Quest for the Primitive Church*, pp. 33–34; George Marsden, "By Primitivism Possessed: How Useful Is the Concept 'Primitivism' for Understanding American Fundamentalism?" in *The Primitive Church in the Modern World*, Richard T. Hughes, ed. (Champaign: University of Illinois Press, 1995), pp. 40–41.

5. Baglyos, "Samuel Simon Schmucker," p. 169.

6. *Christian Register,* 10 April 1841.

7. J. Allen Penniman to the Secretary of the A.U.A., 13 August 1849, A.U.A. Letters.

8. Joseph Gales, "Recollections," p. 174.

9. Gilman, *The Old and the New,* p. 29.

10. *Christian Register,* 10 April 1841; Joseph Gales, "Recollections," p. 174. Also, *Annual Reports,* p. 10.

11. Slavery reform will be addressed in Chapter 9.

12. Gilman, *Temperance,* pp. 24–28.

13. Ibid., p. 10.

14. Eugene D. Genovese and Elizabeth Fox-Genovese, "The Religious Ideals of Southern Slave Society," *Georgia Historical Quarterly* 70(1986): 4, 7.

15. Gilman, *Contributions to Religion* (Charleston, 1860), pp. 172–74, 191–94, 286.

16. Barbara L. Bellows, *Benevolence among Slaveholders: Assisting the Poor in Charleston, 1670–1860* (Baton Rouge: Louisiana State University Press, 1993), p. 21.

17. William Way, *History of the New England Society of Charleston, South Carolina: 1819–1919* (Charleston: New England Society, 1920), p. 9.

18. "Sunday School for Children," *Southern Christian Advocate,* 11 July 1851.

19. [Charleston] *Mercury,* 9 October 1852.

20. William B. Yates, *An Historical Sketch of the Rise and Progress of Religious and Moral Improvement Among Seamen, In England and the United States, With a History of the Port Society of Charleston, S.C.* (Charleston: A. J. Burke, 1851), p. 4.

21. Ibid., p. 5.

22. Eliza Ripley, *Social Life in Old New Orleans: Being Recollections of My Girlhood* (New York: D. Appleton & Co., 1912), pp. 120–23. Stange ascribes no reform activity to the members of The Church of the Messiah in New Orleans. See Stange, "Abolitionism as Maleficence: Southern Unitarians Versus 'Puritan Fanaticism'—1831–1860," *Harvard Library Bulletin* 26(1978): 146–71.

23. *Christian Register,* 16 February 1839.

24. Edwin L. Jewell, "Thomas S. Adams, Esq.," in *Jewell's Crescent City Illustrated* (New Orleans, 1873).

25. For biographies of most of these individuals see Joseph Ioor Waring, *A History of Medicine in South Carolina, 1825–1900* (Columbia: South Carolina Medical Association, 1967).

26. Ibid., p. 222.

27. *Dictionary of American Biography,* vol. 5, pp. 305–6.

28. *Charleston Medical Journal,* 1857, p. 607.

29. Samuel X. Radbill, "Samuel Henry Dickson," *Annals of Medical History,* 3d ser., 4(1942): 382–85, 388.

30. Waring, *A History of Medicine,* pp. 272–75; *Dictionary of American Medical Biography,* p. 882; *Charleston Medical Journal* 12(1857): 827; J. M. Van de Erve, "James Moultrie, Jr." (manuscript, Library Medical College of South Carolina, Charleston).

31. Richard D. Arnold Scrapbook [paper and date unknown], Richard D. Arnold Papers, Southern Historical Collection, Wilson Library, University of North Carolina, Chapel Hill, pp. 140–41.

32. Ibid., *Georgia Telegraph,* 30 August 1859.

33. *Dictionary of American Biography,* vol. 4, pp. 301–2.

34. See Anya Jabour's analysis of female education in the South: "'Grown Girls, Highly Cultivated': Female Education in an Antebellum Southern Family," *Journal of Southern History* 64, no. 1(February 1998): 23–64.

35. Though Elizabeth Fox-Genovese makes this statement of Louisa McCord as a rural slaveholding mistress, the same is also true of urban Unitarian women in the South. See Elizabeth Fox-Genovese, *Within the Plantation Household: Black and White Women in the Old South* (Chapel Hill, University of North Carolina Press, 1988), p. 244. Fox-Genovese concludes for Caroline Gilman: "Caroline Gilman . . . might publish fiction that fell within the general confines of the domestic genre, but [her work] merged with the general culture and fiercely defended the proslavery premises of [her] adopted southern culture."

36. Eaton, "Winifred and Joseph Gales, Liberals in the Old South," pp. 469–70.

Chapter 6. "Our Old and Primitive Faith"

1. Conrad Wright, "The Theological World of Samuel Gilman," in *The Proceedings of the Unitarian Historical Society* 17, pt. 2(1973–1975): 58.

2. Samuel Gilman, *Unitarian Christianity free from Objectionable Extremes; A Sermon preached at the dedication of the Unitarian Church in Augusta, December 27, 1827* (Charleston, 1828), pp. 19, 28.

3. *Unitarian Christian,* March 1831, p. 7.

4. Samuel Gilman to Caroline Howard, 8 March 1812, Gilman Papers, Harvard University Archives.

5. Samuel Gilman, *A Sermon on the Introduction to the Gospel of St. John* (Charleston: Unitarian Book and Tract Society, 1825), p. 5. Hereafter cited as *St. John.*

6. Ibid., pp. 5–6.

7. Ibid., p. 6.

8. Gilman, Reading Notes, November 1813, Gilman Papers, Harvard University Archives.

9. Gilman to W. B. Sprague, in Sprague, *Annals of the American Pulpit* (New York, 1856–1865), vol. 5, pp. 643–44.

10. Holifield, *Gentlemen Theologians,* p. 64.

11. Samuel Gilman, *Revealed Religion: A Dudleian Lecture Delivered in the Chapel of the University at Cambridge* (Boston, 1848), pp. 3–24.

12. Ibid.

13. Gilman, *Contributions to Religion,* pp. 21, 22.

14. Gilman, "For a Unitarian Library," Notes, Gilman Papers, Harvard University Archives.

15. Gilman, *St. John.*

16. Gilman, "Cause and Effect," *North American Review* 12(1821): 395–432; "Brown's Philosophy of Mind," *North American Review* 19(1824); "Character and Writings of Dr. Brown," *North American Review* 21(1825): 19–51; "Brown's Philosophy of the Human Mind," *Southern Quarterly Review* 3(1829): 53–54. All reprinted in Samuel Gilman, *Contributions to Literature* (Boston, 1856).

17. *Southern Quarterly Review,* n.s. (3d), 1(1856):436.

18. Gilman, *Contributions to Religion,* pp. 24–25.

19. G. W. Burnap, "Unitarian Christianity Expounded and Defended," in Gilman, *The Old and the New*, pp. 26–33.

20. Holifield, *Gentlemen Theologians*, p. 64.

21. Jasper Adams, *Elements of Moral Philosophy* (Cambridge, 1837), p. 323.

22. *Southern Quarterly Review*, n.s. (3d), 1(1856): 430.

23. Gilman, *St. John*, p. 16.

24. Gilman, *Contributions to Religion*, p. 358.

25. Holifield, *Gentlemen Theologians*, pp. 111–12.

26. *The Twenty-Eighth Annual Report of the Managers of the Charleston Unitarian Book and Tract Society* (Charleston: Walker, Evans, & James, May 1849), pp. 5–6.

27. Samuel Gilman to Caroline Howard, 8 March 1812, Gilman Papers, Harvard University Archives.

28. Gilman, *St. John*, pp. 15–16.

29. Samuel Gilman to the A.U.A., 22 December 1856, A.U.A. Letters.

30. Cited in Gilman, *The Old and the New*, p. 18.

31. Gilman, *St. John*, pp. 5–7.

32. Ibid., pp. 8–9.

33. Ibid., p. 10.

34. Ibid., p. 11.

35. Charles Wentworth Upham, *A Letter to the Editor of the Charleston Observer, Concerning his Treatment of Unitarians* (Charleston: James S. Burgess, 1827), p. vi.

36. Gilman, *St. John*, pp. 12–13.

37. Ibid., p. 17.

38. Caroline Gilman to "My Dear Children," 16 December 1860, Caroline Howard Gilman Papers, South Carolina Historical Society, Charleston.

39. Gilman, *St. John*, pp. 12–13.

40. Ibid., pp. 8–9. See also *Southern Quarterly Review*, n.s. (3d), 2(1857): 464.

41. W. B. Wellons, *The Christians, South, not Unitarians in Sentiment. A Reply to Rev. John Paris' Book, Entitled "Unitarianism Exposed, as it Exists in the Christian Church,"* (Suffolk, Va., 1860), p. 43.

42. Thomas Smyth, *Complete Works of Rev. Thomas Smyth, D.D.*, edited by Wm. Flinn (new ed.; Columbia: R. L. Bryan Co., 1908–1912), vol. 9, pp. 623–38. John England, *The Works of the Right Reverend John England, first bishop of Charleston* (Cleveland: Arthur H. Clark, 1908), vol. 2, p. 186, vol. 3, pp. 452–518.

43. J. R. Blossom, 12 January 1860, A.U.A. Letters.

44. Stange concludes that this event, along with a similar incident in Savannah, "for all practical purposes terminated that church's life." See "Abolitionism as Maleficence," p. 147.

45. Herbert C. Peabody to Samuel St. John, Jr., 17 December 1858, Peabody Papers.

46. Ibid., 23 January 1859.

47. Eugene Genovese, *The Slaveholders' Dilemma: Freedom and Progress in Southern Conservative Thought, 1820–1860* (Columbia: University of South Carolina Press, 1992), p. 38.

48. *Christian Examiner* 44(July 1848): 83; Gilman, *Revealed Religion*, pp. 10–11.

49. Emerson to Solomon Corner, 1842, in *A Letter of Emerson*, William Reed, ed. (Boston, 1934), p. 18. Samuel Gilman, "Revealed Religion," *Christian Examiner* 45(1848): 77, 80.

50. Joseph B. Lewis to the A.U.A., 28 January 1858, A.U.A. Letters.

51. Wright, "Theological World," pp. 54–72.

52. Conrad Wright, *The Beginnings of Unitarianism in America* (Boston: Starr King Press, 1955).

53. Wright, "Theological World," p. 55.

54. Holifield, *Gentlemen Theologians*, p. 82.

CHAPTER 7. SECTIONAL TENSION

1. "Sixth Annual Report of the Charleston Unitarian Book Society," 20 May 1827, A.U.A. Letters.

2. Ibid.

3. Ibid.

4. Gilman to the A.U.A., 19 August 1827, A.U.A. Letters.

5. Charleston Unitarian Book and Tract Society to the A.U.A., 18 May 1828, A.U.A. Letters.

6. *Christian Examiner* 3(July-August 1826): 352–55. See also, Gibson, "Georgia," p. 148.

7. *Christian Examiner* 5(January-February 1828), *Christian Register*, 19 January 1828; Gilman, *Unitarian Christianity*.

8. *Christian Examiner* 5(January-February 1828), *Christian Register*, 19 January 1828; Gilman, *Unitarian Christianity*.

9. Gibson, "Georgia," pp. 150–51.

10. Stephen G. Bulfinch to the A.U.A., 9 June 1834, A.U.A. Letters.

11. Ibid.

12. *The Georgian*, 13 December 1834.

13. Samuel Gilman to the General Secretary of the A.U.A., 17 June 1834, A.U.A. Letters.

14. J. B. Pitkin to the A.U.A., 7 November 1834, A.U.A. Letters.

15. *Christian Examiner* 55(November 1853): 484.

16. S. G. Bulfinch to the A.U.A., 7 April 1836, A.U.A. Letters.

17. Henry Bright to the A.U.A., 6 September 1835, A.U.A. Letters.

18. Ibid.

19. Stephen Bulfinch to the A.U.A., 11 December 1835, A.U.A. Letters.

20. James Freeman Clarke to H.T.D., 10 February 1836, in James Freeman Clarke, *Autobiography, Diary and Correspondence*, Edward Everett Hale, ed. (1891; reprint, New York: Negro Universities Press, 1968), pp. 112–14.

21. Herbert C. Peabody to Henry W. Bellows, Mobile, 22 December 1838, Henry W. Bellows Papers, Massachusetts Historical Society, Boston. Samuel St. John, Jr., to Charles E. Briggs, Mobile, January 1838, A.U.A. Letters.

22. See Stange, "Abolitionism as Maleficence," pp. 171–227.

23. *Quarterly Journal of the American Unitarian Association* 2(July 1855): 493–96.

24. George Gibson has concluded, "The initiative for establishing additional Unitarian churches in the south Atlantic states arose almost entirely from the Charleston church." George H. Gibson, "Unitarian Congregations in the Antebellum South," *Proceedings of the Unitarian Historical Society* 12, pt. 2(1959): 58.

25. Frederick J. Gray to the A.U.A., 9 August 1830, A.U.A. Letters.

26. *Christian Register*, 10 April 1841.

27. Duffy, *Parson Clapp*, p. 124.

28. Charles Briggs to the A.U.A., 17 February 1837, 18 June 1837, A.U.A. Letters.

29. W. G. Eliot to the A.U.A., 2 March 1837, A.U.A. Letters.

30. *Christian Register*, February 1843.

31. Ibid., 11 March 1843, 1 April 1843, 22 April 1843.

32. Ibid., 18 March 1843, 1 April 1843, 15 April 1843; *Monthly Miscellany* 1843, p. 253. See Stange, "Abolitionism as Maleficence," pp. 187–90.

33. Stange, "Abolitionism as Maleficence," pp. 189–90.

34. Samuel Gilman to the A.U.A., 14 September 1843, A.U.A. Letters.

35. *Nineteenth Annual Report of the A.U.A.*, 1844, pp. 39–42.

36. Gohdes, "Some Notes on the Unitarian Church," p. 364.

Chapter 8. Oil and Vinegar

1. Editorial by A. M. Holbrook, [New Orleans] *Daily Picayune*, 22 December 1850; Theodore Clapp, "A Thanksgiving Sermon, Delivered in the First Congregational Church, New Orleans, December 19, 1850," *Daily Picayune*, 22 December 1850.

2. Clapp, "Thanksgiving Sermon."

3. Richard D. Arnold Scrapbook.

4. Bellows, *Benevolence among Slaveholders*, p. 21.

5. American Sunday School Union, *Union Annual*, 1837, p. 33.

6. John Wells Kuykendall, *Southern Enterprise: The Work of the National Evangelical Societies in the Antebellum South* (Westport, 1982), pp. 39–40.

7. William Ellery Channing, *The Works of William E. Channing, D.D.* (Boston: American Unitarian Association, 1882), pp. 845–46.

8. Joseph B. Lewis to the A.U.A., 28 January 1858, A.U.A. Letters.

9. Thomas Adams to the A.U.A., 31 December 1858, A.U.A. Letters.

10. In addition to John Pierpont, Stange cites the religio-political careers of John Albion Andrew, John Gorham Palfrey, and John P. Hale. John Pierpont (1785–1866), minister of the First Congregational (Unitarian) Church of Medford, Massachusetts, ran unsuccessfully for Congress on the Free Soil ticket in 1850. In 1858 his congregation declared that Pierpont had been "unwisely persistent in preaching politics." Pierpont resigned. John Albion Andrew (1818–1867) of Boston was an antislavery lawyer, a Unitarian minister, and a popular Republican Governor of Massachusetts on the eve of the "Great Unpleasantness," having won the largest vote ever cast for that office up to that time. During his campaign, he filled his speeches with "a profusion of biblical passages and Christian phrases." He taught Bible classes at his church and preached intermittently at James Freeman Clarke's Church of the Disciples and at the "Baptist Church for colored people." He was a vigorous opponent of slavery and was a lawyer for fugitive slaves. Over the years, he moved from the Whigs to the Free Soilers to the Republicans. John Gorham Palfrey (1796–1881) was minister of the prominent and influential Brattle Street Church when he accepted the position of Dexter Professor of Sacred Literature at Harvard Divinity School. In the 1840s he served as a state legislator, as secretary of Massachusetts, and as a Free Soil representative to Congress. John P. Hale (1806–1873), though not a minister, was a religious leader in John Parkman's Church in Dover, New Hampshire. He became a state legislator in 1832 and a U.S. congressman in 1843. In 1846, he was elected to the Senate with the help of Antislavery Whigs, Independents, and

Liberty Party men. He was the Liberty Party presidential nominee in 1848 and the Free Democratic candidate in 1852. He remained in the Senate until 1864. See Stange, "Abolitionism as Maleficence," pp. 100–120.

11. Stange, "Abolitionism as Maleficence," p. 176.

12. John Pierpont, *A Discourse on the Covenant with Judas, Preached in Hollis-Street Church, Nov. 6, 1842* (Boston: Charles C. Little and James Brown, 1842), pp. 29, 32, 34.

13. Pierpont to Pierpont, 21 June 1852, Pierpont Morgan Library, New York.

14. James Freeman Clarke, Young Men's Christian Union lecture, 8 December 1861, in Clarke, *Autobiography, Diary and Correspondence*, p. 103.

15. "Review of *Observations of American Slavery, after a Year's Tour in the United States* by Russell Lant Carpenter, B. A.: Whitfield, 1852" [from the *London Morning Advertiser,* 14 February 1852] (offprint, Estlin Papers, Dr. William's Library, London), printed in Stange, "Abolitionism as Maleficence."

16. Samuel Gilman to the A.U.A., 15 August 1856, A.U.A. Letters.

17. M. J. Rice to the A.U.A., 17 May 1856, A.U.A. Letters.

18. *Annual Reports*, p. 10.

19. Samuel Gilman to Henry W. Bellows, Charleston, 5 May 1849, Bellows Papers.

20. Leonidas W. Spratt, *Speech Upon the Foreign Slave Trade, Before The Legislature of South Carolina* (Columbia: Steam-Power Press Southern Guardian, 1854), p. 4.

21. See Spratt, *Speech Upon the Foreign Slave Trade*, pp. 8–9.

22. See Chapter 1.

23. Clapp, "Thanksgiving Sermon."

24. Charles Chauncy, *Seasonable Thoughts on the State of Religion in New England* (Boston, 1743), p. 327.

25. Isaac Davenport to the A.U.A., 20 March 1836, A.U.A. Letters.

26. Douglas C. Stange, "United for Sovereignty and Freedom: Unitarians and the Civil War," *Proceedings of the Unitarian Universalist Historical Society* 19(1980–1981): 16–38.

27. Miller, *Letters on Unitarianism*, p. 18.

28. Ibid., p. 93.

29. Ibid., p. 92.

30. Howe, *Unitarian Conscience*, p. 295.

31. Miller, *Letters on Unitarianism*, pp. 92, 93.

32. Gilman, *Contributions to Religion*, p. 358.

33. Samuel Henry Dickson, *Remarks on Certain Topics Connected with the General Subject of Slavery* (Charleston: Observer Office Press, 1845), pp. 3, 21, 30. The pamphlet comprises two magazine articles, the second of which originally appeared as a "Letter from S. H. Dickson, M.D.," *Christian Register and Religious Miscellany* 37(November 1844). The editors of the *Christian Register* deleted so much of Dickson's essay that he felt obliged to publish the original essay himself. See also Stange, "Abolitionism as Maleficence," pp. 169–70.

34. Richard D. Arnold Scrapbook.

35. Richard D. Arnold to Col. John W. Forney, Savannah, 9 September 1851; Arnold to Capt. E. M. McGee, Agent for the Georgian Colony in Kansas, 13 September 1856, in Richard H. Shryock, ed., *Letters of Richard D. Arnold, M.D., 1808–1876, mayor of Savannah, Georgia, first secretary of the American Medical Association* (Durham: Duke University Press, 1922), pp. 57, 77–78.

36. Leonidas W. Spratt, *A Series of Articles on the Value of the Union to the South, Lately Published in The Charleston Standard* (Charleston: James, Williams & Gitsinger, 1855).

37. See especially Howe, "A Massachusetts Yankee."

38. Letter of 1856, Samuel Gilman Papers, University of South Carolina, Columbia.

CHAPTER 9. THE FORK IN THE ROAD

1. Richard M. Weaver, "Two Types of American Individualism," in *The Southern Essays of Richard M. Weaver,* George M. Curtis III and James J. Thompson, Jr., eds. (Indianapolis: Liberty Press, 1987), pp. 100, 102.

2. For an elaboration of the Southern world view, see Elizabeth Fox-Genovese and Eugene D. Genovese, "The Divine Sanction of Social Order," pp. 211–29.

3. Samuel Joseph May, *Some Recollections of Our Anti-slavery Conflict* (Boston: Fields, Osgood, and Co., 1869), pp. 335, 336.

4. Genovese, *The Slaveholders' Dilemma,* p. 37.

5. Mitchell Snay, "American Thought and Southern Distinctiveness: The Southern Clergy and the Sanctification of Slavery," *Civil War History* 35, no. 4(1989).

6. Richard D. Arnold to J. G. Robertson, Savannah, 29 July 1865, in Shryock, *Letters,* pp. 108, 124.

7. Eugene Genovese, *A Consuming Fire, The Fall of the Confederacy in the Mind of the White Christian South* (Athens: University of Georgia Press, 1998), p. 88.

8. Charles M. Taggart, "Rev. Mr. Taggart and Slavery," *Christian Register,* 18 October 1851, p. 1.

9. Clapp, *Autobiographical Sketches,* pp. 341, 375–79.

10. Clapp, *Slavery,* p. 66.

11. Dickson, *Remarks on Certain Topics,* p. 9.

12. Notes, Gilman Papers, Harvard University Archives.

13. Caroline Gilman to "My Dear Children," 12 December 1860, Caroline Gilman Papers.

14. Caroline Gilman, *Recollections of a Southern Matron* (Boston, 1836), pp. 235–36.

15. Charles M. Taggart, "Slave Holders and Slaves," *Christian Register,* 29 November 1851.

16. Gilman, *Recollections of a Southern Matron,* pp. 236–37.

17. See Chapter 5.

18. Clapp, *Slavery,* p. 40.

19. Dickson, *Remarks on Certain Topics,* p. 23.

20. Dexter Clapp, "Letter on the Religious Condition of Slaves," p. 207.

21. Shryock, *Letters,* pp. 25, 32, 33, 38, 72, 101, 118, 124; "Last Will and Testament of Maria Cohen, f.w.c. [free woman of color]."

22. Richard Arnold to Jacob McCall, Savannah, 29 August 1849, in Shryock, *Letters,* p. 33.

23. Dickson, *Remarks on Certain Topics,* p. 22.

24. In 1834, South Carolina passed legislation prohibiting teaching slaves to read or write. State of South Carolina, *Statutes at Large,* VII, pp. 459–60.

25. Samuel H. Dickson, *Address of Dr. S. H. Dickson, Delivered at the Inauguration of the Public School, Fourth of July, 1856* (Charleston: Walker, Evans & Co., 1856), p. 9.

26. Samuel Gilman to "Eliza," 14 February 1844, Samuel Gilman Collection, University of South Carolina.

27. Gilman, *The Old and the New*, pp. 28–29.

28. Dexter Clapp, "Letter on the Religious Condition of Slaves," p. 207.

29. Dickson, *Remarks on Certain Topics*, p. 3.

30. See Howe, "A Massachusetts Yankee," p. 206.

31. See Stange, "Abolitionism as Maleficence."

32. "Letters of a Confederate Mother: Charleston in the Sixties," *Atlantic Monthly* 137(April 1926): 514–15.

33. Caroline Gilman to "My Dear Children," 12 December 1860, Caroline Gilman Papers.

34. Larry E. Tise, *Proslavery: A History of the Defense of Slavery in America, 1701–1840* (Athens: University of Georgia Press, 1987).

35. Eugene Genovese, *The Southern Front: History and Politics in the Cultural War* (Columbia: University of Missouri Press), pp. 79–91.

36. Ibid., p. 88.

37. Clapp, *Slavery*, pp. 8–11, 33.

38. Clapp, "Thanksgiving Sermon."

39. Ibid.

40. Snay, "American Thought and Southern Distinctiveness," pp. 314, 318–19.

41. *Annual Reports*, p. 10.

42. Clapp, *Slavery*, p. 33.

43. Gilman, *Recollections of a Southern Matron*, pp. 202–3.

44. Notes, Gilman Papers, Harvard University Archives.

45. Charles Manson Taggart, "The Diversity and Origin of Human Races," *Southern Quarterly Review*, n.s., 4(October 1851): 479–80.

46. Holifield, *Gentlemen Theologians*, p. 82.

47. Notes, Gilman Papers, Harvard University Archives.

48. Channing, *Works*, pp. 835–38.

49. Orville Dewey, *The Works of Orville Dewey, D.D.: With a Biographical Sketch* (Boston: American Unitarian Association, 1883), vol. 2, p. 371.

50. Clapp, "Thanksgiving Sermon."

51. Taggart, "Rev. Mr. Taggart and Slavery."

52. Clapp, *Slavery*, p. 5.

53. Dexter Clapp, "Letter on the Religious Condition of Slaves," p. 207. Also see Dewey, *Works*, vol. 2, p. 366.

Chapter 10. Institutional Decline and the Ghost of Southern Unitarianism

1. Charles Farley to the A.U.A., 26 July 1835, A.U.A. Letters. E. L. Bascom to the A.U.A., 17 February 1836, A.U.A. Letters. Samuel St. John, Jr., to the A.U.A., 10 January 1838, A.U.A. Letters.

2. *Unitarian Christian* 1(June 1831). Gibson, "Georgia," p. 152.

3. *Christian Register*, 18 December 1843.

4. Stephen G. Bulfinch to the A.U.A., 11 December 1835, A.U.A. Letters.

5. [Savannah] *Daily Morning News,* 26 April 1851.

6. J. Allen Penniman to the Secretary of the A.U.A., 13 August 1849, A.U.A. Letters.

7. Samuel Gilman, A.U.A. Letters, 6 April 1852.

8. Pierpont to Pierpont, 11 April 1854, Pierpont Morgan Library, New York.

9. Ibid., 21 June 1852.

10. See Gohdes, "Some Notes on the Unitarian Church," p. 358. Also, W. Asbury Christian, *Richmond: Her Past and Present* (Richmond, 1912), p. 144. Also, Gibson, "Richmond," p. 331.

11. Christian, *Richmond,* p. 149.

12. Gohdes, "Some Notes on the Unitarian Church," p. 358. Gibson, "Richmond," p. 332.

13. Moncure Daniel Conway, *Autobiography* (Boston, 1904), vol. 1, pp. 189–90.

14. "Treasurer's Book, 1858–1881, First Independent Christian Church, Richmond, Virginia," Archives Division, Virginia State Library, Richmond.

15. Ibid.

16. Frank W. Pratt, *The History of the Unitarian Church of Richmond, Virginia* (Mimeograph pamphlet, 1937), p. 1.

17. Gilman, *The Old and the New,* pp. 20–22.

18. Ibid., pp. 28–29.

19. Taggart, *Sermons by Charles Manson Taggart,* pp. xxxiii, xxvi.

20. [Charleston] *Courier,* 18, 11 February 1858.

21. George W. Burnap to Henry W. Bellows, Baltimore, 22 December 1858; Burnap to Bellows, Baltimore, 7 January 1859, Bellows Papers.

22. Taggart, *Sermons by Charles Manson Taggart,* p. xlix.

23. *Yearbook,* p. 420.

24. "The Mission to Charleston, S.C.," *Monthly Journal of the American Unitarian Association* 7(February 1866): 87–98.

25. Ibid.

26. *Yearbook,* pp. 420–21.

27. Wellons, *The Christians, South, not Unitarians in Sentiment,* p. 87; J. R. Blossom, 12 January 1860, A.U.A. Letters; Stange, "Abolitionism as Maleficence," p. 147; Herbert C. Peabody to Samuel St. John, Jr., 17 December 1858, 23 January 1859, Peabody Papers.

28. Butler, "Coercion," p. 1.

Bibliography

Primary Sources

Published Books and Pamphlets

Arnold, Richard D. "Letters of Richard D. Arnold, M. D., 1808–1876." In *Historical Papers, Series XIV,* ed. by Richard H. Shryock. Durham: Trinity College Historical Society, 1922.

Bull, Elias B. *Founders and Pew Renters of the Unitarian Church in Charleston, S.C., 1817–1874.* Charleston: Unitarian Church in Charleston, S.C. Press, 1970.

Channing, William Ellery. *The Works of William E. Channing, D.D.* Boston: American Unitarian Association, 1882.

Chapin, Edwin H. *Duties of Young Men, Exhibited in Six Lectures; with an Anniversary Address, Delivered before the Richmond Lyceum.* Boston, 1840.

——. *An Oration Delivered Fourth of July, 1840, At the Invitation of the Richmond Light Dragoons, the Washington Grenadiers and the Scarlett Guard.* Richmond, 1840.

Chauncy, Charles. *Seasonable Thoughts on the State of Religion in New England.* Boston, 1743.

Clapp, Theodore. *Autobiographical Sketches and Recollections during a Thirty-five Year's Residence in New Orleans.* Boston, 1857.

——. *Slavery: A Sermon, Delivered in the First Congregational Church of New Orleans, April 15, 1838.* New Orleans: John Gibson, 1838.

Clarke, James Freeman. *Autobiography, Diary and Correspondence,* ed. by Edward Everett Hale. Boston and New York, 1891; reprint, New York: Negro Universities Press, 1968.

Cohen New Orleans Directory for 1854. New Orleans, 1854.

Committee of the First Independent Christian Church. *The Faith of the Universalists: Being a defense of this denomination of Christians and their views, against an abusive article published against them by Rev. Wm. S. Plumer, in a paper edited by him, entitled, the "Watchman of the South," of the 28th of December, who declined publishing a reply or correcting the gross misrepresentation.* Richmond, 1838.

Conway, Moncure Daniel. *Autobiography.* Boston, 1904.

Daniel, John Moncure. *The life of Stonewall Jackson. From official papers, contemporary narratives, and personal acquaintance. By Hon. J. M. Daniells [i.e., Daniel], a Virginian.* London, Sampson Low [and] Bacon; New York, Charles B. Richardson, 1863.

Dewey, Orville. *An Address, Delivered Under The Old Elm Tree in Sheffield, With Some Remarks On the Great Political Question of the Day.* New York: C. S. Francis & Co., 1856.

———. *Autobiography and Letters of Orville Dewey, D.D.,* ed. by Mary E. Dewey. Boston: Roberts Brothers, 1883.

———. *Discourses on Human Nature, Human Life and the Nature of Religion.* 3 vols. New York: Charles S. Francis, 1868.

———. *Letters of an English Traveller to His Friend in England on the "Revivals of Religion" in America.* Boston: 1828.

———. *The Works of Orville Dewey, D.D.: With a Biographical Sketch.* Boston: American Unitarian Association, 1883.

Dickson, Samuel Henry. *Address of Dr. S. H. Dickson, Delivered at the Inauguration of the Public School, Fourth of July, 1856.* Charleston: Walker, Evans & Co., 1856.

———. *Remarks on Certain Topics Connected With the General Subject of Slavery.* Charleston: Observer Office Press, 1845.

Emerson, Ralph Waldo. *A Letter of Emerson,* ed. by William Reed. Boston, 1934.

England, John. *The Works of the Right Reverend John England, first bishop of Charleston,* vols. 2 and 3. Cleveland: Arthur H. Clark, 1908.

Eustis, George, Theodore Howard McCaleb, and Christian Roselius. *A History of the proceedings in the city of New Orleans on the occasion of the funeral ceremonies in honor of Calhoun, Clay and Webster.* New Orleans, 1853.

Farley, Charles A. *Slavery; A Discourse Delivered In the Unitarian Church, Richmond, Virginia, Sunday, August 30, 1835.* Richmond, 1835.

Farley, F. A. "Congregational Unitarianism in the United States of America." In *Unitarianism Exhibited in Its Actual Condition . . .*, ed. by J. R. Beard. London, 1846.

Fifth Annual Report Made to the American Unitarian Association. Boston, 1830.

Forster, Anthony. *Sermons, Chiefly of a Practical Nature,* Foreword by M. L. Hurlbut. Raleigh: Joseph Gales, 1821.

Gilman, Caroline. *Recollections of a Southern Matron.* Boston, 1836.

Gilman, Samuel. *Address Delivered at the Anniversary Meeting of the South Carolina Society for the Promotion of Temperance.* Charleston, 1831.

———. *Contributions to Literature.* Boston: Crosby, Nichols, and Co., 1856.

———. *Contributions to Religion.* Charleston, 1860.

———. *The Old and the New: Discourses and Proceedings at the Dedication of the Re-Modeled Unitarian Church.* Charleston: Samuel G. Courtenay, 1854.

———. *Revealed Religion: A Dudleian Lecture Delivered in the Chapel of the University at Cambridge.* Boston, 1848.

———. *A Sermon on the Introduction to the Gospel of St. John.* Charleston: Unitarian Book and Tract Society, 1825.

———. *Unitarian Christianity free from Objectionable Extremes: A Sermon preached at the dedication of the Unitarian Church in Augusta, December 27, 1827.* Charleston, 1828.

Grayson, William J. *Reply to Dr. Dewey's Address, Delivered at the Elm Tree, Sheffield, Massachusetts.* Charleston: Walker, Evans & Co., 1856.

"Historical Sketch of the Unitarian Church." In *City of Charleston Yearbook.* Charleston, 1882.

Jefferson, Thomas. *The Writings of Thomas Jefferson,* ed. by A. A. Lipscomb and A. E. Bergh. Washington, 1904.

Jewell, Edwin L. *Jewell's Crescent City Illustrated.* New Orleans, 1873.

Logan, George W., et al. *Annual Reports Rendered by the Managers of the Charleston Unitarian Book and Tract Society On the Occasion of Its Thirty-Sixth Anniversary, Sunday, August 9, 1857.* Charleston: Walker, Evans & Co., 1857.

Lounsbury, Richard C., ed. *Louisa S. McCord: Poems, Drama, Biography, Letters.* Charlottesville: University of Virginia Press, 1996.

May, Samuel Joseph. *Some Recollections of Our Anti-slavery Conflict.* Boston: Fields, Osgood, and Co., 1869.

Miller, Stephen Franks. *The Bench and Bar of Georgia: Memoirs and Sketches,* vol. 2. Philadelphia: J. B. Lippincott, 1858.

Pierpont, John. *A Discourse on the Covenant with Judas, Preached in Hollis-Street Church, Nov. 6, 1842.* Boston: Charles C. Little and James Brown, 1842.

Priestley, Joseph. *An History of the Corruptions of Christianity.* Philadelphia, 1782.

――――. *Memoirs of Dr. Joseph Priestley, to the Year 1795.* 2 vols. Northumberland, Pa., 1806.

Report of the National Conference of Unitarian Churches. Boston, 1866.

Simmons, George F. *Review of the Remarks on Dr. Channing's Slavery, by a Citizen of Massachusetts.* Boston: James Munroe & Co., 1836.

Smyth, Thomas. *Complete Works of Rev. Thomas Smyth, D.D.,* ed. by Wm. Flinn. New ed., Columbia: R. L. Bryan Co., 1908–1912.

Sparks, Jared. *The Life and Writings of Jared Sparks.* Boston and New York, 1893.

Sprague, W. B. *Annals of the American Pulpit,* vol. 5. New York, 1856–1865.

Spratt, Leonidas W. *A Series of Articles on the Value of the Union to the South, Lately Published in The Charleston Standard.* Charleston: James, Williams & Gitsinger, 1855.

――――. *Speech Upon the Foreign Slave Trade, Before The Legislature of South Carolina.* Columbia: Steam-Power Press Southern Guardian, 1854.

Taggart, Charles Manson. *Sermons by Charles Manson Taggart, Late Colleague Pastor of the Unitarian Church in Charleston, S.C., With a Memoir by John H. Heywood.* Charleston: S. G. Courtenay, 1856.

The Twenty-Eighth Annual Report of the Managers of the Charleston Unitarian Book and Tract Society. Charleston: Walker, Evans, & James, 1849.

The Unitarian Congregational Register for the Year 1846. Printed for the American Unitarian Association. Boston: Crosby, Nichols and Co., 1846, 1854.

Upham, Charles Wentworth. *A Letter to the Editor of the Charleston Observer, Concerning his Treatment of Unitarians.* Charleston: James S. Burgess, 1827.

Wellons, W. B. *The Christians, South, not Unitarians in Sentiment. A Reply to Rev. John Paris' Book, Entitled "Unitarianism Exposed, as it Exists in the Christian Church."* Suffolk, Va., 1860.

Whitridge, J. B. *Calling Things by Their Right Names: A Brief Reply To An Article Under*

That Title, In the Southern Watchman of May 19, 1837. By a Layman. Charleston Unitarian Book and Tract Society. Charleston: Walker and James, 1837.

Yates, William B. *An Historical Sketch of the Rise and Progress of Religious and Moral Improvement Among Seamen, In England and the United States, With a History of the Port Society of Charleston, S.C.* Charleston: A. J. Burke, 1851.

Articles

Gilman, Samuel. "Brown's Philosophy of the Human Mind." *Southern Quarterly Review* 3(1829): 26–54.

——. "Brown's Philosophy of Mind." *North American Review* 19(1824).

——. "Cause and Effect." *North American Review* 12(1821): 395–432.

——. "Character and Writings of Dr. Brown." *North American Review* 21(1825): 19–51.

McFarland, J. R. *Julian, Emperor of Rome, commonly called Apostate: A discourse.* Charleston: Steam Power Presses of Walker, Evans, 1859.

Taggart, Charles Manson. "The Diversity and Origin of Human Races." *Southern Quarterly Review*, n.s., 4(October 1851).

Newspapers

Carolina Gazette, Charleston.
Courier, Charleston.
Daily Morning News, Savannah.
Daily Picayune, New Orleans.
Georgia Telegraph, Savannah.
The Georgian, Savannah.
London Morning Advertiser, London.
Louisiana Advertiser, New Orleans.

Periodicals

Christian Examiner, Boston.
Christian Register, Boston.
Monthly Journal of the American Unitarian Association, Boston.
Monthly Miscellany, Boston.
Quarterly Journal of the American Unitarian Association, Boston.
Southern Literary Messenger, Charleston.
Southern Literary Review, Charleston, New Orleans.
Unitarian, Boston.
Unitarian Christian, Charleston.
Unitarian Miscellany, Boston.
Western Messenger, Louisville.

Unpublished Material

"Treasurer's Book, 1858–1881: First Independent Christian Church, Richmond, Virginia." Archives Division, Virginia State Library, Richmond.

Manuscript Collections Cited

American Unitarian Association Archives, Harvard Divinity School, Cambridge.

American Unitarian Association Letters, Andover-Harvard Theological Library, Harvard University, Cambridge.

Arnold Collection, Richard D. Arnold Papers, Southern Historical Collection, Wilson Library, University of North Carolina, Chapel Hill.

Bellows Collection, Henry W. Bellows Papers, Massachusetts Historical Society, Boston.

Clarke Collection, James Freeman Clarke Papers, Massachusetts Historical Society, Boston.

Dwight Collection, Timothy Dwight II Papers, Massachusetts Historical Society, Boston.

Gales Collection, Joseph Gales Papers, Southern Historical Collection, Wilson Library, The University of North Carolina, Chapel Hill.

Gilman Collection, Caroline Howard Gilman Papers, South Carolina Historical Society, Charleston.

Gilman Collection, Samuel Gilman Papers, Harvard University Archives, Cambridge.

Gilman Papers, Samuel Gilman Papers, South Caroliniana Library, University of South Carolina, Columbia.

Peabody Collection, Herbert C. Peabody Papers, Southern Historical Collection, Wilson Library, The University of North Carolina, Chapel Hill.

Winans Papers, William Winans Collection, Special Collections, University of Mississippi Library, University of Mississippi, Oxford.

Secondary Sources

Published Books and Pamphlets

Adams, Raymond. *The Charleston Unitarianism Gilman Began With,* ed. by Kenneth B. Murdock. Cambridge: Harvard University Library, 1952.

Ahlstrom, Sydney E. *A Religious History of the American People.* New Haven: Yale University Press, 1972.

Bangs, Carl. *Arminius: A Study in the Dutch Reformation.* Nashville: Abingdon Press, 1971.

Bellows, Barbara L. *Benevolence among Slaveholders: Assisting the Poor in Charleston, 1670–1860.* Baton Rouge: Louisiana State University Press, 1993.

Bodley, Edith F. *An Historical Sketch of the First Unitarian Church of Louisville.* Louisville, 1930.

Bremer, Francis J. *Congregational Communion: Clerical Friendship in the Anglo-American Puritan Community, 1610–1692.* Boston: Northeastern University Press, 1994.

———. *Increase Mather's Friends: The Trans-Atlantic Congregational Network of the Seventeenth Century.* Worcester: American Antiquarian Society, 1984.

Brooks, Arthur A. *The History of Unitarianism in the Southern Churches: Charleston, New Orleans, Louisville, Richmond.* Boston: American Unitarian Association, [n.d.].

Calhoon, Robert M. *Evangelicals and Conservatives in the Early South, 1740–1861.* Columbia: University of South Carolina Press, 1988.

Christian, W. Asbury. *Richmond: Her Past and Present.* Richmond, 1912.

Clark, Elizabeth Ann. *The Origenist Controversy: The Cultural Construction of an Early Christian Debate.* Princeton: Princeton University Press, 1992.

Conkin, Paul K. *American Originals: Homemade Varieties of Christianity.* Chapel Hill: University of North Carolina Press, 1997.

Denton, Charles Richard. *American Unitarians, 1830–1865: A Study of Religious Opinion on War, Slavery, and the Union.* East Lansing: Michigan State University, 1969.

Drago, Edmund L. *Broke by the War: Letters of a Slave Trader.* Columbia: University of South Carolina, 1991.

Duffy, John, ed. *Parson Clapp of the Strangers' Church of New Orleans.* Baton Rouge: Louisiana State University Press, 1957.

Eaton, Clement. *Freedom of Thought Struggle in the Old South.* Revised ed. New York: Harper & Row, 1964.

Eddy, Richard. *Universalism in America,* vol. 2. Boston, 1886.

Edwards, George N. *A History of the Independent or Congregational Church of Charleston, South Carolina.* Boston: The Pilgrim Press, 1947.

Fox-Genovese, Elizabeth. *Within the Plantation Household: Black and White Women in the Old South.* Chapel Hill: University of North Carolina Press, 1988.

Genovese, Eugene. *A Consuming Fire, The Fall of the Confederacy in the Mind of the White Christian South.* Athens: University of Georgia Press, 1998.

———. *The Slaveholders' Dilemma: Freedom and Progress in Southern Conservative Thought, 1820–1860.* Columbia: University of South Carolina Press, 1992.

———. *The Southern Front: History and Politics in the Cultural War.* Columbia: University of Missouri Press, 1995, pp. 79–91.

Gibbs, F. W. *Joseph Priestley: Revolutions of the Eighteenth Century.* 1967; reprint, Garden City, New York: Doubleday, 1995.

Greenwood, Francis William Pitt. *History of King's Chapel in Boston.* Boston, 1863.

Holifield, E. Brooks. *The Gentlemen Theologians: American Theology in Southern Culture, 1795–1860.* Durham: Duke University Press, 1978.

Howe, Daniel Walker. *The Unitarian Conscience: Harvard Moral Philosophy, 1805–1865.* Cambridge: Harvard University Press, 1970.

Kuykendall, John Wells. *Southern Enterprise: The Work of the National Evangelical Societies in the Antebellum South.* Westport, 1982.

Marsden, George M. *Fundamentalism and American Culture: The Shaping of Twentieth-Century Evangelicalism, 1870–1925.* New York: Oxford University Press, 1980.

Miller, Perry. *The Life of the Mind in America from the Revolution to the Civil War.* New York: Harcourt, Brace and World, 1965.

Petersen, Henry. *The Canons of Dort.* Grand Rapids, Michigan: Baker Press, 1968.

Rankin, Richard. *Ambivalent Churchmen and Evangelical Churchwomen: The Religion of the Episcopal Elite in North Carolina, 1800–1860.* Columbia: University of South Carolina Press, 1993.

Richmond, City of Churches: A Short History of Richmond's Denominations and Faiths. Richmond, 1957.

Ripley, Eliza. *Social Life in Old New Orleans Being Recollections of My Girlhood.* New York: D. Appleton & Co., 1912.

Scharf, J. Thomas. *The Chronicles of Baltimore.* Baltimore, 1874.

Scudder, Jennie W. *A Century of Unitarianism in the National Capital, 1821–1921.* Boston: Beacon Press, 1922.

Stange, Douglas C. *Patterns of Antislavery among American Unitarians, 1831–1860.* Rutherford: Fairleigh Dickinson University Press, 1977.

Thompson, Ernest Trice. *Presbyterians in the South, 1607–1861,* vol. 1. Richmond: John Knox Press, 1963.

Tise, Larry E. *Proslavery: A History of the Defense of Slavery in America, 1701–1840.* Athens: University of Georgia Press, 1987.

Waring, Joseph Ioor. *A History of Medicine in South Carolina, 1825–1900.* Columbia: South Carolina Medical Association, 1967.

Weaver, Richard M. *The Southern Essays of Richard M. Weaver,* ed. by George M. Curtis III and James J. Thompson, Jr. Indianapolis: Liberty Press, 1992.

Wilbur, Earl Morse. *A History of Unitarianism in Transylvania, England and America.* Boston: Harvard University Press, 1952.

Windrow, John Edwin. *John Berrich Lindsley, Educator, Physician, Social Philosopher.* Chapel Hill: University of North Carolina Press, 1938.

Wright, Conrad. *The Beginnings of Unitarianism in America.* Boston: Starr King Press, 1955.

———. *The Liberal Christians: Essays on American Unitarian History.* Boston: Beacon Press, 1970.

Yacovone, Donald. *Samuel Joseph May and the Dilemmas of the Liberal Persuasion, 1797–1871.* Philadelphia: Temple University Press, 1991.

Articles

Ahlstrom, Sydney E. "The Scottish Philosophy and American Theology." *Church History* 24(September 1955): 257–72.

Baglyos, Paul A. "Samuel Simon Schmucker and the Primitive Church." *Concordia Historical Institute Quarterly* 71, no. 4(1988): 168–83.

Butler, Jon. "Coercion, Miracle, Reason: Rethinking the American Religious Experience in the Revolutionary Age." In *Religion in a Revolutionary Age,* ed. by Ronald Hoffman and Peter J. Albert, pp. 1–30. Charlottesville: University of Virginia Press, 1994.

Carwardine, Richard. "Evangelicals, Politics, and the Coming of the American Civil War: A Transatlantic Perspective." In *Evangelicalism: Comparative Studies of Popular Protestantism in North America, the British Isles, and Beyond, 1700–1990,* ed. by Mark A. Noll, et al., pp. 198–218. New York: Oxford University Press, 1994.

Come, Robert B. "The Influence of Princeton on Higher Education in the South before 1825." *William and Mary Quarterly,* 2d ser. 2(October 1945): 362–94.

Conkin, Paul K. "Priestly and Jefferson: Unitarianism as a Religion for a New Revolutionary Age." In *Religion in a Revolutionary Age,* ed. by Ronald Hoffman and Peter J. Albert, pp. 290–307. Charlottesville: University of Virginia Press, 1994.

Denton, Charles Richard. "An American War that Unitarians Approved: The Civil War." *Proceedings of the Unitarian Historical Society* 17(1970–1972): 46–56.

Fox-Genovese, Elizabeth, and Eugene D. Genovese. "The Divine Sanction of Social Order: Religious Foundations of the Southern Slaveholders' World View." *Journal of the American Academy of Religion* 55(1987): 211–29.

Genovese, Eugene D., and Elizabeth Fox-Genovese. "The Religious Ideals of Southern Slave Society." *Georgia Historical Quarterly* 70(1986): 1–16.

Gibson, George H. "Unitarian Congregations in Ante-Bellum Georgia." *Georgia Historical Quarterly* 54(1970): 147–68.

———. "Unitarian Congregations in the Antebellum South." *Proceedings of the Unitarian Historical Society* 12, pt. 2(1959): 53–78.

———. "The Unitarian-Universalist Church of Richmond." *Virginia Magazine of History and Biography* 74(1966): 321–35.

Gohdes, Clarence. "Some Notes on the Unitarian Church in the Ante-Bellum South: A Contribution to the History of Southern Liberalism." In *American Studies in Honor of William Kenneth Boyd by Members of The Americana Club of Duke University,* ed. by David Kelly Jackson. Reprint. Durham: Duke University Press, 1968.

Hill, Samuel S. "Northern and Southern Varieties of American Evangelicalism." In *Evangelicalism: Comparative Studies of Popular Protestantism in North America, the British Isles, and Beyond, 1700–1990,* ed. by Mark A. Noll, et al., pp. 275–89. New York: Oxford University Press, 1994.

Howe, Daniel Walker. "A Massachusetts Yankee in Senator Calhoun's Court: Samuel Gilman in South Carolina." *New England Quarterly* 44(1971): 197–220.

Jabour, Anya. "'Grown Girls, Highly Cultivated': Female Education in an Antebellum Southern Family." *Journal of Southern History* 64, no. 1(February 1998): 23–64.

Moltke-Hansen, David. "The Expansion of Intellectual Life: A Prospectus." In *Intellectual Life in Antebellum Charleston,* ed. by Michael O'Brien and David Moltke-Hansen. Knoxville: University of Tennessee Press, 1986.

Radbill, Samuel X. "Samuel Henry Dickson." *Annals of Medical History,* 3d ser. 4(1942).

Snay, Mitchell. "American Thought and Southern Distinctiveness: The Southern Clergy and the Sanctification of Slavery." *Civil War History* 35, no. 4(1989): 311–28.

Stange, Douglas C. "Abolitionism as Maleficence: Southern Unitarians Versus 'Puritan Fanaticism'—1831–1860." *Harvard Library Bulletin* 26(1978): 146–71.

———. "United for Sovereignty and Freedom: Unitarians and the Civil War." *Proceedings of the Unitarian Universalist Historical Society* 19(1980–1981): 16–38.

Wright, Conrad. "The Theological World of Samuel Gilman." *Proceedings of the Unitarian Historical Society* 17, pt. 2(1973–1975).

Unpublished Material

Cory, Earl Wallace. "The Unitarians and Universalists of the Southeastern United States during the Nineteenth Century." Ph.D. Dissertation. Athens: University of Georgia, 1970.

Dachowski, Meg. "A Short History of the First Unitarian Church, New Orleans, Louisiana." Manuscript in possession of the author.

Lewis, Frank Bell. "Robert Lewis Dabney: Southern Presbyterian Apologist." Ph.D. Dissertation. Durham: Duke University, 1946.

Pratt, Frank W. "The History of the Unitarian Church of Richmond, Virginia." Richmond, 1937.

Rahn, Milton H. [President of the Unitarian Universalist Fellowship in Savannah]. "Savannah Unitarians' Debt to Dr. Samuel Gilman: An Address to the Unitarian Church in Charleston on July 17, 1966." Georgia Historical Society, Savannah, Georgia.

Weis, Frederick Lewis, Th.D. "List of the Unitarian Churches and Their Ministers in the United States and Canada." Meadville-Lombard Divinity School of the University of Chicago, [n.d. 1950s?].

Index

Mitchell, Edward, 53
Mitchell, J. Clyde, 3
Mobile, Ala., 105; tract societies in, 65; Unitarian activity in, 71–72, 182; Unitarian church in, 39, 46; Unitarian society in, 136–40
Moltke-Hansen, David, 60, 77
Monefeldt, Dr. William S., 61
"monomania," Northern Unitarian abolitionist, 155, 171
Montgomery, Ala., 60
Monthly Miscellany, 141
morality, *vs.* theology, 29
moral philosophy, notion of 'relation' within, 117
Morgan, J. P., 174
Motte, Rev. Mellish Irving, 141, 142
Moultrie, Dr. James, Jr., 61, 62, *83*, 106, 107–8, 109

Nashville, Tenn., tract societies in, 65
Natchez, Miss., tract societies in, 65
National Conference of Unitarian Churches, 16
National Intelligencer, 28, 62
natural law, and slavery, 166
New England: Enlightenment ideals in, 1–2; slavery in, 156
New England phenomenon, Unitarianism as, 17
New England Society, 103
New Orleans, La.: Church of the Messiah in, 47, 52, 93, 105, 177; epidemics in, 99; Episcopal Christ Church in, 49; First Congregational Church of, 51–52, 140; maritime relief in, 105; Mississippi Presbytery in, 51; Presbyterian Church in, 50; rational Christianity in, 6–7; second Protestant church in, 49; social hierarchy of, 59–60; "Strangers" Church in, 7, 92; tract societies in, 65; Unitarianism in, 182; Universalism in, 177–78; voluntary associations in, 97
New Orleans Picayune, 69, 74, 75, 144, 166
New Orleans Unitarian Church, 3, 39, 47, 92; founding of, 48–49; members of, 51–52
newspapers, 111. *See also specific newspaper*
Newton, Isaac, 23
New World, 95
North Carolina Christian Advocate, 94
Northern Unitarianism, Transcendentalism within, 126
Northern Unitarians, 170; abolitionism of, 142, 168; and Association of Southern Unitarians, 135; compared with Southern Unitarians, 125; political activism of, 148–49; politicalization of, 27; "Puritan fanaticism" of, 11, 145; revival meetings of, 154; and scientific investigation, 127; and "sensual" philosophy, 116–17; Southern Unitarian view of, 171–72; Southern views of, 139, 147–48; "spoken word" of, 153

Oakes, Z. B., 59
Oglesby, Joseph, 61
Origenist controversy, 3
original sin, concept of, 48
orthodoxy, Southern: Arian Christology in, 94, 124; compared with Southern Unitarians, 39; Gilman's rational, 29; influence of Southern Unitarianism on, 120; internal divisions of, 78; "like-mindedness" with, 114; and "misunderstandings," 118; realism of, 37; and separation of church and state, 11; and Southern Unitarianism, 4–5, 20, 63, 125; and Southern Unitarians, 173–74, 182; theology of, 119

pacifists, Unitarians as, 155
Paine, Thomas, 113
Palfrey, John Gorham, 198n.10
Palmer, Dr. Benjamin Morgan, 7, 41
Paris, Rev. John, 94, 124, 182
Parker, Rev. M., 45
Parker, Rev. Theodore, 144, 149, 176
Parkman, John, 141–42, 145
Peabody, Ephraim, 137
Peabody, Herbert C., 11, 59, 105, 125, 137, 182
Pease, Jane, 58
Pease, William, 58
Penniman, J. Allen, 57, 100, 173–74
Philadelphia, Pa.: Unitarian church in, 18; Unitarian Society in, 20, 23, 28
Phillips, Stephen C., 142
Picket, E., 65
Pierpont, John, Jr., 76, 149, 174–75, 178
Pierpont, John, Sr., 149, 174, 198n.10
Pike, Richard, 154
Pinney, Rev. Norman, 136
Pitkin, John Budd, 53–54, 55, 75, 135
Pitt, William the Younger, 27
"planter" status, 58–59
Platonists, Cambridge, 30
Poe, Edgar Allen, 62
politics: clergy involved in, 198–99n.10; exclusion of clergy from, 29; and Southern Uni-

tarians, 9. *See also* separation of church
and state
polygenesis, 168–70
Poore, Robert, 72
port societies, 103
postmillennialism, 98
poverty: Northern *vs.* Southern view of, 97;
and sin, 96
predestination: Arminius on, 31–32; Calvinist
doctrine of, 31; English Arminian view
of, 33
Presbyterian Church: of antebellum period, 6;
in New Orleans, 50
Presbyterians: in Charleston, 40, 42; and
Common Sense Realism, 35; in Richmond, Va., 53
Price, Richard, 22
Priestley, Dr. Joseph, 18, 20, 21, 28, 29, 39, 43,
44, 52, *79*, 100, 112, 116; Christological
views of, 24–25; move to Pennsylvania, 22–
23; scientific achievements of, 22; theological treatises of, 189n.4
primitivist movement: American, 100, 101;
ecumenism within, 118; and Scripture, 114
Printing Institution for Blind, in New
Orleans, 105, 106
Prioleau, Dr. Jacob Ford, 61, 106
professionals, urban: among laity, 76; doctors,
61; gentility of, 72–78; growing number of,
59; and planter class, 58; status of, 60; writers, 61–62
"pulpit treason," accusations of, 151, 166
Puritanism: New England, 20; Unitarianism
from, 2

racial dictatorship, 160
racial differences: W. E. Channing on, 170;
S. Gilman on, 169
Raleigh, N.C.: tract societies in, 65; Unitarians
in, 21, 60
Raleigh Register, 27, 28, 62, 65
Ramsay, David, 37, 40, 43, 97
Randolph, John, 158
Rankin, Richard, 6
rationalism: Christian, 9, 30; Enlightenment,
183; "religious," 1, 6, 72; "Supernatural,"
112, 126
reason: and emotionalism, 152; revelation and,
113, 115; "unassisted," 112–13
Recollections of a Southern Matron (Gilman),
162, 168
reform, 78, 97; benevolent, 98; benevolent so-

cieties for, 102; educational, 110; maritime
aid, 101, 103, 104, 140; nineteenth-century,
104; slavery, 162; Southern Unitarian approach to, 101, 158–59; temperance, 101,
104, 105, 140, 146; and written word, 111.
See also social reform
reform, medical: in education, 106, 108; in febrile diseases, 107; licensing power, 109; and
"racial" aspects of disease, 163; Society for
the Relief of Families of Deceased and
Disabled Indigent Members of the Medical Profession, 108
reform societies, 95–96
Reid, Robert Raymond, 7
Reid, Thomas, 34, 35, 116, 117
religion: enlightenment, 2, 5; Natural, 112; science and, 169. *See also* Enlightenment religion
religious journals, 111
"Remonstrance," of followers of Arminius, 32
Remonstrants, 32. *See also* Arminianism
republicanism, and proslavery ideology, 165
resurrection: S. Gilman on, 122; importance to
orthodoxy of, 125
retirement, for slaves, 162
revelation: perceived role of, 117; reason and,
113, 115; slavery and, 167
revival meetings, 154. *See also* Great Awakening
Revival of 1858, 154
Rice, M. J., 122–23, 150
Richardson, Henry D., 59
Richmond, Va.: First Independent Church of,
54, 55, 175–77, 191n.12; lyceum movement
in, 77; Unitarian laity in, 72; Unitarian-
Universalist Society of, 53; "Uni-Uni"
Church in, 47
Richmond Examiner, 62, 74, 175–76
Richmond Unitarian Church, 52–53
Rittenhouse, David, 22
Roman Catholic church, 139
Roman Catholics, in Richmond, Va., 53
Roper, Col. Thomas, 61, *85*, 106
Roper Fund, 106
Roper Hospital, 85, *86*, 106
Rose, Dr. A. B., 61
Roselius, Christian, 61, 74
Ross, 160

Sabbatarianism, 101
Sabbath observance, 102
Sabbath School, slaves in, 164. *See also* Sunday
school movement

Sailor's Home, 104. *See also* maritime aid

St. John, Samuel, Jr., 137, 171

Saunders, Samuel S., 72

Savannah, Ga., 57; Sunday school established in, 103; tract societies in, 65; Unitarian laity in, 76–77; Unitarian society in, 141; voluntary associations in, 97

Savannah Bible Society, 105, 140

Savannah Medical College, 90, 109

Savannah Unitarian church, 46, *91;* beginnings of, 133; demise of, 172–75, 196n.44

savings bank for laboring poor, 105

Schmucker, Samuel Simon, 99

science, and religion, 169

"scientific racism," 169

Scottish Common Sense Realism, 8, 11, 20, 25, 29, 43, 120; in America, 34; characteristics of, 35; of Charleston church, 45; and discrepancies between science and theology, 36; ecumenical possibilities of, 119; and slavery, 166, 167; in South, 36–37

Scripture: and Christian unity, 119; for Southern Unitarians, 127; and support for slavery, 160–61

seaman's welfare group, in Savannah, 140

Seaton, William Winston, 28, 62

secession: and Richmond church, 176; Southern Unitarian support of, 157

sentimentalism, and liberal religion, 152

separation of church and state, 29; and abolitionism, 149; W. E. Channing on, 147; controversy over, 10–11; ideal of, 25–27; reform and, 101; and republicanism, 165–66; and slavery question, 141, 143, 150; for Southern Unitarians, 34, 100; W. Tennent on, 40

sermons, publication of, 68–69. *See also* writings, clerical

servitude, personal, 160

Sheldon, Rev. Dr., 119

Sherman, Gen. William T., 173

Shrigley, James, 176

Simmons, George Frederick, 125, 137, 142–43

Simpson, Lewis, 165

sin: original, 48; and salvation, 118; and social change, 96; for Southern Unitarians, 123

Skepticism, 1, 6, 29, 36

Skinner, Otis Ainsworth, 54

slaveholders, in Unitarian churches, 162

slaveownership, status afforded by, 59

slavery: capitalism and, 102; defense of, 168; Northern Unitarian opposition to, 149;

Northern *vs.* Southern approach to, 158; and Southern Unitarians, 142–43; Southern view of, 161–62. *See also* abolitionism

slaves: care of, 162; education of, 101, 163–64; traffic in, 163

slave trader, 59

Smith, Daniel D., 175

Smith, Samuel Harrison, 28

Smith, Rev. Thomas Hirst, 181

Smyth, Rev. Thomas, 124, 182

Snay, Mitchell, 167–68

social reform, 10; and benevolent societies, 102; for Northern Unitarians, 159–60; of Southern Unitarians, 159; and written word, 67–68. *See also* voluntary associations

society, hierarchical, 59–60

Socinian, label of, 9

Socinianism, 21

Socinius, Faustus, 24

the South: Arminian tradition in, 161; hierarchical world view of, 117; invisible religious institutions in, 4; religion in, 2, 102

South Carolina, Medical College of, 84, 106–7

Southern Christian Advocate, 103

Southern Pioneer and Gospel Visitor, 54

"Southern principles," ideals of, 110

Southern Rose, 62, 109

Southern Unitarianism: in Alabama, 136–40; appeal of, 60; characteristics of, 112; evolution of, 12; Gilman ministry, 45–46; influence of, 123–27; "invisible" presence of, 78; non-New England origins of, 39; origins of, 20, 27–29; research on, 187–88n.13

Southern Unitarians, 2–5; on abolition, 16–17, 155–56; Arian Christological position of, 25; associations of, 4; in Augusta, 172; in Charleston, 178–81; and Common Sense Realism, 36; compared with Northern Unitarians, 125; defense mounted by, 65; and denominational differences, 155; doctors among, 106; in Georgia, 131–36; historical role of, 183; intellectual pursuits of, 78; invisible tradition of, 63, 146, 147; libertarianism of, 27; local churches of, 4; in New Orleans, 177–78; north-south differences of, 38–39; orthodoxy and, 120–21; proposed Association of, 80, 134–36; proslavery ideology of, 165–70; reform efforts of, 10, 101, 146; respectability of, 8; in Richmond, 175–77; in Savannah, 172–75; and scientific investigation, 127; Scottish philosophy for,

117; and "sensual" philosophy, 116; and sepa-
ration of church and state, 11; slavery de-
fended by, 143, 151, 163, 168; toleration of, 9;
voluntary associations of, 98; women, 111;
written word for, 67–68, 152–53
The Southern Watchman, 64, 72
Sparks, Jared, 27, 28, 29, 37, 45, 64, 65,
73–74, 132
"spirit of improvement," 78, 98
"spiritual swindling," 146
Spratt, Leonidas W., 62, 151, 156
Stange, Douglas C., 18, 148–49, 153, 164
Stebbins, Rev. Calvin, 181
Stevens, Dr. Joseph, 61
Stewart, Dugald, 34, 116, 117
Stewart, Samuel, 59
"Strangers' Church," in New Orleans, 7, 92
Stringfellow, 160
Sunday School movement, 103, 106, 111, 146
Synod of Dort, 30, 31, 33

Taggart, Rev. Charles Manson, 62, 68, 75, *82*,
161, 174, 178, 179–80; on slavery, 162, 170;
slavery defended by, 168–69
Tannehill, Wilkins, 65
Tebbetts, Theodore, 154
temperance, 101
temperance movement: in Charleston, 104; in
Savannah, 105, 140
temperance unions, 146
Tennent, William, 37, 40, 43
Thacher, William Vincent, 75, 76
theology: of natural science, 127, 169; and sanctity of individual conscience, 10, 67, 158;
skepticism, 1, 6, 29, 36. *See also* biblical
criticism
Thomas, Charles B., 178
Thoreau, Henry David, 158
Thornwell, James Henley, 6, 8–9, 37, 116, 117,
160, 169
Tise, Larry, 165
Touro, Judah, 50, 93, 177
Touro Free Library Society of New Orleans, 105
towns, growth of Southern, 58. *See also* urban
areas
tract societies, 63, 146; American Tract Society, 64; in Augusta, 65, 66, 71, 138–39;
in Charleston, 66, 67, 71, 138, 179; in New
Orleans, 65; in the South, 65
Transcendentalism, 126, 127, 158, 176

Transylvania University, Ky., 36–37
Trinitarianism, 14, 23–24
Trinitarians, 114, 121, 122
Tuckerman, Joseph, 45
Tusculum College, Tenn., 37

Unitarian, 54
Unitarian Book and Tract Society, 128. *See also*
tract societies
Unitarian Christian, 67
*Unitarian Christianity free from Objectionable
Extremes* (Gilman), 132
Unitarianism: Charleston's, 55–56; compared
with Universalism, 47; denominational
splits in, 15–17; English, 18–30; first-
generation American, 9; New England,
19, 20, 37; non-New England stream of,
19; "religious rationalism" of, 1. *See also*
American Unitarian Association
Unitarian Miscellany: agents of, 64–65; publication of material from, 65–66
Unitarians: attacks against, 64; Boston, 35;
compared with Trinitarians, 122; Deist,
23, 25, 26; and doctrinal consensus, 114;
first American church of, 188n.15; first-
generation, 113–14, 126; New England, 26;
in Richmond church, 54; in social hierarchy, 60
Unitarian Theological School, Meadville,
Pa., 179
Uni-Uni Church, in Richmond, Va., 53
Universalism, 139; compared with Unitarianism, 47; in New Orleans, 47; in Richmond, 47
Universalists, in Richmond church, 54, 175
universities, in South, 78
Upham, Charles Wentworth, 122
urban areas: antebellum, 5; impact of capitalism on, 102–3; rational Christianity in, 8;
reform societies in, 96; of South, 57–58. *See
also* towns

Vaughan, John, 23
Virgin Birth, 122
Virginia tidewater, latitudinarianism in, 33
voluntarism, 101
voluntary associations, 78, 97, 145, 159. *See also*
benevolent societies

Walker, Alice, 181
Walker, Joseph, 181

• About the Author

John A. Macaulay is an independent scholar in American History and the History of Christianity. He earned an M.T.S. degree from Duke University Divinity School and a Ph.D. from the University of South Carolina.